E-Mails From The
Church Dog

Lessons From A Therapy Dog For The Ministry

*To Lorraine —
Enjoy our book.*

Lynda Fisher

LYNDA REYNOLDS FISHER

WestBow Press
A DIVISION OF THOMAS NELSON

Copyright © 2011 Lynda Reynolds Fisher.

All rights reserved. No part of this book may be used or reproduced by any means, graphic, electronic, or mechanical, including photocopying, recording, taping or by any information storage retrieval system without the written permission of the publisher except in the case of brief quotations embodied in critical articles and reviews.

WestBow Press books may be ordered through booksellers or by contacting:

WestBow Press
A Division of Thomas Nelson
1663 Liberty Drive
Bloomington, IN 47403
www.westbowpress.com
1-(866) 928-1240

Because of the dynamic nature of the Internet, any web addresses or links contained in this book may have changed since publication and may no longer be valid. The views expressed in this work are solely those of the author and do not necessarily reflect the views of the publisher, and the publisher hereby disclaims any responsibility for them.

Any people depicted in stock imagery provided by Thinkstock are models, and such images are being used for illustrative purposes only.

Certain stock imagery © Thinkstock.

ISBN: 978-1-4497-3094-9 (sc)
ISBN: 978-1-4497-3093-2 (e)

Library of Congress Control Number: 2011960334

Printed in the United States of America

WestBow Press rev. date: 11/15/2011

Who else could I dedicate this book to, but my patient, VERY supportive husband? Even though we've downsized our living quarters, there's still a lot of housework to be done, and Larry does a lot of it. There's a two-pronged reason: one is that I suffer from Chronic Fatigue, which makes any small physical exertion a reason for not moving even a finger for the rest of the day—not even knitting or typing! The second reason is to free up my time to spend it on the computer writing this book, even though much of it has already been done by the many reports that Mosby has e-mailed to Pastor Debbie and his Uncle Jack Holmer. Pastor Debbie is Mo's direct connection to his Boss (God), and Jack was working on securing funding for Mosby, from a legacy to be used for support of town activities, so both of these people have been included in Mosby's e-mails regarding his activities.

So—a book is dedicated to my husband—Mosby's favorite person in this whole wide world. I know I'm the one whose picture is included on our NEADS photo ID card, along with Mosby, but a dog doesn't always choose its favorite person by man-made assumptions. How can a dog compare Mom's weekly grooming chores with two-mile daily walks, and not choose the walking companion? Larry and I equally feed Mo, and we both toss the Frisbee and put him through his agility equipment, but it's mostly Larry who gets up from his recliner chair and lets him out, then in, then out again, and in again. At bedtime, it's Larry's side of the bed—on the floor—that Mosby chooses to lie on. Once that's said, how could I not dedicate this book—Mosby's and mine—to Larry?

Mosby Mac Fisher, Therapy Dog for the Ministry

ENDORSEMENTS

E-mails from the Church Dog

This is the tale of three souls: a vibrant, long married couple who find a renewed purpose for their life when they are matched with Mosby, a trained Therapy dog for the Ministry—and a pretty self-assured one I might add! God brought them together and set them on a faith journey that has brought great joy, compassion and purpose, not only for the three of them, but for all those whom they have touched. It is a true story of how everyday folks live out a life of faith, serving both God and neighbor with their time and creativity. Lynda, Larry and Mosby Mac Fisher continue to inspire me and their story is guaranteed to keep a smile on your face and occasionally make you laugh out loud.

Rev. Deborah J. Blanchard
Minister
First Baptist Church of Littleton

And—a book co-written by a dog should have an endorsement from another dog's perspective:

This is a true story of my good friend Mosby Mac Fisher, a silky-haired Golden Retriever, who is a ministry dog at my church in Littleton, Massachusetts where my mom, Pastor Debbie, is the minister. Mosby brings his parents, Lynda and Larry Fisher, to church on Sundays as well as to nursing homes, hospitals, grocery stores, special events, and to NEADS, a special college for puppies and dogs. Wherever Mosby goes he loves everybody equally and brings comfort and cheer to many humans. Mosby is an excellent storyteller who has put pen to paw upon these pages to spread the word and spread the love from our Boss above. I am proud to call Mosby my friend and know you will enjoy his tails.

Mr. Gibson,
Black Labrador Retriever and regular dog
As dictated to Pastor Debbie

FOREWORD

In almost every book I've read when the main subject is a dog, the last chapter talks about the death of that creature, and I cry buckets of tears while reading it. No matter how meaningful a life, how spiritual and enlightening the story is told, the loss of a dog always brings me to tears. You, the reader of Mosby's experiences, will be reassured that this book will not end with the finish of Mosby's life here on earth. Mo has so many stories to tell that this book will only cover the first three years of his life with Larry and me. Please know that you'll be closing this book with the happy thought that Mosby Mac Fisher is still here, walking his Dad around town, sleeping under our pew on a Sunday morning, and happily visiting people in hospitals and nursing homes, to say nothing of his other adventures. I promise.

Lynda

IN APPRECIATION

Many thanks, first, to NEADS for training Mosby, and for realizing his Calling to work for God, and to Mosby's Puppy Trainers for all their many hours and personal energy that went into Mo's training. My deep appreciation is gratefully extended to our Pastor Debbie Blanchard for encouraging and supporting Larry and me in our many church-related efforts with Mosby.

Also, many thanks to our church people who all love Mosby and enjoy his warm presence in our church programs. My apologies to those few who are allergic to dogs, and those who just don't care for dogs.

Lynda J. Fisher

Chapter 1

OUR LIVES BEFORE MOSBY

Our married life has been blessed with some really fine dogs, all with different admirable traits and qualities, and the whole family loved each and every one of them. We had thought one time about adopting a rescue dog, but had read too many stories about families who had acquired a dog from a shelter, background unknown, and that dog bit or turned on a family's small child. We felt that risk wasn't worth taking, even before we had any children. Also, we felt that having a pure-bred dog meant that, with a little research on our part, we'd know the eventual size and temperament of the adult dog. No guess work for us! We wanted to know—would that breed be a yappy barker? Would it be too timid to bark at someone at the door? Would it be happy playing with a small child, yet not try to dominate that playmate? We both knew that there were many successful matches of rescue dogs with human families, but we didn't want to take a chance on perhaps not having a good match. So—we definitely agreed that we'd purchase a pure-bred puppy from a good, reliable breeder.

Coincidentally, since Larry's sister Mary was breeding Collies in the early years of our marriage, she graciously offered us a pup as a wedding gift. So—our first dog was a large rough-coated tri-colored Highland Collie, whom we named George, partly because he was born on the birthday of our nation's first president, George Washington. Reflecting back, we were really ignorant dog owners. We never had him neutered, even though we had no intentions of ever breeding him. Back in the early 1960's, most people didn't neuter their male dogs, believing that just spaying the females was enough. Neither did we keep George in a fenced-in yard, but allowed him the freedom to roam around his neighborhood. When I think back on it, I'd NEVER do it that way again! George loved both of us, and newborn Scott also, seeming not to play favorites with any of us, but enjoying his life with all of us. George was really a homebody, and after an early morning foray around his neighborhood, he'd stay pretty much in our yard. But—his roaming habits ended his life, tragically too soon, when he somehow jumped a barrier fence onto busy Interstate Route 495, a good mile away from our home, and he found he was no match for a hurtling vehicle. We were all devastated by his loss, especially in such a brutal way, at only five years of age.

After a suitable mourning period, when we were ready for another canine companion, we bought Cindy, a fawn colored Boxer, reminiscent of Rebel, the family dog when I was a teenager. Cindy was the only one of our dogs who was MINE! Really mine. She doted on me, following me all around the house and yard when I was gardening. I was quite pleased by her love for me—she'd play quite willingly with our kids, Scott and Laurie, and any of their friends who were playing with them, but when I appeared on the scene, she'd happily trot over to me and sit beside my chair. Cindy was spayed at the appropriate time in her life, but she was never fenced in, even though she didn't stray far from our yard.

By then, Scott and Laurie were pre-teens and we were into family camping, which included Cindy and Ching, our beloved Siamese cat, both of whom traveled with us on their leashes. One particularly hot August day at a campground in Maine, eight-year-old Cindy suffered from Bloat and died before we could get her to a veterinarian, who might not have been able to save her anyway.

We waited, a sad family without a dog, until the next spring, when Brandy came to join our little family, a wee, tiny seven-week-old Golden Retriever. On the first few nights of her life with us, Scott and Laurie, both in sleeping bags, slept with Brandy on the kitchen floor, but still that little baby whimpered for her seven littermates for a few nights until she accustomed herself to living with all humans and one Siamese cat, who disdainfully kept her distance from "that alien creature."

By then, we had acquired enough sense to fence in our back yard, almost a half acre, so that our new puppy grew up either running freely in the yard or walking sedately on a leash with a human on the other end. Laurie and I took Brandy to obedience classes, so that Laurie could earn a Girl Scout badge, and to make Brandy a better behaved family member, although she already was very well behaved naturally, as all Goldens are. (Can you sense a certain bias already developing in me?) Even though I was the one who mostly walked Brandy, she chose Larry over everyone else in the family. She loved us all, almost equally, but she favored Larry over the rest of us. That was okay with me, because I had experienced that same adoration with Cindy, and I could understand it. That brings to mind the winter that our whole New England area received an overabundance of snow, which meant our four-foot dog retaining fence became a one-foot laughable fence. Brandy's little buddy from next door used to jump the fence to play with our dog, and when she tired would jump back out and trot home. We watched with trepidation as Brandy chased the short-legged dog over to the fence and stopped short of it with her chin on the other side. Amazing! She could have just walked over the fence, but she knew where she belonged, and she stayed on her side! We had many wonderful years of companionship and love with Brandy, and after 14-and-a-half years, we carried our beloved ailing Golden

Retriever to the veterinarian's office for her final visit and patted her and told her how much we loved her, while the needle was slipped into her leg and her life was peacefully ended. We had no regrets, except that she couldn't have lived for another ten years or so, but knowing that so many years with a large dog is a good testament to our caring of her.

Larry and I had talked about downsizing with our next dog, remembering how the arthritis in Brandy's aging hind quarters had made it difficult for her to walk up steps without a little boost. Larry had even built a little platform for Brandy to stand on before gradually easing up the steps to our back deck. On one occasion poor Brandy had slipped on the ice-covered snow in the back yard and didn't have the strength to get up, necessitating Larry to have to lift her up and carry her over to the steps. It was then that we decided our next dog would be a smaller breed, since we'd also be senior citizens when it became a senior canine citizen, needing help with those tough stairs.

Doggy homework once again! We knew we wanted/needed a smaller size dog, we knew that we leaned toward the hunting/retrieving/ working dog breeds, because we had read they're mostly happier to be trained (please, no arguments on this, we've heard it all from fans of the other dog groups), and we didn't want the terriers because they tend to be more active, energetic, noisy breeds.

Finally, the Brittany (upland game bird dog) won out, because they're a smaller package (40 lbs. maximum), don't tend to be yappy, and have the soft, bird-dog retriever mouth. Lucky for us, when we finally had decided to search for a Brittany pup, Fran Phillips had just had a "litter on the ground" in Petersham, a one-hour drive for us. After talking for over an hour on the phone to Fran, we traveled out to Petersham to be checked out by Fran, and to look at the three-week-old babies. Of course, I wanted ALL of them, but in the next four weeks, with advice from a professional consultant, Fran sold us seven-week-old Jessie, who would become our grand-dog for the next 15-and-a-half years.

Oh, did we ever enjoy our years with Jessie! By then our kids had grown and left our home, and we were ready to enjoy this puppy and take part in many activities with her. I immediately signed Jessie up for puppy Obedience classes, and took her on age-appropriate long walks. We found Jessie to be everything we wanted in a companion dog—bright, quick-to-learn, and just a happy, lovable dog to live with. We had been encouraged by Fran to go into Breed competitions, but after going to puppy classes and learning that every weekend there'd be a different dog show to attend (mostly in different states), we just didn't want to tie up our weekends and lives in that manner, since our recreational time was devoted mostly to square dancing, to say nothing of our various church-related activities. We continued with Obedience classes until the next phase would be matches and competitions, again requiring us to travel long distances to far-off states, and at that time Jessie retired from classes and continued to be our much-loved four-legged family member, eager for long walks and fun events. By then I had retired from my secretarial job and was only working part-time, and Larry was headed in that direction. Even though I was around the house and yard more than Larry was, Jessie loved him dearly, although she showed me much affection too. But Larry was her God, and I acknowledged that I placed a close second.

Then came that dreaded day—the final trip to the veterinarian's office, after a year of slowly failing health. As long as she seemed happy and eager for her walks, we kept her going on meds, but there came the day when she wouldn't come out from behind Larry's chair for food or water, and we knew it was time, for Jessie's sake. Her euthanasia was just as peaceful as Brandy's had been. In those intervening 16 years, the procedure had advanced from Brandy lying on the hard metal examining table, to a blanket being spread on the floor for Jessie to lie on, with us holding her head, patting her, talking to her, our tears slowly soaking into the blanket. She was ready, it was time, but we weren't ready, as reconciled to her loss as we were.

However—on the lonely car ride home that day, we started talking about our future with dogs. We had talked many times about not bringing up another puppy who might outlive us, if it lived its normal span, since we were both in our 70s. We had decided to bring up and train a Service Dog puppy, even though we knew we'd have to give it up after a year or so. It seemed to us the right thing to do, since we'd been blessed with four wonderful dogs in our married life.

Chapter 2

BECOMING PUPPY WALKERS

We turned to the Guide Dog Foundation for the Blind, out of Long Island, New York, and amazing as it seems, circumstances were right, and we had a new little puppy two weeks after losing Jessie. Amazing timing! Georgie, a wee ten-week-old Golden Retriever puppy, entered our lives. And what a beautiful baby he was! His coat was a pale gold color, and he wore the traditional Golden Retriever black-rimmed eyes and nose leather, reminiscent of our Brandy. As arranged by the Foundation, we would have the puppy for about a year, taking him to classes to learn to become a Guide Dog for a blind person. We were called "Puppy Walkers" and walk we surely did! Much of the training involved walking our little guy and teaching him all the different commands he'd need to follow in his life of serving a blind or visually impaired person.

We still missed Jessie, but our days were occupied with training this new little life with the guidance of Arlee, the Foundation's trainer who ran the puppy classes. Larry was Georgie's chief trainer, even though I had my hand in his lessons, too. Larry found out that Georgie was very headstrong, VERY headstrong! I thought, in the beginning, it was because Larry had never had much to do with training our other dogs. I was the one who took them to obedience school and mostly walked them, not Larry. Soon I found out that Georgie really was a handful, and we both complained to Arlee. Arlee responded with, "He's just a puppeeee!" to which we responded that we'd never had a puppy like that before, but we acquiesced to Arlee's vast experience of training so many puppies. The next Spring, however, the Foundation had apparently questioned Arlee on how Georgie was doing, and she told them that we were having difficulties with him. Turns out that Georgie's parents were both excellent, proven breeders of successful Service Dogs, so the Foundation decided to breed them together and get a really great litter of intelligent, highly trainable pups. What turned out was a whole litter of headstrong, untrainable puppies whose only interest in life was to do what THEY wanted to do, and not on anyone's command. As Arlee expressed to us, "Breeding dogs is a crap shoot." The whole litter was recalled early, to be turned over to the professional trainers for one last chance to be Service Dogs. Georgie was placed in a trainer's home and after a few months, was rejected from the program, as were his littermates. Georgie was placed with a lovely young family on Long Island, and is a happy, contented much-loved family member now. We're very pleased that Georgie's human mom e-mails us pictures of his activities with his forever family.

What happened to us, dealing with our perceived "failure" of raising a Guide Dog puppy? Larry decided that he didn't want to try another dog right then, much to my chagrin. He gave a million reasons for his refusal to consider another puppy—he was too busy—the house had to be painted, the swimming pool needed constant maintenance, the back yard needed lots of work, etc., etc. I knew that wasn't a valid reason because most of these things never got done anyway, dog or no dog. My otherwise wonderful husband is, and always has been, a procrastinator, and I knew he wouldn't change. He readily starts projects, but has trouble completing them. I will say that the aging pool, with all its leaks popping up to be taken care of, WAS maintained perfectly so that all I had to do was swim laps in it for exercise. Can't fault him for that! However, the painting of the house had been postponed for a couple of years already, and I didn't see it being done this summer, either. I went into a tailspin of despair because I saw that his excuses were just that—excuses, and I couldn't see ahead to any time in the near future that we'd again have a dog in our lives. Georgie left us in May, amid many buckets of tears on my part.

I was lost without a dog in the house, a dog to walk, a dog to sit beside me in the evenings when I was reading or knitting. If you, the reader, aren't a "dog person" there'll be no understanding of this concept, but if the person reading this story IS a "dog person," you'll understand exactly where I was coming from. I was complaining to a couple of women during coffee hour one Sunday after church, and Vera spoke up and said, "You can walk my dog anytime you want. She likes walks and I can't do it anymore." So that started my relationship with Missy, a sweet little mixed-breed something-or-other. I had to drive to Vera's house to walk Missy around the narrow streets of the lake area, and, while I enjoyed the time spent with a dog, we both realized that she didn't belong to me. Something was lacking. Then came the day that Vera said Missy had gone to live with her daughter, and that was the end of my relationship with Missy. About that time, Larry had been talking to a neighbor on our street whose son had found an abandoned husky-type dog and the family took him in. A husky. With no walking manners, no leash manners, nothing except the desire to "keep on mushing" with me being his "sled" at the other end of the leash. I finally got him to walk like a gentleman on my left side, but he always wanted to be tugging at the end of the leash, so it wasn't a very enjoyable walk. This relationship continued through the winter, broken up with many New England-type snowstorms and below-freezing temperatures, not to mention colds which seemed to pull me down to not enjoying the outside temperatures, so it ended that I handed the house key back to the owner and said goodbye to that hairy guy, with no hard feelings on either side, I think. I still wanted my own dog again.

Finally in December I started taking matters into my own hands, working around Larry's reluctance to commit to another dog. I suggested adopting an older dog from a breeder. I looked into many different breeds of dogs, and looked into some rescue organizations, but nothing really "called to me."

I had been e-mailing to our niece, Jackie, who has a Spanish Water Dog, about maybe adopting an older dog whose family could no longer keep it. Hmmm. Maybe that would work for us? If it were older, it probably wouldn't outlive us. During these e-mails Jackie asked if we'd like to watch Tucker for a week when they were planning a vacation where dogs weren't allowed. I was tickled at that prospect. Tucker is about 40 to 50 pounds, is well behaved, and we'd have another dog, if only for a week, to take care of and to take on walks. What an enjoyable week that was! We found Tucker to be a gentleman, and a powerhouse of energy. Accustomed to living with three small kids, he constantly wanted to play, and sometimes we older folks just wanted to sit and relax, but we certainly gave Tucker his exercise, and we enjoyed having a dog in the house again. But still, contemplating an older dog, that route just didn't seem to be a good fit for us.

Chapter 3

ENTER MOSBY

Do you believe that God can work His Way into your life? I believed it before, but now I have proof. I got the idea of having a Ministry Dog through my minister, I called NEADS, and here we ended up with Mosby, the most wonderful dog we've ever owned. I do believe that God was leading us to this wonderful Calling of serving others through a dog. I've never been so gushy about God before, but now I am. I believe that we had to go through the grief of giving up Georgie, the emptiness of having NO dog in our lives for almost a year, to finally experience the joy of living with Mosby. Believe me, I suffered mightily when I bleakly looked forward to living a life with no dog in it. Canines were too important an issue to not have one, for such flimsy excuses as I was getting from my otherwise thoughtful husband. Larry later told me that, even though none of my other thoughts on acquiring a dog appealed to him, as soon as Debbie and I started talking about a Ministry Dog, he felt good about it, and wanted to go ahead with that idea, right from the beginning.

INTRODUCTION TO NEADS
(National Education for Assistance Dogs Services)

My initial phone call to NEADS sounded something like this:

Ring, ring. "Good morning, NEADS, how can I help you?"
"I'd like to inquire about getting a Therapy Dog for the Ministry."
"Well, the Ministry Dogs are only assigned to members of the clergy. Are you a clergy person?"

"No, but, I'm a Deaconess in my church, and one of my duties is to visit sick people and shut-ins, and I thought that a Therapy Dog for the Ministry would help me in that work. Besides, our minister says that we're ALL ministers in our faith!"

"Oh, well, let me see. I'll have to speak to someone about that. We've never had this before." Phone call put on hold. "Hello? I was told that you might be considered, since you do some work that a clergy person would do. Let me have your name, address, and phone number and I'll send you an application form." At least they didn't say NO outright! I felt that I had my foot in the door, so to speak.

E-Mails From The Church Dog

The mail box was scrutinized thoroughly every day until I found the envelope from NEADS, filled it out immediately, and mailed it back, then waited anxiously for the next step in the procedure, which didn't take that long, actually, although at the time it felt like an eternity. My interview appointment was scheduled for February 29th, and I don't remember being that nervous and anxious about any job interview that I can recall.

When I entered the Princeton building at NEADS for my interview with a Kathy Forman, I must admit I was a little bit nervous. What if they decided that I wasn't suitable? After reading about the NEADS program, I really wanted to be a part of it, particularly the Ministry Dog program. It would add so much to our visitations, and a dog would be a part of our lives again, which we both needed so very much. I made up my mind that I had to sell myself to this Kathy Forman and make her see that I really was a reliable, well-qualified person to be entrusted with one of their dogs.

I met with Kathy in a conference room, where she reviewed my application, shuffling the papers on her side of the table while I sat opposite her, trying to keep my knees from knocking together in nervous anxiety. Kathy, a middle-aged lady with a kind face and warm voice, asked me how I'd use a dog if I were to receive one. I told her that it would go to church with us for regular Sunday Worship Services, for special Sunday School programs, any of the church programs where it would be appropriate, but mostly we'd be fulfilling one of my obligations as a Deaconess in my church by visiting patients in hospitals, nursing homes, etc., and a dog would be such an asset, bringing another dimension to our visits and offering some cheer and/or comfort to the sick people. I had heard that for some people, just touching a dog, besides cheering them up, could also lower their blood pressures. Don't know if I bought into that, but surely putting a smile on a sick person's face is a good quality.

Kathy then explained a little about the training process, at which time a dark-haired, slender young lady entered the room and was introduced to me as Christy, one of the dog trainers. I was immediately put at ease by her easy, friendly manner and felt that she'd make a good dog trainer if she was that calm with the dogs. When asked about my past experience with dogs, I told them that we'd had dogs most of our married life, and I'd taken the last two to obedience school and enjoyed that work with the dogs. One, our Golden Retriever named Brandy, was a particular love, although our last one, Jessie, a Brittany, would always hold a special place in our hearts, since she was our "grand-dog", not having any grandkids at that time. I mentioned that I really liked most dogs, but I felt that Goldens might be my favorite breed.

Kathy explained that there are mostly two types of dogs. One dog will enter a room and immediately take charge of the situation, approaching a person with enthusiasm and energy. The other type of dog will meekly enter with its handler and wait to be greeted before approaching anyone. That made sense to me, and I was looking forward to meeting both types of dogs, to see which type they'd think would be best suited for me.

I do believe in love at first sight, although it didn't happen to me in my human relationship with Larry. We met at a stag dance and Larry often said that when he saw me, he first was attracted to my long, dark hair and after dancing with me, he knew I was someone special to him. All I knew was that I enjoyed dancing with him! For me, love grows gradually, it didn't burst on my being with a clap of thunder; instead there was just a gradual warming of the heart, until I knew that he was someone special and I wanted him to be a part of my life forever.

But—when I met Mosby, I heard a thousand angels in Heaven singing the Hallelujah chorus. I said to myself, "Lynda, you've been too long without a dog!—you're a little loopy. This isn't the dog that you'll end up with, so don't fall in love with him. Kathy had said that he was just an example of the kind of dog I might be matched with."

When Christy went to the kennels and returned with this great big Golden boy, I couldn't get out of my chair and over to him fast enough. He was a large dog, with a broad male head, large ears, and his long nose ended with the blackest leather nostrils I've seen in a Golden, matching his black lined eyes. On a Sit command from Christy, his front legs showed what a strong boy he was—they were large, wide, sturdy, and ended in really huge paws. He showed me his Golden smile, tongue hanging down an inch or so in the most appealing way. I approached him quietly, because he didn't know me, extending my closed fist for him to sniff, then I scratched him under his chin for a moment, gradually extending my hand to the top of his head for a good patting and scratching behind his ears. All through this, his doggy smile captivated me. I rubbed his big shoulders, then he surprised me by rolling onto his back for a good belly rub. How wonderful was that! During these heavenly moments, I kept up a patter of talk, telling him how handsome he was, and his smile widened considerably. In too short a time, Christy suggested that we walk up to the training room so that I could walk with him and see what kind of a personality he had and handed the leash over to me. Actually, I knew it was so that they could check me out, how I handled a dog. Up the stairs we went, Mosby walking like a gentleman beside me, as he had been trained to do. As we approached the doors to the large training room, Christy told me that he'd been trained to allow his handler to enter first, then enter only on my command. She said if the opening were large enough to accommodate both of us, he could enter with me.

Once in the room, Kathy suggested that I walk around, giving him commands to Sit, Stand, Walk forward, etc., whatever I wanted him to do. Oh, it was so easy. I felt as though I were floating on a cloud, I was so happy with this big guy. And—I think I was walking to the rhythm of the Hallelujah chorus, still humming in my mind. It was so wonderful, this well-trained dog keeping pace with me. Whatever speed I walked at, he automatically set himself at the same pace, never tugging to surge ahead, or lagging behind. We walked around the perimeter of the room a few times, occasionally doing a "Sit" or "Down" and I never wanted to stop, but all too soon Christy approached me to say that she'd take Mosby back and bring up another dog, a quieter, calmer type. I hugged Mosby and kissed him goodbye on top of his velvety soft head and a little bit of my heart went with him. Yes, Goldens really were special to me, and particularly this one. Chatting with Kathy while we waited for Christy to return with another dog, my mind went back to that gorgeous (no, handsome) Golden dog, and it was hard to pay attention to what Kathy was saying.

Christy soon appeared with a small black mixed-breed dog she called Nora, and as I took the leash from Christy, I was thinking to myself that I wished it were Mosby I was walking with. As little black Nora and I walked along together in the training room getting acquainted, I could hear those angels faintly humming, and I couldn't get the song out of my mind. I tried to concentrate on Nora's personality, but my mind kept skittering back to big, golden Mosby. Nora was a perfect lady, as Mosby had been a gentleman, and I marveled at the training that had gone into the behaviors of these two dogs. If I hadn't met Mosby first, I would have been very happy to think about a dog such as Nora. But Goldens have always held a special place in my heart.

Soon, we headed back down to the conference room for a brief while, and Kathy mentioned that she'd put on my application that I'd prefer a Golden Retriever. I wasn't quite looking at her, but by the tone of her voice, I had the distinct impression that, if I were approved for the program, I'd definitely have a Golden. Little did I know that it would be Mosby, my Hallelujah dog. We ended the meeting with hand shakes and I was told that I'd be informed of their decision in a week or so. Lord, I prayed all the way home that I'd be accepted, and that I'd be matched with a Golden Retriever, just like Mosby.

When I told Larry about the meeting and my experience with Mosby, he smiled as much as I did, and we both hoped that I'd hear from NEADS very soon. Much to our surprise, that actually happened. Christy was the one who called me and told me that I'd been accepted and would come to the Princeton facility for a week of training, including one overnight, and to bring a lunch with me every day, along with comfortable walking shoes. She told me the date and I eagerly said I could come sooner than that, but she said it was OK, but that it was set up already. And, oh, by the way, I'd be matched with MOSBY!!!

As soon as I hung up the phone, I shrieked in utter joy! God is good! All the time!

What a long month that was, waiting for that last week in March when I'd go to "doggy school" and learn everything that Mosby already knew. Every day I woke up thinking that in a month we'd have a wonderful dog in our lives again. Could any month drag by as that seemed to do? It was similar to waiting for a baby to be born, although with this arrival into our lives we knew the exact due date.

Mosby, Three Months Old
Photo by Bonnie Pansa

Chapter 4

MY TRAINING WEEK

Soon (not soon enough, though) that Monday finally arrived when I drove to Princeton, on pins and needles the whole drive, to meet Mosby again. Christy greeted me at the door and led me up to the Training Room to meet Karen, another trainee, who already had her dog, J.R, a black standard poodle. I soon learned that J.R. would be a Therapy Dog for the Classroom where Karen worked with special needs children on the South Shore. (That's the shore line in Massachusetts, south of Boston, for you readers who aren't from Eastern Massachusetts.)

All during that week, while Karen and I learned the commands that our dogs already knew, Christy would intersperse her teaching with talks about keeping our Alpha dominance over the dogs, as their wolf ancestors experienced in the wild. The Alpha wolf (always a male) is the boss, the leader, and all the other wolves in the pack submit to him, just as these dogs would recognize that we humans are their Alpha leader and would be happy to obey us.

Christy said, "In the wolf pack, the Alpha wolf sleeps highest, in a cave or hollow. That's why the dog should never be allowed to sleep on a human bed, but on the floor beside his human, in a lower position."

"The humans should eat their meals first, then feed the dog, because the Alpha wolf always eats the kill first, taking the choicest part for himself."

"When entering a house or walking through a doorway, if it's too narrow for dog and handler to pass through together, the human goes first, then the dog, as the Alpha wolf leads the pack in the wild."

"Don't use his name and then scold him. His name should be used for positive actions, not negative. If he does something inappropriate, say, "eh, eh" in a low, disapproving tone. When it's something positive, then use his name, as in, "Mosby, come." Use an upbeat, higher tone, rather than a low, disapproving "no."

"Don't call him to you for something negative, like bad tasting medicine that you know he won't like. Instead go over to him and bring him to where you want him."

Christy told us to always end the play time on OUR command, not the dog's. When he doesn't want to chase the ball or Frisbee any more and drops down, make it one more time, then end it, so that he knows it was MY choice, not his. I'm always Alpha.

On the recall, unlike the Obedience command I had learned with Jessie and Brandy, Christy told me to keep my hands down in front of me and he'd come up and touch my hands before he sat. This would be critical for someone in a wheelchair, I could see. It was hard for me to remember to keep my hands in front, since I was used to keeping them at my side and not moving them as my dog approached me.

The "up" command is used for placing two front legs on someone's lap or bed, the "jump" command is used for jumping with all four feet, as in jumping into a car. Easy to remember—"up" has two letters, and the dog uses two front feet, while "jump" has four letters and is used when the dog jumps with all four feet. I've never forgotten those commands.

The "My Lap" command is used by a person sitting in a wheelchair or bench, when they want his paws on their lap, instead of when I tell him "up" for another person. The result is the same—a person has dog paws in their lap and dog tongue close enough to wash their face! We had to watch out for that, with our friendly, people-loving guy.

As we entered the training room, I saw a lovely black and white cat casually sauntering across the large floor. Since Mosby didn't pay any attention to it, I assumed that they were quite familiar with each other. Christy explained that he was the training room cat and he lived there. His food and water dishes were on the floor near the refrigerator, always amply supplied with fresh water and kibbles. On that first day, I felt sorry for the poor kitty, not living with a loving family but in this training room. But as the week progressed and I watched the situation closer, I became aware of all the people he encountered during the day. Some of the offices were on this floor, and there was a constant stream of coffee break and lunch break people coming in to use the small kitchen area set off to one side. Each time a person would encounter the kitty, there'd be a pat on his back or under his chin, and some small talk, which kitty seemed to enjoy. I had laid my jacket on a convenient table located near the door, and kitty soon jumped on it, turned around a few times, and made it his bed. Christy told us that he frequently used coats to sleep or lounge in, and if someone didn't want that, they hung their coats on the backs of chairs which were placed along the long side of the room. All that week, I carefully placed my fleece-lined jacket on the table for kitty's bed, and when he saw it placed there, he'd immediately make it his bed, then look up at me for his required patting and love talk from me. If I did it to his liking, then he'd purr me his thanks. During the week I learned that classes were held just about every evening, so I knew the kitty had company then, too. Probably by the time the evening classes were over and the people had left, kitty was happy so see them go so that he'd have some time by himself.

I soon got the message, though—the kitty was helping in the training process of the dogs. He was Christy's co-coach. He kept to the sidelines when the dogs were using the center of the room—sometimes lying on a table, using my coat as a soft mattress, sometimes lounging on the wide window ledges, or occasionally walking around the perimeter of the room to go to his food or water dish, completely ignoring the dogs. Of course, the dogs were supposed to ignore kitty, as they would any interesting thing when they might be working with a human.

I had thought that this week spent at NEADS' training room would be just a review of all the things that I had already learned at Brandy's and Jessie's Obedience classes, but not so at all. I learned so much about "dog psychology" and how to handle many different occasions that might arise when out with a service dog. Even though our two dogs would be used as Therapy dogs and not Service dogs, we were taught everything the people learned whose dogs would be their Service dogs. Interspersed with all the obedience lessons were many helpful tips to make us more aware of how to handle different situations.

On Tuesday morning I arrived prepared to sleep overnight with Mosby always at my side. In addition to my lunch for that day, I brought a covered dish for supper that night. In another building, a nice cape-style house, I was shown the complete layout—an eat-in kitchen, fully equipped, a warm, inviting living room complete with television, jigsaw puzzles to work on, and a bookcase filled up with books for casual reading. Beyond the dining room were three or four small rooms, just large enough to accommodate a single bed, night table, and a mattress on the floor for the dog to sleep on. Tiny, but for one night, fine. The bathroom was fully equipped for a wheelchair person with grips beside the toilet and an extra-wide walk-in shower to accommodate a person in a wheelchair.

I met John, who was leaving the next day to go home to California with his Hearing Dog. John could understand me when I spoke directly to him, but felt that a Hearing Dog would allow him to be alerted to doorbells, telephones, and alarms, which made a lot of sense to me. We chatted on while eating our suppers, then went into the living room after feeding our dogs and walking them to their "fresh-air outdoor bathroom," a fenced-off area specifically designated for dogs, complete with "pooper-scoopers" and trash barrels, conveniently situated equal distance from the training building and the overnight residential house.

I can't say that I spent the entire night sleeping, since I never do in a strange bed, but each time I awoke, I'd reach my hand down beside the bed and feel Mosby's soft fur as he slept on his bed beside me, and it generated such warm, happy feelings, just to know that he was there and always would be, for his entire life.

On Wednesday, because of the sleepover on Tuesday, I went home to Larry with Mosby. I approached the side of the car, as Christy had instructed, opened the door, and gave the prompt "ready?" then the command, "JUMP!" in a firm voice, and before I could take a breath, Mosby was up on the back seat, sniffing all over it, finally settling down before I told him, "Down." He behaved like a perfect gentleman in the half-hour car ride, as I expected he would. I wondered what was going through his mind—he'd been on so many car rides in his short life, sometimes to do errands with his trainers, but sometimes to go to a new place to live for another phase of his training. I told him, "Don't worry, buddy, you're not going anywhere now except to visit your forever home." He reached his head over to the front seat when he heard my voice, just as if he understood what I had said. Who knows? Maybe somehow he did understand.

Arriving in our driveway, I opened the rear door, took his leash, and told him, "Let's go." He promptly jumped down and started sniffing the strange smells on the lawn and plantings, which I allowed for a while. After all, he was here for the first time and had to familiarize himself with these strange surroundings. I spotted Larry in the open doorway and quickly led Mosby in to meet his new "Dad" and to sniff his new home. Our new guy promptly answered Larry's "hello" and started wagging his tail enthusiastically. This started their lifelong love affair. We allowed Mosby to wander around to his heart's content, sniffing out every room, spending more time in some places than others, and we soon realized he was intent on sniffing the places where Georgie and Jessie had spent the most amount of time. We showed him his crate, which had been placed in the back bedroom/computer room, since it was too large to fit anywhere else. I showed him the opened crate, he promptly went inside and just as promptly turned around and walked out! I didn't insist that he should stay in it, but let him wander around and settle in to the new house. That night, and the next morning, as apprehensive as I was about him settling in, it was as if he had always lived there. He knew where his water and food dishes were, he went to the back door to enter the fenced-in back yard, and just made himself right at home. What a guy!

On Wednesday morning Mosby and I drove back to NEADS for more lessons (for me, anyway) and Karen and I learned how to groom our dogs, our legal obligations, and, most comforting, we signed forms that if we became incapacitated and couldn't care for our dogs, that NEADS would find a good "retirement home" for them.

Christy taught us how to recognize the different behavior signals that other dogs we might encounter would use—submissive, as well as aggressive attitudes, and how to handle our dogs successfully in different situations. The training room kitty seemed not to be bothered when Christy would bring in different dogs with different attitudes. He just chose a high perch from where he could lie down and survey the activities.

Sometime during that training week, I had asked Christy if it would be OK to change our dog's name. Since both Larry and I had such a strong affinity for our Scottish roots, and knowing that Goldens originated in Scotland, we thought we'd like to name the dog "Mac" in celebration of his Celtic roots. However, she emphatically replied, "No." The dogs have been named sometimes for various purposes, they've grown accustomed to their names since they first arrived at NEADS, and the name should never be changed. I later learned that sometimes people would donate money in memory of someone, and a puppy would carry that person's name, and in Mosby's case, he was named in memory of a much-loved dog. Don Irving, husband of Karen, who worked in the NEADS office, was a Civil War history buff and had named his dog Mosby, after Colonel John Mosby, whose unit, Mosby's Raiders, would raid and harass the Union lines, capturing arms and supplies as well as soldiers. Colonel Mosby was known as a gentleman in his dealings with his prisoners and others, treating them fairly and with respect and Don named his dog Mosby in tribute to Colonel John Mosby. Since Don annually donated a substantial sum of money to NEADS, he could choose a puppy's name. In memory of his dog Mosby, Don continued that name with our Mosby, hoping that the same good qualities would be carried on in this NEADS puppy. When I heard that, there was no way I would consider changing our dog's name, even though my ancestor fought on the Union side in the Civil War.

We could, if we chose, rename any of the training commands we used, though. Christy said sometimes people would like to use a different language other than English, or a command name they were more familiar with. In my mind was the command "Better Go Now" which NEADS used for the dogs' bathroom call. We had been used to "Get Busy" from when we were training Georgie, the Guide Dog pup. We had used it enough times, Lord knows, trying to get him to do his business on pavement! So I was glad that at least we could use the command that we were more familiar with, even though his name would have to remain "Mosby" and not "Mac."

During that training week, I'd tell Mosby "better go now—get busy" and for a while longer until he settled into our home. Then I just dropped "better go now" and just used "get busy" and he settled right into it as if he had always known that command only.

Christy told us that, although the training would end on Friday with a field trip to a mall, there'd be a "meet-and-greet" on Saturday morning, when we'd get a chance to meet the puppy raisers who played such an important role in our dogs' early training. Needless to say, I was looking forward to meeting them. During the week, I met Karen Irving, when she was working in the office, and she told me the story of their Mosby. Looking back now, both Larry and I can affirm that our Mosby does have some of those characteristics of Colonel Mosby and their dog Mosby—most of the time! Karen was surprised that I knew who Colonel Mosby was, even though I didn't know the full story, but she told me that she and Don would be at the Meet-and-Greet so that Don could see Mosby again, and I was looking forward to meeting Don.

On Friday morning, after my co-trainee Karen and I had signed many papers which basically transferred ownership of our dogs from NEADS over to us, and committing ourselves to always treating our dogs conscientiously and respectfully, we drove our individual cars to a nearby mall for our last lessons and for Christy to make final corrections, if needed. She watched us get our dogs into our cars appropriately, after showing them their outdoor bathrooms, and then we followed Christy to the parking lot at the mall. She explained that we should always try to park near a grassy place, if possible, to give the dogs a last chance to "Better Go Now" (or "Get Busy") before entering the mall building. She watched as we gave our dogs the command to exit the car and walk over to the grassy area. I was reminded of trying to train Georgie, the Guide Dog puppy, to use paved areas, with very little success, and how much easier it was with Mosby on the grassy strip.

Soon we all entered the building and we walked around quite a bit in and out of the little shops, all the while being scrutinized by Christy for our correct behaviors. She knew the dogs would behave correctly, but it was us humans who might need some corrections. Then it was time for the food court, to grab a quick lunch and to use more commands. Both dogs quickly crawled under the tables on command, but of course Mosby was so large that, while his head and

E-Mails From The Church Dog

shoulders were under, his rear end and tail were spread across the narrow aisle to the adjacent table! Christy showed me how to gently use my foot to nudge him a bit more under the table, which, of course, left no room for my feet. Oh well, that's life with a big dog, and I didn't mind the inconvenience one bit. We chatted briefly while eating our lunches, with both dogs quietly resting. They were both good examples of the excellent training they had received as puppies.

After exiting the mall and returning to our cars, Christy watched us place our dogs into their cars, congratulated us, and with hugs all around, we two were on our way to our respective homes, with our wonderful canine companions. The reality of actually having such a handsome, well-trained and loving dog hit me on the way out of the parking lot, and I shed a few tears of happiness, almost missing the ramp to the highway. I sang praise songs all the way home, and I was so eager to see Larry, with this marvelous dog, our own dog!

After waiting for my enthusiasm to bubble over, during supper Larry told me that he had a small medical problem relating to his Coumadin dosage for his atrial fibrillation, which necessitated a call to his doctor with the resulting order, since this was Friday afternoon, that Larry should go to the Emergency Room at the hospital to be checked out.

Of course, all my enthusiasm and bubbling-over joy with Mosby was immediately deflated, with the prospect of Friday evening spent at the hospital. We both decided that Mosby, being so new to us, should stay home from this trip, even though I was encouraged to take him everywhere that I might go.

As expected, Larry's trip to the Emergency Room resulted in an overnight admission to the hospital for observation, and I would pick him up the next morning. Larry was very firm that he wanted me to go to Princeton the next morning for the Meet and Greet, and I did acquiesce, since he was so adamant about this.

On the car drive Friday night from the hospital back to Littleton, I felt reassured that I wouldn't be spending the night alone, but would have Mosby for company. Hey, this would be Mosby's first official function—keeping my spirits up!

Saturday morning found Mosby and me on our way back to Princeton, which I was eagerly looking forward to. We arrived on the campus a bit early, so had our choice of parking spaces, and I firmly offered Mosby his outdoor toilet facility, commanding him, "Better Go Now, and Get Busy" figuring I'd say both commands and eventually lose the first one in preference to the second command.

The Meet and Greet occurred in the overnight house where Mosby and I had stayed on Tuesday night, and as I sat at the kitchen table, Mosby crawled under it, all by himself. Almost as soon as we were settled, Bonnie Pansa and her husband Mike Carbone arrived, with a gift bag for us. In it was something more precious than diamonds—an album of Mosby's baby pictures and all his activities with Bonnie, Mike, and Leah, their teen-aged daughter. What an adorable baby he was! Of course! Leah had compiled the album with little titles and funny adjectives for each picture. I had been told that Mosby had been a prison pup in the Rhode Island prison system, so on the weekends he went to live with Bonnie and family for exposure to events that a prisoner obviously couldn't offer. Sometime in his Rhode Island stay, after going through two released inmates, Mosby finished his stay there full-time with Bonnie, Mike, and Leah, who had painstakingly cataloged each event in Mo's training, even when he was her date for one of Leah's middle school dances. I learned that Bonnie was a teacher at the school where Mike was the principal, so it was a natural occurrence that not just Bonnie's class, but the whole school, was involved in Mosby's training.

Sometime mid-way in Mosby's training, he went to live in Lebanon, New Hampshire, with Ginny and Glyn Reinders, who arrived next for our Meet and Greet. I thought Mosby was excited to see Bonnie, but it was nothing to his reaction to Glyn! After a moment of quiet recognition, our great big golden guy became so excited I thought he was going to puddle on the floor! He tried to jump on Glyn, but remembered his manners, tail wagging furiously, and just about turned himself inside-out in his ecstasy, all the whole time yodeling his joy at seeing Glyn. Glyn said, "Hey, my Frisbee guy! You remembered." Glyn said that he had taught Mosby to catch the Frisbee, and Mo was the best Frisbee dog he'd ever seen. Mo certainly remembered Glyn and Ginny, who, I learned was also a teacher, like Bonnie. I always knew that teachers were special people, but for these two, busy with the school children, to find time to train puppies, I thought was fantastic. Ginny also turned over to me a picture album of Mosby's activities and events while living with them, and it, too, brought tears to my eyes. It reminded me of all the pictures I had taken of little Georgie, our Guide Dog puppy, and how much satisfaction it was for me to send it to Georgie's forever family. What goes around, comes around.

Mosby at 6 months old
[Photo by Ginny Reinders]

Mosby's First Christmas, Duchess, Mosby and Brody
[Photo by Ginny Reinders]

Chapter 5

MOSBY'S FIRST HOSPITAL VISIT

As much as I loved meeting these important people in Mosby's puppy life, I kept thinking in the back of my mind about Larry in the hospital. Soon I extended my heartfelt thanks to these great people and hurried to my car with Mosby for the return trip to Littleton and then straight to the Emerson Hospital in nearby Concord.

This time when I went to Emerson, Mosby was with me. I proudly went to the receptionist's desk, Mosby beside me wearing his Service Dog vest, and asked for Larry's room number. One woman standing in the office doorway walked over to us and asked permission to pat Mosby, which I allowed, of course. After all, this was his job—to make people happy and comfort them where needed. As we walked down the corridor to the elevators, we were stopped a couple of times by people just wanting to pat our golden boy. Mosby entered the elevator just as he had been trained at NEADS, entering with me, then turning around to face the front doors without being told. A man beside us kept eyeing Mosby, and when I told him Mosby could be patted, he smiled and reached out a hand. I learned right away, on our first visit, that it would take more time to get to our destination than we'd spend visiting someone. I couldn't walk by anyone who had that look of wanting to pat Mo but not quite daring to.

Larry was all dressed and waiting for us as he picked up his overnight tote bag. He introduced us to his roommate, who, he said, needed some attention from Mosby. So—this was Mosby's first official act—and he fully lived up to our expectations and hopes for him. We approached John slowly, Mosby sat beside the bed, and on command he put his paw on the bed for John to pat. When that was achieved, I told Mosby, "up" and he put both paws on the bed so that his head could be petted, bringing a large smile to John's face.

When I thought enough time had elapsed, we all said goodbye and good luck to John and headed out of the room and down the corridor to the elevators, constantly being stopped so that someone could reach down and pat Mosby. Outside the hospital, on arriving at the curb to our parked car, I opened the door to the back seat, told Mosby to "jump" and he immediately landed on the seat. He stayed there like a perfect gentleman all the way home. No moving around and trying to jump into the front seat, as our little Jessie used to do!

Chapter 6

SETTLING IN

The next week was a settling-in time for Mosby. I often wondered if he ever considered that this might be his forever home, that he wouldn't just be living with us for a short time and then be transported to someone else's house. After all, in less than two years' time, he'd been taken from his littermates and mom and delivered to the puppy house at NEADS headquarters, then to the Rhode Island prison with weekend breaks with Bonnie Pansa and family, then full-time with Bonnie. From there our intrepid traveler lived in upstate New Hampshire with Ginny and Glyn Reinders, and from there back to NEADS for further evaluation. Did Mosby ever think (if a dog IS capable of that thought process) that his whole life would be spent traveling from home to home to yet another home? I doubt it, but still, I hope he realized somehow, on some level, that our place would be his forever home, and we'd be his forever family from now on.

During Mosby's first week with us, we noticed that he didn't bark when someone came to the door. We were so used to Jessie's furious barking to let us know that someone was there, that it surprised us not to hear anything from Mosby. That lasted just about a week. Apparently Mo thought he was a guest in our home, and then when he figured out it was his home also, he started alert barking. Just as with Jessie and Brandy and Cindy and George before him, the alert barking included anyone walking by on "their" street. But, just as with all his predecessors, Mosby soon learned that when either Larry or I said, "OK, that's all" it was time to stop. We had been alerted, and the canine task was completed. Time to wag the tail at the interloper at the door and make friends.

Part of my e-mail message to my e-mail distribution list announcing Mosby:

"Many of you know that Georgie, the puppy that we raised for the Guide Dog Foundation for the Blind, was returned last May to the Foundation for advanced training. I was looking forward to receiving another puppy to raise, but just before Georgie left us, Larry announced that he wanted a break from puppies and had too much outside yard work to do to devote all the necessary time required in raising and training a puppy. His reasoning was accurate from his point of view, but NOT FROM MINE!!! I disagreed heartily with him, but couldn't budge him. It made me very angry, and cranky—Larry will testify to that, if you ask him. That summer we learned that we weren't getting into the over-55 condo units being built in Littleton, and that was another blow for us. Then—the final straw that broke my camel's back was when our daughter moved back home with two-year-old Mikey. Larry said no way was he going to bring a little puppy into the house with Mikey's inevitable toys strewn all around, just the size for a little puppy to chew on and possibly choke. At that point, I wasn't just angry, but depressed. We have never lived so long without an animal in our house, and for two animal lovers, it was a heavy sentence. Christmas was extremely hard, with no gifts under the tree for either cat or dog. It looked like it was going to be a looong time before another dog came to share our lives.

"It is said that when God closes a door, he opens a window. Our pastor, Debbie, had e-mailed me a picture of a colleague of hers, Renee Kaufman, with a Ministry Dog she had acquired from NEADS (National Education for Assistance Dogs Services). Sometime after the first of the year, when I was cleaning out some old e-mail files, I came across that picture and realized that it had been in the back of my mind for some time. Now, I thought more of it. Larry and I had already been doing some home visitations of shut-ins from our church, along with nursing homes and/or hospitals, to take some of the responsibilities of that off Pastor Debbie, to ease her heavy workload. Then I went into the NEADS website and read about all the different service dogs they train, one of which is Ministry Dogs, trained to go with clergy on their visits to people, also to take part in certain areas of the church ministries.

"After the interview process, and the week of training with Mosby, I finally reached that perfect time in my life—a dog in the house, finally, again!

"Looking back on this whole experience, I felt that the door that God closed had hit me in the face, but I saw the opened window and jumped through it, feet first, and landed upright, on my feet."

Chapter 7

HONORING OUR SCOTTISH HERITAGE

On Sunday afternoon, April 6, Mosby experienced the lovely music of the Great Highland Bagpipes, probably for the first time in his life. We had been planning for some time to attend a Kirkin' o' the Tartans ceremony in Taunton, about a half hour from Littleton. Tartan Day, which is celebrated on April 6th, not by chance, falls on the day the Declaration of Arbroath, a document declaring Scottish independence, was prepared at Arbroath Abbey in the year 1320. It was in the form of a letter submitted to Pope John XXII, dated 6 April 1320, intended to confirm Scotland's status as an independent, sovereign state and defending Scotland's right to use military action when unjustly attacked. Many Scots and people of Scots descent gather to show their pride in their clan tartan by bringing them to a worship ceremony (kirk is Scots Gaelic for church). Many say this declaration was the model for our own American Declaration of Independence. Unfortunately for Scotland, it didn't work out so well for them, and Scotland is still part of Great Britain.

Upon arriving on a side street by the church, I opened the car door and told Mosby, "Let's go." Of course, he immediately jumped onto the sidewalk and started looking around. A piper was nearby practicing his tunes, Mosby saw and heard him, and didn't blink an eye. Of course, he was too interested in all the activities near him to Get Busy, but he had done his business in the back yard prior to our leaving Littleton, so I wasn't concerned. We followed many tartan-wearing people into the church and took a pew in the back because I wasn't at all sure of Mosby's reaction to the bagpipes inside a rather small building. Mosby, clad in his NEADS Service Dog vest and a doggie scarf made from my Clan Sutherland tartan, immediately laid down at our feet, claiming the space under the pew directly in front of us. I was thrilled to see that he remembered his training and related the pew seats to tables, knowing that he should lie quietly underneath.

Very soon after our arrival, the kilted clan representatives, all wearing their clan tartans and bearing their clan flags, gathered in the back of the church, following a proud piper. Soon the bagpipe tune of *Scotland the Brave* could be heard as the piper led the procession to the altar area of the church, where they remained for the short ceremony honoring the clans and Scotland. I looked around me at the gathered people and saw very few who were not wearing some sort of tartan, whether it was a man in a kilt, or woman in a kilted skirt or scarf, or at least a pin. I was quite pleased that Mosby was showing his Scottish roots by wearing his Clan Sutherland tartan scarf, matching my own Sutherland scarf and pin. I was also pleased with his manners—he never barked when the pipes and kilts proceeded up the aisle almost under his nose! He was very alert, but not noisy, much to my relief. During the social time afterwards in the church hall, I had to be careful to steer Mosby away from the dropped crumbs on the floor. Apparently he didn't remember his training about not taking things from the floor, especially not when those enticing crumbs smelled of Scottish shortbread or scones!

So—Mosby's first Scottish-related outing, and he certainly lived up to my expectations. In the church hall he behaved like a perfect gentleman when the people would approach him and inquire about his vest or why he was there and either Larry or I would tell them of his job of comforting people and giving them a lift. "Well, he certainly does that. I just love to pat him!" one woman said, as she balanced a cup of tea and shortbread cookie with one hand while patting Mosby with the other. I was holding my breath for fear that Mosby would try to grab that cookie that was so close to his long nose, but he didn't, although I noticed that his eyes never left the cookie until the woman walked away with it. Both Larry and I were so relieved to see that Mosby behaved well "under fire" more or less.

Chapter 8

GINNY'S PHOTOS

I found Ginny Reinders to be an excellent photographer—in addition to being an enthusiastic puppy raiser. Each time I opened an e-mail from her, there'd be photo attachments of all her current dogs in action, or all lined up to celebrate something—Easter, Christmas, St. Patrick's Day, a birthday of one of the dogs. They'd all be sitting in a row wearing party hats, costumes, doggy tee shirts, and all would be so patient together to have their happy moments captured by the camera in the hands of their foster mom. I was amazed at the patience it must have taken to get them all to cooperate! Until Mosby arrived in our lives, I couldn't get one of our dogs to wear a party hat for more than two seconds. As soon as I stepped away from her, Jessie would paw at her head and shake it until the hat would drop off. No matter how patiently I'd say, "Stay, stay, stay" that darned costume would leave the dog. And here Ginny has six dogs all patiently sitting in a row, waiting for that flash of the camera to light up their eyes! I'm forever grateful for Ginny for her patience in teaching Mo because he's the first of our dogs to be happy about wearing a party hat or antlers at Christmas time, and a tee shirt for the Souper Bowl Sunday celebration after church, when he helped raise food for our local food bank on Super Bowl Sunday. Thanks, Ginny!

Duchess, the Easter Bunny
[Another Ginny Reinders photo]

Chapter 9

MOSBY GOES HI-TECH

Our church has a beautiful, informative website with links to a variety of interesting facets of the church, both ongoing programs and single events. Our talented pastor, Debbie, gave Mosby his own page on this website, and since that time many of Mosby's happenings can be found on his own page.

Very soon after his arrival in our home, Mosby acquired his own e-mail address and started writing his own messages to people. I should say, Mosby dictated his messages to his Mom, who did the actual typing, prompted by his remarks to her. Mosby's first e-mail message was an article for the church newsletter informing everyone of his Commissioning Service, which was held during a Sunday morning worship service:

Mosby's Commissioning Service

Hi—I just wanted you-all to know how much I appreciated the Commissioning Service that Pastor Debbie led for me and my mom and dad (Lynda and Larry Fisher) on Sunday, April 13. This was a milestone in my life.

Many of you don't know that after I left my mom and brothers and sisters, I went to prison in Rhode Island. Sounds bad, but it wasn't. This really great inmate taught me all sorts of things I'd need to know in later life, and I'm grateful for the knowledge I acquired while living there. On the weekends, I lived with a family outside the prison walls where they did all kinds of neat things with me, to get me used to all sorts of experiences—grocery shopping, trips to the hardware store, visiting an animal petting zoo, train rides. The list goes on and on. Then, after a while I lived with a family in northern New Hampshire, where I learned to be a Frisbee boy. So, you see, I had a pretty interesting early life. When I had matured enough to be over the teenage rebellious stage, I lived at a place called NEADS (National Education for Assistance Dogs Service) in Princeton, where I really learned things—like college stuff, where before I was just learning elementary and high school lessons, all in preparation of a lifetime of serving someone in some capacity which NEADS would decide I was best suited for.

Then—my most wonderful experience—I was introduced to Lynda! It was love at first sight for both of us. We both could tell it was a forever connection, that we were destined for each other, and that God had a Hand in this. After a while, Lynda came to the NEADS headquarters so that she could learn everything I already knew, and we even had an overnight together. I heard her tell her classmate that I was the only guy she'd ever spent the night with, other than her husband, Larry (now my dad).

We went home together at the end of that week, and immediately I was immersed in my life's work—serving people. Dad had an emergency trip to the hospital that night, and we went to take him home the next day—my first hospital visit. I could tell Dad's roommate needed a sympathetic touch, and I visited him for a while, offering my paw which he readily patted, and he even needed to pat my silky head.

I've been to the monthly ham and bean suppers that the church puts on and made the rounds of all the tables, chatting with the folks who wanted to pat me. They're all such nice folks! I've been to the church worship service, and I can tell you, I love the friendly people there, especially the kids. They ask for my paw, and I'm happy to oblige them, offering them a silly grin, too.

My first assisted living visit brought me to Ayer, to Kaarlo and Elsa Manni, who just loved me, almost as much as I adored visiting with them. As we were leaving, my mom told Elsa to pat her lap (she was sitting in her wheelchair) and say, "my lap" which she did, and I immediately responded as I was taught, and placed my two front paws on her lap. The unexpected thing was that when she grinned happily and giggled, I lost control for a minute and licked her face. We all ended up laughing about that. I can hardly wait to return to visit them, but I know there are lots of other folks in the church that I can visit and spread some of my good cheer.

The Commissioning Service was really moving, and I got right into the spirit of it. I gravely listened to Pastor Debbie ask us to minister to people who need us, and when my folks responded to her charges, I silently agreed also. I was quite happy and felt really accepted when she asked Mom and Dad what name I was given, and Mom responded, "Mosby Mac Fisher." Debbie explained that Mac is Scots Gaelic for "son," which is what I am to them, now. Since my ancestors originated in Scotland, probably alongside their ancestors, I'm quite proud to have Mac as my middle name. This naming is done, I understand, when new parents bring their little ones to church to be Christened and Dedicated to God, and I felt especially welcomed when Pastor Debbie took my leash and walked me up and down the aisle so that people could see me up close and reach out and pat me, just as she does with the newly dedicated human babies.

My emotions are just overflowing right now—I know my adopted family loves me, and I know that I'm truly loved and accepted by my church family. Somewhere in the Bible, there's something said about "Your people will be my people, and your God will be my God." Well, even though I'm not of their race, these church people have taken me, a Golden Retriever, into their hearts and made me feel so welcomed, that I'm going to work my tail off to be deserving of their love and esteem.

Arf,

Mosby Mac Fisher, Therapy Dog for the Ministry

And dedicated Baptist Canine

Chapter 10

MOSBY MAKES THE NEWSPAPER

We have a terrific local weekly paper, The Littleton Independent, full of local news and many character stories. One of the contributing writers is Jeanne Bracken, a published author, whose wit and fine humor show through in every one of her articles. Jeanne had interviewed us when we had Georgie, so I called her to see if she wanted to write something about Mosby. Of course, she did! We were thrilled, because it would give Mo some excellent publicity for his role of Therapy Dog for the Ministry, and people reading the article might give us some leads on people to visit in hospitals, nursing homes, etc. We knew our own church folks would eventually run dry and we'd need some additional people for us to keep on with our visitations.

On April 30 Jeanne appeared at our door, to be greeted enthusiastically by Mosby, who turned on his charm and completely captivated Jeanne. Her article was just as I expected it to be—casually informative and full of humor. Mo's story was published and out to the public one Thursday, and then the phone started ringing. But it was from people we already knew, and who already knew about Mosby! Since that time, though, we have spoken to different people at some local events who mentioned the article, so I knew that others, also, knew about Mosby and would spread the word about him and his service. Good publicity for Mo!

Chapter 11

FROM HOUSE TO CONDO

Sometime in this summer, we found we really could move into one of the condos which we had been looking at last year, with a possible moving date in September. This set us in a whirlwind of sorting out things we couldn't keep in smaller digs, packing, taking items to the consignment shop for sale, or the Council on Aging thrift shop for donations to that cause, and much paperwork. The accumulation of 46 years of living in the same house was amazing!

The grounds had to be spruced up, some plants dug up and discarded or moved around, and we hired a company to paint the house. Ah, painting the house. Larry's main reason, when he said he didn't have time to train another puppy, because the house had to be painted. As I knew would happen, the house never did get painted, and some pros were hired to do the work this year. I had to bite my tongue not to mention it at the time, but I never forgot this was the main excuse for not acquiring another dog after Georgie left us. But maybe God had hatched a devious plan—maybe God figured that'd keep us dog-less until Mosby was ready to be born? After all, if we had taken another Guide Dog puppy at that point, we'd never have turned to NEADS, and Mosby would never have entered our lives. Terrible thought!

Chapter 12

GRADUATION DAY

NEADS holds graduations three times a year for the teams of dogs and handlers who've just gone through their program, and Mosby's and my turn came on June 22nd, in Boston. We don't miss too many Sundays of worship service at First Baptist Littleton, but on this day we had to miss church to be able to ride on the bus with some of the other NEADS teams and assorted support people.

On the drive to the Princeton campus where we'd board the bus, I remarked to Larry that Mosby didn't seem as excited as we were for this big day. Mo did his usual dog-nap on the ride, waking up just as we entered the driveway at NEADS. Immediately he became alert, hearing and smelling the other dogs already there. NOW—he was excited! The bus was already there, being boarded by dogs and their humans.

First, I offered him his outdoor bathroom, knowing it would be a long drive into Boston and not knowing what kind of landscape might be there, suitable for a toilet. Of course, as I expected, with all the excitement, he had no interest in his outdoor toilet facilities. I told him, "OK, big guy, you might have to hold it for a long while!" As we boarded the bus, I let Mosby enter first, so that I could climb the stairs without an enthusiastic dog behind me, and Mosby immediately made friends with the driver while I encouraged my reluctant knees to make the steps. I thought, how am I going to get him down the aisle now? He's turned around completely, facing me! Then I remembered the command that Christy had taught me—"Back!" I firmly and authoritatively told him, "back" not knowing if that command would be remembered. Amazingly, Mosby didn't hesitate, but took two steps backward down the narrow aisle of the bus, ignoring the dogs sitting on the floor beside their handlers! Amazing! We "backed" halfway down the bus until an empty seat appeared, and I pointed to it, commanded "under" and immediately Mosby nosed under the seat, as if he had been doing it every day since he'd left NEADS! I was completely amazed. Didn't think it would work, really. I then decided that, yes, my dog was really smarter than I was. Or, at least, his memory worked better than mine.

Mosby continues this story, since his memory actually IS better than mine:

"Before our graduation ceremony, all the graduating pups were gathered together for a group photograph, taken by Win Handy, whom I remembered from my training days in Princeton. Wherever Mom and I went that week, Win followed us around, snapping impromptu pictures of us doing various duties, even our outdoor bathroom duties. I understand these snaps are used by NEADS in promotional material, and probably other uses, too. Now here we were, all together, for our formal graduation picture, all posed on a wide staircase, some sitting, some lying down, so that we all were visible. Randy Price, our emcee, was sitting at the top, holding his own personal pup, whom we welcomed into our midst, even though she wasn't receiving a diploma that day.

Later in that month when Mom and Dad received the picture in the mail, Mom requested two extra copies so that she could send them to my puppy raisers, Auntie Bonnie Pansa and Auntie Ginny Reinders. This resulted in the following e-mail from Auntie Ginny:"

Hi Lynda—

YES—we received it on Thursday. THANK YOU! . . . . On Friday I helped a friend do a private dog consultation—Saturday Brody had agility class—then today Blue had his agility class. I haven't been on the computer much as we've been sooooooooooo busy. I'm getting my house organized (a <u>never</u> ending process)—my classroom set up and storing things for my parents who are in the process of moving up here to an assisted living place from Florida.

Glyn still misses the Mos so much. He likes Blue a lot—but Mosby and he really bonded together.

Please let us know if you're ever up this way. We have plenty of empty rooms and would love to have you ALL.

Thank you again for the graduation picture of the Mos!

Ginny & Glyn

To Ginny Reinders—Aug 18 2008

I'm so glad that you did receive the graduation picture—the Mos is the handsome guy in the front row.

Larry and I agree with Glyn—Mosby is a special guy, definitely. I can appreciate where Glyn is coming from, but he should be assured that we well realize what a special gem we have, and that we appreciate his presence in our lives. We do feel that God gave us a special gift, and we treasure him most definitely. And, Mosby has made a large impression in our church family, and actually the Town of Littleton. Everybody knows him by name (even though they don't know ours), and he's a minor celebrity in town. But, in the evening, when we have him to ourselves in the living room, we feel we are so blessed with his head and paws resting on our feet. We've had lots of dogs in our lives, not as many as you folks have, but still a goodly number, and Mosby is far and above the most unique guy with all his many talents. As our minister says, "God is good." To which we reply, "All the time."

We have our house on the market to sell, since we're moving into a small over-55 condo development going up in Littleton, and are busy packing up 46 years of accumulation in our present house, which will keep us VERY busy this whole summer and probably into the fall, so we're not taking any trips this summer.

In September we'll take an extended weekend trip to the New Hampshire Highland Games in Loon Mountain, and that's the only time we'll be away from the house. The best thing about this condo association is that we own the land (quite unusual), so we can install a fence for Mosby. It won't be a large area, but at least he can run free off-leash and chase his beloved Frisbee.

I'll keep in touch with you and will probably send many pictures of Mosby at the Highland Games.

ljf

To Ginny—Aug 23, 2008

Today, while a realtor was showing our house and we had to leave the premises, we took a drive down to Gemini Dog Training, which is just down the road and around a corner from us. There are usually a couple of dogs being walked from their doggy day care, so we thought we'd see some dogs, but to our surprise, we discovered that Gemini was hosting some sort of Agility competition. All sorts of campers and tents were strewn all around the grounds, and we HAD to stop to shmooz with the dogs.

We chatted with someone with a couple of Brittanys (we're sort of drawn towards them, in memory of our beloved Jessie) and it turns out she's a trainer for NEADS and works with the prison systems.

As luck would have it, nothing was going on with the competitions, but it was fun to chat with the different dog owners, and Mosby had a rare opportunity to meet different dogs. He's a little bit lacking in his doggy skills, just because we don't have many dogs in our neighborhood, and he doesn't have much of an opportunity to see other dogs.

We're going back tomorrow and hope we get to see some Agility competitions.

When we get to our condo, we'll own the land, so we can put up a fence surrounding our property, and Larry was talking about getting some agility equipment to work with Mosby. If all goes well, we might take the courses that Gemini offers. You folks KNOW that the Mos loves that kind of stuff!

ljf

Chapter 13

NEW HAMPSHIRE NATIONAL GUARD DEPLOYMENT

9/3/2008

Subject: A Military Ministry Dog Event

Hi, Pastor Deb—I hope all is well with you. I'm writing to you about my most interesting day yesterday.

It was my brother-in-law Steve's Deployment Ceremonies at the New Hampshire National Guard Armory in Concord, NH. We all rode up together in Laurie's car—Laurie driving and Mom in the navigator's seat in front, the three guys (Dad, Steve, and little Mikey) in the back seat, and I, in the place of honor—the wayback. They gave me the most spacious part of the car, and I did take advantage of it, sprawling out and taking up all the space. I had wanted to try out our "way back" before, but the time never was right. I found it quite comfortable and plenty roomy. Stretching out fully and relaxing, I found it to be a luxurious way to ride, and I wish my folks would let me ride there in their car, instead of the back seat. After all, I've pretty much covered that area with my wonderful dog hairs, in spite of the quilted cover they've placed there. Now it's time to cover the wayback with my beautiful hairs.

When we arrived at the entrance gate, I was snoozing a bit, but woke up when I heard Mom explain, "Hey, this must be the right gate—it says 'Alpha Gate' and we're all Alphas except for Mosby." I was hoping I wouldn't have to find another gate to enter, but I guess the guard thought there were enough Alphas in the car to let us through. Doggone, it was a close call, though.

We arrived with time to spare because Steve had to be there early, so I had ample opportunity to cruise around, spreading my personal good cheer to everyone, mostly the kids. They all wanted to pat my silky head, and Mom had to tell their parents that I was the kind of guy they could pat, unlike my Service Dog buddies, who are untouchable. I thought, because of the reason for the ceremonies (departure), that it would be a solemn time, but the kids kept everything in a light mood, and the leaders did on purpose, I think, just so the kids wouldn't feel sad.

Lynda Reynolds Fisher

The ceremonies themselves were fairly short, over in well under an hour, and I was glad. There were so many Alpha-type people up there on the stage giving speeches that I felt I was the only one who wasn't Alpha. There were Lt. Colonels, Sgt. Majors, etc., and I was afraid they'd start barking orders at me any moment. I stayed pretty close to Mum's chair and she said I behaved very well during the talks, just as I do in church. When everyone stood for the singing of the Star Spangled Banner, Mom had me stand, too, and I know she was pleased that I stood so still.

Afterwards, Governor Lynch made many photo-ops with the military personnel and their families, and I wanted to get in on it, but Mum kept me back, telling me it was a time for the families and that didn't include me. Mikey actually was carried around to the flags on the stage by the Governor, and his picture will be in the Union Leader (a NH newspaper).

Some of the guys and gals in uniform came over to pat me and talk to Mum, and I felt good about that. After all, that's the main purpose I was there—in case somebody needed a little lift to their spirits. The day went well, overall, even though I didn't get to partake of any of the snacks that the ladies of the volunteer organization had laid out for the military personnel and their guests. Geez, I was a guest, too, but Mum didn't see it that way!

The ride back to Massachusetts and Townsend was a good snooze time for me, then we hopped into our car to get me home for my overdue supper. And then—they left me home and went out the door to go to Steve's Mom's house for a late pizza supper! Something was said about Nana's sick kitty not dealing well with me, which I totally don't understand. I'm the friendliest guy around, and anyone will tell you that, but they didn't see it that way. It was just as well I stayed home, because I was pretty tuckered out, and I have to conserve my energies because tomorrow we have to get up early and go to Manchester Airport to see Steve and his buddies off on a plane.

So—that was my day yesterday—my first military event. Except for having too many Alpha types all in the room, it was very nice, and I think I did my duty by giving so much of my love to everyone.

Mosby Mac Fisher
Military Ministry Dog

E-Mails From The Church Dog

In a message dated 9/3/2008:

Hi Mosby,

You are a busy dog and you have a great sense of humor. I am glad to hear you kept your Alpha tendencies in check with all those military personnel around. It was very touching to hear about the service men and women coming over to see you before you left. Do you have any pictures of that? I would like to see those.

Mr. Gibson said he is proud of you!
Well, keep up the good work
Pastor Debbie

Sept 4, 2008

We all drove up to the Manchester, New Hampshire airport to say goodbye to Steve. His mom came with us, and I graciously allowed her to use my back seat, next to Mikey's carseat. I'd rather ride in the wayback anyway so that I can fully stretch out and relax, getting a little snooze time in. I find it best to just take a dognap when the humans are driving anywhere.

We arrived at the airport before Laurie, Steve, and Mikey, but had to wait at the Southwest ticket counter until Steve arrived to show them his travel orders and check us all in. While we were waiting, I did my job and cozied up to a few people to offer them my love and affection.

I could spot the departing military personnel right away, even though they wore civvies instead of their uniforms, because those military haircuts stand out. The only ones who wore uniforms were the Alpha guys,—the leaders—Major General Clark and three or four others. They weren't leaving, but were there to send the guys off.

Eventually, after we had showed the ticket person our identification, we were all issued passes and walked upstairs to the security area. I really wanted to try the escalator, but Mom said no, she'd rather I did the stairs with her. There was a really huge German Shepherd Security dog escorting his human, and I wanted to let him know that I was Alpha and that I also had a Mission to accomplish today, but Mom told me to "stand down" and mind my p's and q's, whatever they are.

The looping line for the Security check took forever to move forward, and I spotted a little girl there, about ten years old, crying her little eyes out. I decided that I'd give her some of my comforting presence, but—*my first failure*—she didn't want any part of me and turned away towards her mom for comfort, still softly crying. I could tell my Mom felt badly for her, so I offered Mom my paw, which she accepted and then patted me. I know I wasn't there to comfort her, but at least I did my job on someone. But that was my only failure. Everyone else was happy to pat me and left me with a smile on their faces.

My opinion of the Security check is not that great. I was truly insulted when the officer asked Mom to unsnap my leash to have it X-rayed. Yikes! What do they think I could smuggle in with that? But it has a metal clasp, so they had to check it out. Then I had to walk, unleashed, through the X-ray gate and I surprised them when I kept on walking ahead. Laurie grabbed my collar, though, because she could see I was just a tad confused. Mom followed right after me and quickly attached my leash again, to everyone's relief.

We had a bit of a wait for departure, so there was a lot of shmoozing around with everyone, and I could see they were getting a little bit tense as the time for departure neared. Then the announcement came that everyone was dreading to hear. "Would the military personnel who are departing for duty please form a line to enter the plane first?" Steve hugged and kissed everyone goodbye, and as he walked into the line, he turned back for one last kiss on top of Mikey's head. When it was her turn, I heard Mom tell him to "keep safe" and "go with God." I looked up at Mom in time to catch the glimmer of a tear in her eye.

The uniformed Alpha leaders lined up beside the entrance tunnel and each soldier shook hands with the lineup as a few words were passed from the Alphas to the departing warriors before they were swallowed up in the tunnel. I stood at attention, as directed by Mom. Then, as Steve shook the first extended hand, Mom started clapping, and pretty soon everyone standing around was applauding too. I heard Mom tell Dad afterwards that she thought of clapping earlier, but wasn't sure if it was the right thing to do, and wondered if she'd be alone, and that would be embarrassing. But then when it was Steve's turn, she couldn't help it, and she clapped as long as he was in sight, until he entered the tunnel to go to the plane. I think everyone was choked up with emotion at that moment, until the last soldier had passed out of sight.

We wanted to wait until the plane taxied off, just so that Mikey would know that Daddy was actually on his way. Of course, there was a bit of a wait, but soon the workers drew the entrance tunnel away and a special truck pushed the plane into the taxi lane. Then the plane started slowly on its way until it was out of sight.

The car ride home to Littleton was filled with subdued riders. We all had our own thoughts to deal with about this departure. I've decided that it's probably almost as hard for the loved ones who are left behind as it is for the warriors who are traveling in harm's way. Different, but still hard. I think I have my Ministry Dog work cut out for me.

Mosby Mac Fisher
Military Liaison Ministry Dog

Chapter 14

VISITS TO LIFE CARE CENTER OF NASHOBA VALLEY, IN LITTLETON

9/12/08

Hi, Pastor Deb—

My schedule has become just as busy as my Mom and Dad's! I've only now been able to pause in my busy day to write you about my Ministry visits. On Wednesday, I took Mom and Dad to Life Care Center on Foster Street. I was hoping to see Coda and Charlie, but the receptionist said they were on vacation this week. Doggone! It's always a good time when I can chat with other four-footed people, especially Golden Retrievers, my own kind.

We found Phyllis Wallace and had a good time with her. Mom kept me a little further back from Phyllis than I liked, but she didn't want me to accidentally step on the bad foot, and we didn't know what other sensitive areas Phyllis might have because of her fall. In spite of the fact that she looked thinner and more frail than last time, Phyllis appeared to be in good spirits, and right on top of things mentally, which was a blessing. She kept on forgetting people's names that she was talking about and blamed it on the drugs she's taking, but Mom told her that she and Dad have the same problem sometimes, without any drugs at all! Personally, I never have problems like that.

We feel that Phyllis will be there for a while for physical therapy alone, but we do hope that she'll eventually be back home at the Mill Pond site. She's such a nice, cheerful person! Our visit was just starting to wind down, when Aunt Bobby appeared in the doorway, which startled me a bit, and I let out a little whuff when I recognized her and had to wag my tail at her and try to grab her hand with my teeth, which is just a little love nip for me, but Mom doesn't like it. Of course, I recognized her from church and also when she brings granddaughter Errika over to play with me, so I felt like we were having a little party. But Mom and Dad decided it was time to leave to give the two ladies time to chat.

Our next visit was to Jo Adam in the Alzheimer's wing. After an attendant let us in, we found our way to the dayroom where a lot of the folks were sitting in their *wheelchairs watching television. Jo was pointed out to us, so we went over to her, and found it was a sad visit. She's failing enough that she didn't recognize any of us, and my feelings would have been hurt when she didn't recognize me, but I know it's just her illness. Mom said later that she said a little faux pas (whatever that is) by asking Jo if she remembered us, which of course she didn't. That little slip won't be repeated. Then the attendant asked us to stay and visit with some of the others, which I was quite eager to do. I saw some looking at me with smiles on their faces and outstretched hands, so Mom led me over to them and they patted and smiled, and some tried to talk to me, even. When we stepped back out of the room, by the nurse's station, a very old lady was sitting in a wheelchair, and we were told that "Granny" was 109 years old! She smiled when she saw me and didn't want to stop patting my silky head. When she told me that she had had a dog when she was young, Mom asked her the dog's name, but she just kept repeating that she had a dog, and that's all. I felt sad about that, but Mom later reminded me that I was doing her a little good just by sitting still and letting her pat my head. Mom didn't want to leave her as long as she was enjoying me, but the attendant looked like she was waiting to take Granny somewhere, so off we went, after we were unlocked from that wing. The nurse told us to come back anytime, because even if it's just for a short visit, I bring a spark of life back to some of the folks there.*

While driving home, Dad told Mom that he liked the visit to the Alzheimer's wing, even though it was sad, because the folks there really seemed to enjoy our visit, so we'll probably go there again when we visit Life Care Center.

Sometimes I feel that God is really leading me where He wants me to go, because there are times when I don't feel inspired to go, but afterwards I'm so glad I did! Mom and Dad feel the same way, I know.

Mosby Mac Fisher—Arf!!!

Chapter 15

NEW HAMPSHIRE HIGHLAND GAMES

Date: 9/24/2008

Ministry Dog Mosby Mac Fisher Goes to the Highland Games

Och! Such a bonnie weekend! The pipes, the drums, the braw laddies strutting proudly in their kilts brought joy to my heart and a wag to my tail. And the ladies weren't far behind their men—all demonstrating their clan pride by wearing tartan scarves, kilted skirts, and clan pins. The weather, unlike that in Scotland most times, was sunny with a cool breeze blowing, and I, aah, I, was beside myself in my own Scottish pride.

You see, many, many years ago, Scottish Lord Tweedmouth desired a certain kind of retriever for his hunting estate on the River Tweed, so he crossed a curly-coated retriever with a yellow dog, and the resulting pups were my ancestors, so the stories tell. Yes, I, a handsome Golden Retriever, descend from Scots ancestors also, just as do my Mom and Dad, Lynda and Larry Fisher, their son Scott, and their daughter Laurie and her son, Mikey. So—we all had something to celebrate at the 33rd New Hampshire Highland Games held on the slopes of Loon Mountain in Lincoln, New Hampshire, on the weekend of September 19-21, 2008.

Of course, my humans had all visited there many times in past years, but for me, being only two years old and adopted by them this past spring, I experienced this wonderful weekend for the first time, and all the activities will remain in my mind forever, just as my heart beats in time with the pipes and drums. Poetic phrasing? Aye, but it's the truth.

There was no problem as I entered the shuttle buses each time to be taken to the mountain, because even though the driver emphatically stated, "no pets allowed" my Mom would say, "he's a Service Dog" which turned the driver's frown into a smile, and we were welcomed onto the bus. Disembarking and then walking over the bridge spanning the tumbling Pemigewasset River and onto the grounds brought me to the most awe-inspiring weekend of my young life.

We walked all over the area, visiting the vendors' many tents, the sheep dog trials held on Friday, the Athletics Heavy Events on Saturday and Sunday, and stopping at the clan tents. Of course, as my Mom and Dad have found out, they can't walk anywhere without pausing to talk with folks about my service as a Ministry Dog. People would hesitate, knowing they shouldn't pat a working Service Dog, but desiring to touch me. My Mom would tell them that I'm the only Service Dog that can be patted while working, because my work IS to give them a little joy, just as when I'm working and we visit sick humans in the hospital or nursing home, spreading my comforting love all over.

This weekend, besides my working vest, I wore my red backpack containing my collapsible water bowl and drinking water, plus a packet of little plastic bags for when I have to "do something" and my responsible owners pick up after me. This was all topped off by my Clan Sutherland tartan scarf which I proudly wore around my neck.

Of course, Mom had to head to the Sheep Dog Trials first thing, and we made it with only a few stops for people to pat my silky head. However—and I don't understand this—when I showed my enthusiasm by barking at the Border Collies herding the sheep through the obstacles, it displeased my folks to the extent that they decided to leave the hill. Gee—I was only cheering my cousins on!

The vendors' tents were placed all along the walkway road, and Mom and Dad took turns holding my leash so that I wouldn't get squeezed with all the folks looking for bargains. Very considerate of them, I thought. Every time Mom would break away from a tent, there'd be Dad holding my leash and surrounded with folks patting me and talking about the NEADS program, where I was trained for my life work as a Service Dog for the Ministry.

A little lassie approached us, her long hair pinned up on top of her head, sporting some makeup on her already-beautiful face, and wearing a traditional Highland dancing dress and shoes. I could tell she was a little nervous, so I reached my head to her and when she patted my shoulder, she broke out into a timid smile. When asked if she had competed yet, she replied, "No, and I'm a little nervous about it." I was glad I was there to comfort her a little. As she walked away with her parent, her step was a little lighter, I think.

Seeing this encounter, a young lassie approached us and asked if her grandmother could pat me, and that was another Service moment for me. Grannie was in a wheelchair, and I almost put my front feet on her lap as I was trained to do on command, but Dad held me back, feeling that my feet might be dirty, and the lady might not be happy. But the smile on her face as she patted me told us that she was delighted to see me.

It took us quite a while, what with all the stopping for folks, to make our way to the Clan Sutherland tent, but eventually we found my Mom's clan. Nice folks! I could tell they were dog people right away. This was a rest stop for us, while the Sutherlands, Bob and Barb, and Peter, John and later Jane, tended to the many folks who stopped by our tent. I say "our" because they say I'm a special member of Clan Sutherland. The next time my mom pays her dues, she says she'll make it a family membership and include me as well.

Lynda Reynolds Fisher

Imagine that! If there were a Clan Tweed, I'd want to join that one, too. This year, Bob was able to have a double tent, which was ample room for the Saturday pot-luck lunch, and it was so great to meet other Sutherlands, too. There was more than enough food for everyone, but I wasn't allowed to have any, even though there were many leftovers, and I did try once, but was discouraged by Mom from actually taking any.

At the Parade Ground, Mom and I, along with Laurie and Mikey, sat in the bleachers for the Clan Parade and Roll Call, and was I ever thrilled when "Sutherland" was announced and we shouted out the clan yell, "To the Bridge!" along with the Sutherlands who carried in our clan flag. I barked it, but nobody heard me.

On Sunday morning, I got the thrill of the weekend, from my point of view. My Mom took my picture with Rev. Dr. John Turner of Virginia, the Chaplain for the Games, just before the Worship Service. Imagine, two "men of the cloth" together, one with two feet, the other with four feet and a tail. I wanted to sing along to Amazing Grace, but Mom didn't think it was a good idea.

One picture we didn't get was of the police officers proudly wearing their kilts in the New Hampshire tartan. They were always so busy directing traffic and helping out folks that we didn't want to bother them. We'll try for that picture next year.

Another pawsitively pleasant aspect of this weekend was to see the volunteer workers busily employed all over the mountain, moving platforms and helping set up other things. We could tell who they were by their tee shirts which stated, "Clan Mac Crew" in large bold letters across their backs. And yet another Clan added, possibly, to the roll call?

I heard Barb telling Mom that next year, WE, the Northeast Region of Clan Sutherland of North America, get to host the Annual General Meeting of the clan. I'm hoping they'll include me in that, also. Jane is getting menus for the clan dinner and I hope, at this event, I'll get a little piece of meat from somebody. I'll still attend, anyway. It's doggone nice to be a part of such a warm, friendly group.

All too soon came the Closing Ceremonies with the Massed Bands once again marching on to the Parade Ground and prizes given out for the top performers—the Heavy Athletes, the Kilted Mile winners, the drawing for the winner of the Trip to Scotland. None of Clan Sutherland was a winner, but I'm pawsitively hoping for next year.

Och Aye,

Mosby Mac Fisher, Therapy Dog for the Ministry

(and proud of his Scottish roots)

(as dictated to Lynda Fisher)

With the Chaplain for the Games, Dr. Turner

Chapter 16

A VISIT TO A CUB SCOUT DEN MEETING

Nov 7, 2008

I had another "first time" visit a while ago. And a very enjoyable visit, too. I took Mom and Dad to Mr. Mackersie's Cub Scout den meeting, to tell them what service I give to people. Their theme this month is "serving others" or something like that, and Mr. Mackersie had asked Mom and Dad if I could tell the cubs about my kind of service. Well, I don't mind going to visit kids, not at all, but I'm pawsitively not going to speak to them, so Mom helped me out with that.

When we entered the house, I was quite interested in the cat food that was on the floor in the kitchen, because in our house, the only food on the floor is for me. They let me drink the cat's water after Mrs. Mackersie had removed the cat food dishes. Darn! I should have been quicker! I will say, though, that cat water tastes very similar to dog water, although there is a slight fish aftertaste.

The first thing was taken care of right away—greeting the boys (only five of them) with tail wags and sloppy kisses. Then we settled down to business after Mr. Mackersie opened the meeting with a Pledge of Allegiance. I was so happy that they still say, "Under God" because, as a Ministry Dog, I'm really tuned in to God.

Mom told the kids all about the NEADS training program, and asked the kids if they knew of any services that dogs do for people. Of course, the first hand that shot up belonged to a cub who said, "they lead blind people who can't see" which was a funny way of saying it, and Mom had to tell them that the NEADS pups do everything else but—even though it was a good answer. Then the next kid said "they rescue people from avalanches" and then Mom explained about stability dogs, hearing dogs, and helping wheelchair-bound folks as well. Mom put me through my paces to show how obedient I am—sit, down, stand, stay, come. She tried "my lap" with some of the kids sitting in chairs, but I was confused because she held my leash, and their voices were so timid. So Mom had to sit and demonstrate it, and of course, because I was sure of her command, I immediately put both front legs on her lap. Some of the kids did "paw" with success, because I knew what they wanted me to do when they reached out their hands.

After I was done, Mr. Mackersie introduced Dad to the boys and told how Dad had been a Cubmaster for this very same Scout Pack, and Dad told them how everything was done 40 years ago. Learning about how Scouting used to be done was a requirement for another badge that the boys were working on, so our little family served two purposes in one visit—serving others and Scouting history. Hot dog—we're getting pretty good at this visiting!

Mosby Mac Fisher, Ministry Dog (as dictated to Lynda Fisher)

Chapter 17

ON BEING THANKFUL

November 24, 2008

To: Donna Laconti; Bonnie Pansa; Ginny Reinders
Cc: Debbie Blanchard, Larry Fisher, Jack Holmer
Subject: I'm Thankful

I'm so thankful for all the help I received along the way to becoming a really great Service Dog. In this season of Thanksgiving (for the humans, anyway), I had to take time to thank everyone.

First, I'm thankful to my two sets of foster parents, the Pansas and Reinders. Bonnie and Leah, I don't have a clear memory of the prisoners who trained me, but I do remember the weekends with you guys, and then when I stayed with you all the time. I'm grateful for the hours I spent at school, and loved all the kids I met.

Glyn, my mom and dad are so grateful for your lessons on Frisbee catching, and Ginny's Agility lessons. I love my flexible Frisbee, which everyone throws for me, and Dad loves to show off to visitors my talents on grandson Mikey's climbing "castle" which I use more than Mikey does, jumping in through the many holes, and sliding down the slide.

The lessons I was taught at NEADS will stay with me forever. Mom puts me through my commands which she uses a lot, and even the odd ones that we don't really use every day, but just so I'll remember. Last night at a church meeting, she had to get me out of a pew backward, and I heard her tell someone she didn't know if I'd remember "back" but OF COURSE I remembered, even though I hadn't heard it since the trip to Boston for my graduation ceremony! Christy trained me well, and I'll never forget those sessions with her. Especially when she brought her own dog, even though we didn't get along all that well.

I found out that we in Littleton have a wonderful all-church ecumenical Thanksgiving service the Sunday evening before Thanksgiving, and all the townspeople (a lot, anyway) attend to hear lay speakers from the five churches talk on a pre-determined subject of interest. The combined choirs sing, and it's a wonderful time of fellowship with others of different faiths who come together to worship and thank God for His many blessings. The nice lady from our church (she likes to pat me) was suddenly taken sick, in the hospital in Boston, so when Mom found out on Saturday that nobody had taken her place, she volunteered to speak for our church—about me! I heard her tell Dad that it's a great opportunity to "expose" the townspeople to me, and maybe they'd tell her about people I could visit. That way, I'd be serving the town, not just our church. Even Pastor Debbie wouldn't be there, because her father-in-law had died and she was busy with that family responsibility, out of town.

After church on Sunday afternoon, Mom started cranking out a little talk, and I helped her by poking my nose onto her lap occasionally and cheering her on. With my encouragement, it came together very well. Father Clifton, of the host church, had told Mom Saturday night that the theme was "Giving Thanks in a Time of Need" which mom was struggling with, to put some words down on me, but then Father quoted the Scriptures to be used—Lamentations, Chapter 3, Verse 17:

*"my soul is bereft of peace,
I have forgotten what happiness is."*

Wow! It was like God had tapped her on the shoulder and told her what to say!

As usual before speaking, she says a quiet little prayer asking for God's help to keep her from messing up and making a fool of herself, because she's so nervous, but with me at her side, I calmed her down and we both walked up to the lectern and she put me on a "down" while clearing her throat to start her talk.

First, she told about me and who NEADS is and what NEADS does—all the different training that they do for different purposes. She always likes to get a plug in for NEADS, wherever we go. Then, she quoted the scriptures, emphasizing "I have forgotten what happiness is."

She told the following story:

"About a month ago, we were visiting at the Life Care Center on Foster Street and asked at the nurse's station where Josephine was, since she wasn't any longer in her room where we were accustomed to visiting her. The nurse told us she was now in the Alzheimer's wing and proceeded to escort us down there and unlocked the door for us to enter. I had never been there before, and didn't know what to expect. Would any of them even WANT a dog visit? We were told to go to the day room to find Jo, and I pawsed in the doorway to take in the whole room. All the residents were sitting in wheelchairs, four rows deep, facing a television sitting on the wall. They were facing the television, but it didn't appear that any of them were watching it; in fact most of them were dozing or slumped over, with their heads leaning forward. Then, one of them spotted Mosby, nudged her neighbor, and soon the whole room was

looking at him, heads raised, sitting erect, smiles on their faces, and beckoning us with their outstretched hands. What I thought would be a five-minute visit with Josephine stretched into twenty minutes, at least! We couldn't leave until each outstretched hand had patted Mosby and talked to us. As we left the room, we could hear the murmur of animated voices, certainly talking about the dog who had visited them. I'm sure that they soon returned to their former state of silence, but for these few minutes, they had come out of their slump and returned to a resemblance of what they had been.

"I had forgotten what happiness is."

Mom ended by saying, "For a short while, these patients remembered what happiness is, and it was all due to our Ministry Dog, Mosby Mac Fisher."

Amen.

And a happy Thanksgiving to everyone!

Mosby Mac Fisher, Therapy Dog for the Ministry
(as dictated to Lynda)

On Mon, Nov 24, 2008, Pastor Debbie responded:

Mosby,
That was so beautiful . . . . it made me cry. Is that what you did at the service last night?

Mosby replied to Debbie:

"I don't think anyone cried last night, but at one point, they all laughed out loud at something Mom said—something that she didn't think was funny at all, but it surprisingly tickled their funny bones. Mom was saying that I'm not just a Baptist dog, but a Littleton dog, and that we want to visit everyone in town who needs my loving paw. All she got out was that I'm not just a Baptist dog—and she couldn't continue because they were laughing so loudly. She continued by saying that I attend church more faithfully than some of the humans, and they all nodded in agreement that it happens in all the churches. But she was really surprised that her unintended funny remark got such a response.

There were some sober faces, though, when she finished up with the Alzheimer story. I think it touched some of them.

MMF"

Chapter 18

A BUSY CHRISTMAS SEASON—VERY BUSY!

Thu 12/4/2008

To: Bonnie Pansa, Ginny Reinders
Subject: Your Addresses

Hi, Foster Moms—

I need your addresses so that I can send you Christmas cards. I wanted to surprise you and your families with my new expertise in doing this, but my mom can't find your addresses anywhere, so we have to do it this way.

We're packing up and getting ready to move to new digs—over-55 condo living, still in Littleton, but because they're downsizing, Mom and Dad expect to have more time to devote to ME! More walks, more hospital visits, etc. I'm going to miss the half acre that I run around in, but down there the small yard will be fenced in so that I can still run around a bit.

I hope you-all had good Thanksgivings—I stayed at home because Mom and Dad went to their niece's home and since there were six kids plus many adults, they thought my beautiful tail would be stepped on too many times. Turned out, besides Tucker, the resident dog and my best buddy, one of the families brought their rescue dog, who did get in the way a bit, and tried to eat the turkey off the counter. I would NEVER have done that! I've been trained too well, thanks to you guys. My mom said she's amazed that I never even sniff the food that's left on a kitchen counter, and she credits that to my excellent childhood training.

Merry Christmas!

MMF
(as dictated to Mom)

Lynda Reynolds Fisher

12/5/08
Mosby's message to Ginny Reinders:

Hi, Mom #2—

Funny thing happened yesterday—my mom had just helped me send the e-mail request to you and Bonnie, and when Dad went out to get the snail mail, he brought back a big folder from NEADS. When Mom opened it, she laughed. It was a nice printout with all the names and addresses of everyone who had a paw in my early puphood training. My two foster families, and all the vets, and the New Brunswick breeder. Wow! All in one package! Funny how things happen.

My mom thinks she and Dad must be a bit younger than your parents, because they're just about to move into a 55-and-older new condo community that's going up in Littleton. But—it's been very frustrating. The original move date would have been December 6, and we would have missed the Christmas Tree Lighting ceremony at the town Common and our church's open house with cocoa and gingerbread men for the kids—none for me. Now we can go to that. The second move date would have been December 13, which would have knocked out the All-town Christmas Concert with the combined choirs, which I wouldn't have attended since it's always jam-packed full of humans with a definite risk of someone stepping on my tail. So now they can go to that.

The third and final move date (they hope) is December 20—FIVE DAYS before Christmas! Mom is definitely not happy with that.

I'm looking forward to the move, because even though it'll be less of a house for Mom and Dad to clean and tend to, it'll have a fenced-in yard for me to play in and practice frisbee-catching, and they'll both have more time to give me long walks along the walking trail that abuts the property. So—even though e-mail is quicker (and cheaper, so they say), you now have our new address.

Love, Mo

p.s.—Give Brody and Duchess a couple of big licks from me.

On Sat, Dec 6, 2008 at 6:47 AM, Bonnie Pansa wrote:

Oh I can't wait to see the Christmas card! You can send it either to me at home or at school (I will definitely show the kids!)

12/13/08

Gotcha! I'll pawsitively send it to one of those addresses. I'm wiggling all over, especially my tail, in anticipation of Christmas in our new digs. The fence guy is coming next week to install the fence so that I'll have a secure place to romp around in, in addition to the many walks I take with my mom and/or dad. Life is good! And, on top of that, I get to see so many folks in hospitals, nursing homes, etc., that I'm constantly on the go. To say nothing of all the folks I see most Sundays at my church. I went to the Town Christmas Tree Lighting Ceremony and then took my mom over to our church, which is right on the corner of the Common and has an open house for everyone, complete with hot chocolate, cookies, etc. They laid out some yummy gingerbread men on some tables with lots of frosting and trimmings in dishes so that the kids could decorate their own, but Mom kept me away from that activity because she doesn't think I have enough will power to resist a little lick or two. Dad was busy running the trains for the kids, and once, when he had me on a long down/stay, he had to correct a little kid who put his hand on the tracks. He used my correction—eh eh—and it surprised him when I looked up at him with my face all confused because I hadn't done anything wrong, and I knew it. Then Dad had to tell Mom how I thought for a minute it was ME he was correcting, instead of the kid. And, of course, the kid didn't know what that "eh eh" meant—he wasn't a dog!

I hope you and all the kids have a Merry Christmas (or whatever holiday they celebrate), and a wonderful new year.

Love,

Mosby Mac Fisher

In front of the altar, enhancing the poinsettias.

Chapter 19

THE MOVE—AT LAST!

After the third delay in moving into our new condo, the buyers finally lost patience and said they were purchasing our house NOW, or never. I don't blame them—they had been more than patient with two delays, and I could understand how they felt. There was going to be a lot of work done on our old house before they moved in, and they were anxious to get started. So this left us homeless! Betwixt and between houses. Luckily, the condo was completed enough that we could move our belongings in, but there was no occupancy permit signed, so we couldn't live there. A lot of the work had been delayed by a huge ice storm which killed the power to most of the homes in Littleton, and, naturally, the Light Department crews were busy re-establishing downed lines all over town. Areas with established occupied residences were their prime concern, and our area, with very few occupants, was low on their priority list. I could understand that, but it was very frustrating. Matt, our builder, haunted the offices of the Light Department, but with no success on moving up our re-installation. We did move in many boxes, and more were put into commercial storage facilities, so we were left, in our old house, with just the bare essentials. And my plants. Can't put them into storage or a condo with no heat, so they stayed with us.

Our expected move date arrived, with the threat of yet another snowstorm due in hours. The time was moved up from 8 a.m. to FIVE O'CLOCK in the morning! Five o'clock? I didn't know there WAS such a time. I thought the morning started much later than that. Didn't it? That meant that we had to get out of bed at 4 o'clock—in the MIDDLE OF THE NIGHT! I'm not sure what Mosby thought about that, but when his breakfast dish was laid down on the kitchen floor, he didn't question it, but got right to town on eating it up before we discovered our mistake and withheld it for a more humane hour. Wayne, our best friend any family could ask for, arrived shortly before five, and we all waited for the arrival of the moving vans—two! After a call to the mover's office which resulted in a message left on their answering machine (who gets to work at 5:30 a.m.?), we were told that both vans were on their way. Sometime after six a.m., just as dawn was breaking in the east, they finally arrived and they got down to business. Mosby was a great hand after he had met all the team; he was kept busy telling them which rooms to do in which order, I think. Actually, he stayed with us in the house and was a gentleman throughout the whole process. As the guys would return to the house from the vans and would pass us in the kitchen, they'd exclaim, "No snow yet!" much to our relief.

Soon our little caravan was driving down the road, Larry and I with lumps of nostalgia in our throats. When we had moved in to that house, we had a toddler son, a large Highland Collie dog, one black cat, and not much furniture. We left, with two vans' worth of belongings and a different dog, plus two adult children long moved out.

Immediately upon arrival at our non-electrified condo, the moving guys started unloading the first van. I had marked all the boxes with the room they should be deposited in, and I found it easiest to just stand in the living room and play traffic cop—bedroom—no, upstairs bedroom, loft, downstairs bedroom, living room, kitchen, hall closet, etc. The movers worked steadily and both vans were actually unloaded in less time than it had taken to load them up. I had made sure that Mosby's food and dishes were at the top of one of the kitchen boxes so that we wouldn't have to scramble at the end of a long, exhausting day to feed our hardworking guy. He stayed pretty closely to us all during this process, but there was no time for his usual many naps, since he just didn't know when he might be called upon for some work, or to make sure that nobody except movers entered the condo. All this was taking place while the inside carpenters and workers were busy putting finishing touches on the kitchen, and on the living room floor, assembling shelving for the many closets.

Soon the lead mover had been paid, complete with tips for all, and the vans pulled out for their home base. As they left Jeannette Way and entered White street, the horn sounded, and I looked out the living room sliders to see one of the guys hanging off the back of the second van and pointing to the sky! Looking closely, I could just see the first light fluttering of snowflakes descending from the gray sky overhead. Amazing timing! So then we turned around to face the mess and to start putting things in order.

Then the reality really set in—we were homeless! Laurie had generously offered her house in Townsend to us, which we readily accepted. The alternative would be to live in a local hotel until we could move into our condo, and that didn't suit Mosby particularly well. This was his opportunity to live with his little pal, Mikey. Each day would find us at our cold, powerless condo, unpacking boxes and storing things where we hoped they belonged, trying to stay out of the way of the carpenters who were still finishing up their work. When the early dusk would settle down on us, we'd leave for the 40-minute drive up to Laurie's house in Townsend, with a stop at the post office to pick up our mail. Each day we'd hope for the clearance to be able to move in to the condo, but each day came and went with no inspection sticker in evidence. At least we ate well, since the contents of our cellar chest freezer were stored in cooler chests on Laurie's three-season porch. The three seasons did not include winter because there was no heat on that porch, which made it an ideal place to store food at freezing temperatures. As something looked like it was starting to get soft and no longer frozen solid, I took it into the house to continue thawing, and that's what we ate that night! It saved me from starting from scratch in preparing supper, and Laurie didn't have to lift a finger when she arrived home from work.

Christmas Day was spent at Laurie's place, celebrating with our son Scott and my brother Charlie. When Charlie arrived, he asked if we were into our new condo yet, to which I replied, "No." "Oh, he remarked, "Where are you staying?" "Here." "How long?" "Who knows?" I grumbled.

We were concerned about Mosby's accepting so many moves in his short life-time, but there was nothing to worry about. We soon realized that, wherever his humans are, there's where "home" is, to him. Every evening when we were settled on the couch, he'd sit down beside one of us and warm our feet with his huge head and front paws, and I think he felt comforted by the fact that, even though his house had changed, his humans remained the same.

My computer had been packed up at the old house and taken to the computer repair store for a good cleaning out (mostly of dog hairs) and update of some programs. That left me with idle hands in the evenings, so I mostly read or knitted, which helped to relax me, even though I was still "on edge" about the condo delays.

On December 31, the very last day of 2008, as we were driving out of the post office parking lot, headed for Laurie's house in Townsend, Larry's cell phone rang. It was Matt, informing us that the occupancy permit had finally been signed, since the electricity had been turned on! Wow! We could finally stay overnight in our new home! Immediately, after phoning Laurie at work, Larry pointed the car back down to Jeannette Way instead of onto Route 119 to head for Townsend. Unbelievably, as the car turned into Jeannette Way, the cell phone jingled again, and this time it was our attorney's office informing us that the purchase and sales papers were finalized and as soon as we signed them, we'd be home owners again! "Wow!" I exclaimed, "We won't be homeless anymore!"

We left the lawyer's office in a small state of euphoria—we didn't have to go to Townsend because we had a legal home to sleep in. One of us turned to the other and reminisced, "It was 46 years ago to the day, in 1962, that we signed the ownership papers in Cambridge for the house on New Estate Road. What are the odds of that? Especially because we traveled back to Littleton in an ice storm, with baby Scott in his car seat. This time, we just had to travel the quarter-mile down the road to Jeannette Way, in another snowstorm! Life is full of these little ironies.

Again, Mosby was fine. His water bowl was in the kitchen alongside of his food bowl; we had laid out his blanket beside the bed, and he spent his first night sleeping contentedly beside our bed, just as if he had always been there!

Chapter 20

RINGING IN THE NEW YEAR, IN A NEW HOME

1/20/09

To Donna at NEADS:

Donna, I'm sorry I haven't responded to your e-mail message, but my family has been SO busy with the big move they've made, that they haven't had time to help me log on to my e-mail account. Darn! If only God had blessed me with opposable thumbs instead of dewclaws, I could do my own typing. Anyway, the computer went to the computer hospital while the humans were busy with the move to over-55 condo living, and it just returned and was put on-line last week, and I heard Mom grumbling about the 300+ e-mail messages she was reading.

Humans make life so complicated! As long as I have my water dish, food bowl, toys, and comfy mattress to sleep on, I'm happy. They're very pleased with how easily I've accepted condo living. They don't realize that wherever my humans are, that's my home. I'm very pleased that Mom and Dad paid extra to have our piece of yard fenced in so that I wouldn't run wild and get hit by a car. So thoughtful of them. I have a friend already, faster than Mom and Dad are making friends here. We're only the fourth family to move in, but the builder has this cute little mixed breed, Reggie, who comes with him every day to lend a helping paw and advise him. Dad opens the gate, Reggie bounces in, and we have play time until I wear her out and she stands by the gate to be let out. Life is good! I heard Mom tell Dad that we'll get back to our Ministry visits soon, when they've unpacked everything and are really settled in.

I'll let you know how it goes.

Arf,

Mosby Mac Fisher, Therapy Dog for the Ministry, NEADS graduate

Chapter 21

A WELCOME RETURN TO HOSPITAL VISITS

Feb 9, 2009

To Deb

Today, after a looooong dry spell, I took Mom and Dad to Life Care Center of Littleton, to visit Phyllis Wallace and Jo Adam.

Mom and Dad kept on putting the visits off, claiming they still had unpacking to tend to, the temperature was too cold, the weather was too snowy and/or rainy, until I was quite annoyed. Nothing to complain about, but I was making that observation. I heard Mom tell Dad that they'd still be unpacking, arranging books, trains, china and crystal until it would be planting time out in the yard, so she thought they should listen to me and JUST GO! So, that's what we did today.

The first stop was with Phyllis, who is always a joy to see. She's so friendly and delighted to see us, and we had a nice little visit, until a nurse stuck her head in the door to say that she needed some time with Phyllis. So, we said hi to her roommate, goodbye to Phyllis with a promise to return soon, and then we were on our way to the opposite end of the building, to the Alzheimer's wing to visit Jo. We found Jo in the dayroom with lots of other wheelchair-bound folks, who all were happy to see us. So we made the rounds of the whole room, once we'd had a few words with Jo. Mom and Dad think it's sort of depressing to be there, but I thought it was great because there were so many wrinkled old hands reaching out to pat me, and I couldn't pass up anyone. Of course, I tried to steal the cookies they had in their hands, but Mom wouldn't let me. She told them that I only eat dog food, not people food, but that's just her thinking. Try me.

Soon we were out of there and on our way out the doors, and I hi-tailed it to the car, because I know they always give me a puppy treat once I'm in the car.

I heard Dad tell Mom that it really felt good to be out visiting folks again, and now that we've started again, we'll try to make at least one visit every week. I hope so!

Arf,

Mosby Mac Fisher, Ministry Dog

Chapter 22

MR. POPULARITY GOES TO EMERSON HOSPITAL

February 2009

Doggone, I should be blushing, if you could see it under all my gorgeous golden fur, but I must let everyone know how popular I was on Thursday when I took Mom and Dad to visit Joanne Dates at Emerson Hospital. Whenever we visit anyone, Mom and Dad realize now that it'll take three times as long as they plan on, because we have to stop in corridors so that all the doggy people can get their fill of patting me and talking about how gorgeous I am.

We walked down the long corridor to get to the elevators and had to stop on the way so that some nice ladies could pat me, and of course, while they were getting their fill of me, another lady walked by and had to stop, too. She soon walked through a door to an office and almost immediately out popped another lady who had heard about me and just HAD to meet me! She was an experienced dog person, because when I got excited with her and tried to jump (much to Mom's dismay), she knew enough to turn her back to me, which stopped me dead in my tracks, of course.

Mom had been taught by NEADS to tell people to do just that when I lost control and tried to jump on them, but Mom has found that usually people aren't listening to her, so she or Dad just pull me off. I saw so many people on that corridor! And they all loved me, of course. One man came up to us while the girls were patting me and he said to Dad, "I passed you earlier and wanted to pat him, but thought he was working and I shouldn't, but now that I see others are patting him, I just can't resist coming back!" He went on to tell us about his Golden Retriever, as so many folks do who just HAVE to stop to pat me, and it made me feel very proud of my kind.

When we exited the elevator on the sixth floor and were looking for Joanne's room, a lady came up all smiles to ask us who we were to see, and I could just tell she wanted to pat me but thought she shouldn't. Dad told her it was OK to pat me, and she knelt down and gave me a big hug! That's why I love visiting folks in hospitals—most of the nice people who work there seem to be dog people, which is just the kind of humans I love. The nice lady said she'd be just a minute while she checked with Joanne's roommate to see if she had a dog allergy, since she had breathing problems. It was not the case, so she waved us on in, and the room contained, besides the two patients, three hospital folks who just wanted to visit with me! Imagine that!

After they had their fill of me, Mom brought me over closer so that Joanne could reach me. I could tell she needed my special attention, especially after she told mom that she was scheduled for surgery in about an hour. First, Mom asked Joanne if it'd be OK with her if I put my front paws beside her on the bed, and when Joanne thought it'd be all right since her pain was on the other side, Mom gave me the command, "up" and I promptly put my handsome, sturdy front paws beside her so that she could reach me better to get a really good hug. I licked her hand a bit, just to comfort her, until Mom pulled me away. I'm so glad to bring some cheer and happiness to people! I definitely help them to feel better. Joanne's roommate couldn't get enough of hugging and kissing me, and after a while Austin came in to see Joanne, so we left them with best wishes, good luck, and a promise of prayers for a successful surgery and speedy healing. The roommate couldn't stop talking to Mom, and I could overhear some of their conversation, as Dad and I pawsed outside the room. I heard her tell Mom that we three were a real blessing, and Mom assured her that I, Mosby, was a blessing to everyone, and that she and Dad feel that they are also receiving blessings from our experiences. In the car on the way home, I heard Mom tell Dad what a joy our visits are to her, and Dad agreed. They both have a really good feeling about all these visitations we do, and even though people say that WE three are a blessing, Mom knows that it's really ME. I heard Mom tell Dad that she'd have to call Pastor Debbie when we get home to let her know about Joanne's scheduled surgery, since it was just planned today and Debbie might not be aware of it.

So—another busy week for me—It's good to get back to visiting people who need to see me!

Arf!

Mosby Mac Fisher, Therapy Dog for the Ministry

Chapter 23

April 29, 2009

Hello, Debbie—

Hmmm. Where do I start? A couple of weeks ago, Mom and Dad were so busy with the new place that I couldn't get them to go to anyone for a visit. Then, last week, in spite of an arfully busy week, I got them to go to Life Care Center on Foster Street. Phyllis Caldwell had told us that her daughter Marian would love a visit from me, so they rushed through some things to go over on Friday.

In the late morning, after shopping and errands, I took Mom and Dad to Life Care Center. Well, did we see Marian? No. She was off learning how to make pasta! And we didn't even get any to sample. On the way in, we had to stop a few times so that folks could pat me and talk to me, and Mom forgot which room Marian was in. She started reading the names next to the rooms' doorways, and she came across Elsa Manni's name! We saw Elsa sitting in her wheelchair at the same time, so we made a beeline into that room to chat with her. Doggone, I just love Elsa—she's always so happy and always glad to see me, and I her. I was wagging my tail off as she patted my head and talked to me. Mom found out that Elsa was on her way back to Assisted Living in Ayer, and she'd been at Life Care Center for a week, but nobody knew, so nobody visited her. I felt bad about that, but Elsa was her usual cheerful self, so I guess she didn't miss a visit from me.

When we couldn't see Marian, that meant a longer visit with Phyllis Wallace, who is another of my favorite people, even though I have to stay away from her sore feet. We all thought that Phyllis was tired of being there—she wasn't her usual pleasant self, and was complaining about the food, misplacing her Bible, etc. So I avoided her feet but let her pat my head as we headed on the way out.

So—this week we headed back to the Life Care Center in the late afternoon with a determined goal in mind—get there when Marian would be sure to be in her room! Of course, it didn't turn out quite that well because the Director saw us and had to speak to me and tell my folks that another resident, Alberta White, used to raise my kind and would love a visit. OK. As we were walking towards the middle circle with the round table placed in the center, a lady reached out her hand to me, so we had to visit with her. Turns out she was Alberta, and she was talking to a woman whose mother was the head of the Yankee Golden Retriever Club of Massachusetts, so we had to look at pictures and chat of mutual acquaintances. That lady couldn't get enough of me!

Finally, I pulled Dad away from them and high-tailed it down the corridor to Marian's room, leaving Mom to finish her conversation and follow us. Mom recognized Carolyn Webster coming down the hall, and at Mom's question to Carolyn, she replied that, yes, she had just stopped in to see Marian, and then Mom joined us as we were schmoozing with Marian and her mom, Phyllis. I've pawsitively found another nice person to visit. Marian is a dog lover also! We really had a nice long visit and only left when it was time for the residents to get ready for dinner.

So this brings us up to date on visits.

Next Monday Dad goes for day surgery at Emerson Hospital for his knee which has been bothering him for so long. He didn't want to bother you about it because you've been so concerned (and busy) with Eddie's far more serious medical issues, but I told Mom that you would want to know, so I'm telling you now. I'll be taking him to the hospital early in the morning, dropping him off, and probably I'll decide to stay home when Mom picks him up at the end of the day. That way, he can hobble around on crutches without my help, and I'll be waiting impatiently to greet him when he arrives home. But, I have no doubt, I'll have to be petted by some needy folks on our return trip home when I drop Dad off there in the morning. That might be my only visitation next week, depending on how well Dad does.

I'll let you know how that goes.

Arf!

Mosby Mac Fisher, Ministry Dog
(as dictated to Mom)

Chapter 24

MOSBY'S "BARK AND ROLL" MIDDLE SCHOOL DANCE

On Friday, March 6, I took Mom and Dad to Rhode Island, to the school of my first foster Mom, Bonnie, where I spent many hours of my puppyhood, happily playing with the students. When we arrived at the fund-raiser dance, I was so excited to see my foster Dad, Mike, there. I not only wagged my tail and wiggled all over, I sang my greeting song to him, which Mom tells people I only do for folks I really like. When the kids asked my name and Mom told them, "Mosby," they said, "Wow! Is that Mosby? He's gotten so big!" They only remember me as a little guy, not even a teenager. There were three other dogs there, all pups, service dogs-in-training, wearing their blue vests, and since I was the only graduated, working dog, I had to set the pace for them. But, actually, I was so excited to see everyone that I was just as goofy as they were. We all had a ball, and after a while the moms took us to the back of the room because the music was so loud, as it should be for a middle school dance.

Of course, knowing the occasion was such an important dance, I was all duded out in my tux and top hat, but Mom quickly found out that the kids wanted to pat me more than anything, so she removed my clothes (gasp) to give them free access to my wonderfully soft fur.

I've found that NEADS fundraisers are a fun place to be, and I look forward to going to many more. On the long drive home, I heard Dad tell Mom that he was glad we went to this dance because the kids were so happy to see me again, and I thought it was great to visit the school of my childhood where I spent so many happy hours learning how to be a great Service Dog.

Mosby Mac Fisher

To Bonnie Pansa 3/7/09

Hi, Bonnie—

I just wanted to let you know how much fun I had yesterday at the school. When we started out in the car, I had no idea where my mom and dad were taking me, and even when I got out of the car in the parking lot, I still wasn't sure where I was. But, when I got near the school entrance, I KNEW, and I was so excited! Lots of kids wanted to pat me on the way in, and I let them, but I wanted to get to where the action was, and the folks that I remembered.

I was so excited to see Mike that I gave him my little song, in addition to the wagging tail and wiggly body. It was so good to see him again! I'm glad I met the new dogs going through training, just as I did last year, when I was with you folks. I wish I could have seen Leah, but I guess I couldn't have everything I wanted. It was enough that some of the kids remembered me, and I was so happy to see you with another dog, although I did have a slight flash of jealousy.

My mom and dad want to thank you for the thoughtful gift bag you gave them as we left. It was full of nice things, and Dad says every time he drinks coffee from his mug, he'll remember what a nice time we all had at the school. I heard him tell Mom as we were headed home on Route 495 that he's so glad we went to Rhode Island to help support the fundraiser for NEADS. I'm dying to see the pictures that Mike took.

Love,

Mosby

Chapter 25

MOSBY'S WEIGHT

When Mo left NEADS in March 2008, he weighed 68 lbs. At a veterinarian's visit in December of 2008, he weighed 78 lbs., but when Christy said that was too much, he had a vet visit in the spring of 2009 and he weighed **87 lbs**.!

Without even trying!

That's with no extra people food, only dog food in dish, plus training treats. Dr. Kilgore said to try Purina One, Healthy Weight Formula, and reduce the 4 cups a day to 3-1/2 cups. We reduced it to 3 cups daily, half in the morning and half in the evening. Training treats are limited to 1 or 2 per session, or action, when he receives treats. Daddy was walking him a couple of miles daily, but with knee problems which resulted in surgery, that was curtailed to my ½ mile walk most days.

Now Mosby is back up to a couple of miles a day with Dad, not much with me. On March 2, he checked in at 79 lbs. The vet said she'd be happy to see him at 74 or 75 lbs., so that's what we're aiming for.

Chapter 26

BACK TO KAARLO AND ELSA

3/13/09

Dear Debbie:

I thought you would like to know that I took Mom and Dad over to Ayer yesterday to visit Kaarlo and Elsa Manni again. Doggone, they're such nice folks to visit! I don't know who enjoyed the visit more—them or us. When we first entered the building, while Mom was signing us in, some ladies were sitting in the parlor knitting away on some projects and hollered at Dad to bring me over to visit them. At first, they thought I was a girl because I was so beautiful, they said. Yuck—how could anyone mistake ME for a GIRL? Anyone could tell, seems to me, with my handsome-looking head and manly chest hairs, to say nothing of my graceful tail, that I'm definitely a guy dog. In spite of that reception, I was nice to them and went over to each one in turn so they could pat me and tell Dad how silky soft I am. I really made their day, I think.

Then it was off to visit with Kaarlo and Elsa, who were equally as happy to see me. Elsa almost hopped out of her wheelchair to get to pat me, and Kaarlo reached far over from his chair to give me a pat—I almost thought he was going to fall off his chair. Finally I settled down on Mom's feet and let the humans chat a while. It was fun for me to listen to them talk about "the old days" in Littleton. My memory only goes back to last year, but Kaarlo and Elsa remember way back to when my gr-gr-grandfather was a pup.

All too soon it was time for me to take my folks home, so we left the Assisted Living facility with a promise to return soon. It's really nice for me to do my job when it's such a pleasant thing to do. I feel so good afterwards, and I know my folks do, too.

They're planning, next week, to visit Gloria and Mel Morris, who used to work with Dad and they've lived in town all their lives. I heard Mom talking to Dad about branching out and visiting folks in town who aren't Baptist folks, and Gloria and Mel fit the bill, since they're both dog lovers and go to another church. I'm beginning to realize that there are folks who go to church, but not ours. There are lots of churches in town, I'm finding out, and there are folks in them who could use a visit.

So—next week—a different venue for us.

Mosby Mac Fisher, Ministry Dog Extraordinaire

Chapter 27

HELPING OUT A GOLDEN IN NEED

Most times we make a definite decision to do "some good" for someone. Other times, however, we just fall into a situation where it becomes necessary to lend a helping hand, and we can ignore the situation or choose to help. Such a situation happened to us through our daughter, Laurie.

Even though no longer married to Steve, Laurie was still actively involved with the organization which gives support to the families of the deployed military personnel. It opened my eyes to just how many ways some people might need help while their loved ones are overseas. Laurie's e-mail contact was Bea, who sent out notifications of upcoming events and some needs that some families might have that could be solved by other families of deployed personnel. It's a great way of keeping in touch and helping each other out. One of Bea's e-mails informed the readers of a young woman about to be deployed and had nobody to take care of her dog, a female Golden Retriever named Indie. Could anyone help? This soldier's daughter would be living with her grandmother, but the living arrangements could not include a dog. Because of my many contacts with NEADS, Laurie had forwarded the message to me, with the subject line stating—"Mom, Can You Help?" My heart went out to this Goldie, her human mom, and even the little girl, who would surely miss her dog, at a time in her young life when she'd be without a mother's caring arms. Grandmas count big-time, but nothing can replace a mom. So I put on my thinking cap. Should I forward the message to NEADS? Through their many links with so many dog people, maybe they'd know of someone who could take in a dog for a year.

Wow! I suddenly realized that I had that contact myself, with Ginny Reinders! On every holiday, Ginny would send out pictures of all her dogs of the moment, starting with Duchess, the Reinders' St. Bernard, and going through pups of varying ages, whom Ginny was raising for NEADS. If she could find room for multiple dogs, I thought perhaps she could find room for one more dog for just a year, a needy dog who would be missing her family and who would benefit from Glyn and Ginny's love, but also the pluses received from being one of a pack of dogs to play with and sleep with.

So I fired off the e-mail to Ginny, who responded immediately with questions that I hadn't thought to ask: "How old is the dog, has it been neutered, how much training has it had, any health issues?" I forwarded Ginny's questions to Bea and asked her to contact Ginny directly, which obviously she did. Wanting to help in a small way, if I could, I said that we'd be willing to pick up Indie and transport her to the Reinders' home, across to the other side of New Hampshire and kick in with some food money, if Ginny would be willing to take care of Indie for a year's time.

Dog people are wonderful people, without a doubt. I knew of Bonnie Pansa's dual compassion for dogs and Special Needs kids, and how hard she worked for both of those special interests of hers, and obviously Ginny's heart also was wide open for dogs, with her small pack of dogs at any given time. The next thing I knew, I received a picture of Ginny's pack, naming the dogs, starting with Duchess, and in the middle of the dogs was Indie! Wow! How great was that? Ginny and Glyn had traveled across the state of New Hampshire to retrieve Indie, and that girl was comfortably living with the Reinders pack. I sat at my computer with the emotional tears of gratitude welling up in my eyes. Immediately I sent off a check to help with Indie's food bill.

On Mon, Mar 16, 2009, Ginny wrote:
Her daughter Chloe is 8 years old!!!!!!!!!!!!!!!

Give the Mos a BIG kiss from us. We'll need to get together somehow this summer!

And yes, Indie is the golden who belongs to Kat. At the moment she is in NJ training but will be deployed soon to Baghdad for a year! Her daughter lives in Manchester so I told them I would try to get down there a few times with him.

How far away from Manchester are you?

Ginny

To which I replied:

We drive 1/2 hour to go shopping in Nashua, so I think it's about 45 minutes for us to reach Manchester. In fact, I know it is. Our son-in-law, former son-in-law, I should say, is in the National Guard stationed out of Manchester, so we've been there for a few of his ceremonies. He's now in Afghanistan, so we worry about him, even though he's no longer officially part of our family. He's still the father of our wonderful grandson, so he'll always have a place in our hearts. Steve's unit went to Fort Riley, Kansas, for his deployment training last summer, then went to the remote mountains of Afghanistan and will be returning sometime this summer.

Larry and I talked about bringing Mosby up to see you-all sometime next summer. We'll plan it around our mutual calendars.

And then Ginny responded:

Hi Mosby & Lynda!

Thank you so much for your support for Indie. It was so thoughtful of you to do—but you don't need to do it! It's funny how those who give continue to give. A para in our school had this dog living under her trampoline all winter long. She tried to find a home for her—we even looked at her but she was a bit too timid for our gang. To make a long story short—they're keeping her—but they have a low income. Glyn and I are paying for the spaying but they don't know it's us!

So thank you for your support! We need to get together with our pups this summer!

Ginny

My response to Ginny:

What goes around, comes around. I have a firm belief that when I do someone a favor, they don't have to repay me, but to pass the good deed on to someone else who might need it, or appreciate it. If everyone did it, eventually the world would be a better place.

ljf

April 27

Hi, Indie—

I can well remember my first few days when I was a kid and went to live with the Reinders clan. Of course, I was a little nervous, but Duchess, the queen, soon put me at ease and took over the role of my foster mom, teaching me a lot of things, just as I'm sure she's teaching you now. Be sure to always listen carefully to her, and for goodness' sake, stay on her good side—she's a big girl, and she can really pack a wallop if she needs to! Watch out for her tail.

I'm sure by now you're all settled in up there, but I did want to tell you what a great family you're in. Auntie Ginny is a really, really good teacher, I can tell you, fur sure.

I'll bet she's got you doing some of the agility work—she's famous for that! And be sure to have Uncle Glyn toss the Frisbee for you—I used to love that! Doggone, that was lots of fun, and I have my own forever family hurl it for me now. I haven't forgotten how much fun it is. My folks think I'm the greatest dog they've ever had, and they say it's all due to my early training I got, first in Rhode Island, and then in Lebanon, NH. I really lucked out with all the good teachers I had, and my folks are forever grateful for all the work that went into my becoming the great guy that I am. I hope to meet you this summer, and renew my acquaintance with Madame Duchess.

Mos

At this writing, in 2011, Indie has long since been reunited with her mom and little sibling, Chloe, and everyone is happy about the outcome. So—this valiant mom has served her country, the grandmom has helped out her daughter and has had the pleasure of enjoying her granddaughter for a year, Ginny and Glyn have the knowledge that they did yet another good deed for a pup and family in need, and we are just so grateful that we had a small part in bringing this all together for a happy ending. It's a win/win experience!

L to R: Izzy, Indie, Duchess, Brody, with Frankie the cat supervising
[Photo by Ginny Reinders]

Chapter 28

PHYLLIS ACCEPTS THE LOSS OF HER NIECE

March 23, 09

Hi, Pastor Deb—

This morning I heard my mom and dad talking about who needed a visit, and they weren't sure which way they should go. If Don Mayer hadn't been released from the hospital yet, they thought they should go there, but most likely he has, so they decided to visit Phyllis Wallace, who would probably need a visit from me more than Don. They didn't know if Phyllis had been told about the death of Marcia, her niece, so were on their toes not to blab it out. When we arrived in her room, Auntie Bobby Holmer was already there, perched on the bed and Phyllis was in her wheelchair. Phyllis obviously had heard the news already, so we felt free to talk about it. I wanted to go right over and give her a doggy kiss but Mom held me back since those bare, sick toes were facing me, right down at my level, and Mom didn't want me to touch them. They kept me back the whole time I was there, so I took a nap since I couldn't put my head on her lap to cheer her up.

As is her nature, Phyllis was taking the loss of her niece stoically, saddened by it, but accepting. She told us that you had already been to see her and had given her a new prayer shawl, which she had placed on her lap and was constantly fingering. It seemed, to me, that she truly was receiving some small bit of comfort from it, and Mom told her how many prayers were crocheted in the shawl.

Next Tuesday is her 92nd birthday, so we'll go there again and maybe bring her a little flower.

We said our goodbyes, saying we were headed to the Alzheimer's wing, but walking down the corridor, Mom suddenly felt tired, so we all came home instead. We'll go there another time, when Mom isn't so wiped out.

So—let us know when Don is settled in at home, and we'll go over to see him.

Arf,

Mosby Mac Fisher, Ministry Dog (dog about town)

Chapter 29

COUSIN TUCKER

Our niece and family have a wonderful Spanish Water Dog, Tucker, and since Tucker is family, Mosby has been to their house to meet him, and Tucker has spent some time at our place when his family goes on vacation to a place where dogs are not welcome. What a terrible thought! A vacation place that doesn't want dogs! What kind of a vacation is that, anyway?

Since Mosby doesn't take to little dogs, and not being sure how he'd react to Tucker, being mid-size, we arranged for the two boys to meet for the first time on "neutral" ground. Jackie drove over to our house with Alec, the toddler, while the two older kids were in school, and on their arrival, I had asked her to stay on the road, Tucker on leash, and we brought Mosby out, on lead, too. That way the two boys met on fairly neutral ground, not in Mosby's house or back yard. They greeted each other, stem to stern, and seemed to feel that each one was acceptable to the other. We opened the gate to the yard and Mosby, of course, galloped in, with Tucker following along hesitantly, sniffing around at all the strange, alien smells that he encountered. Soon the two guys were chasing each other, then rolling around, and happily they were bonding perfectly.

I had hoped for this happy outcome, but didn't want to take any chances with a bad first encounter. This set the scene, later on, for Tucker's week staying with us. The two boys played together, slept together, and had a ball. Mosby shared most of his toys with Tucker, but his favorite toy was off limits and he let Tuck know that he couldn't have it with a warning growl, no teeth showing. Tucker backed off and didn't touch it again during his visit. We had picked up Tucker at his home so that he'd know that HE was leaving his family, not his family abandoning HIM. At the reverse, when the family returned home, Jackie drove to our place and retrieved Tucker, with the expected joyous reunion. We told Jackie that Tucker could come back anytime he wanted to, since he was such a well-behaved house guest.

To Jackie, 3/31

Hi, Jackie—

Please pass this message on to Rosa, my new baby cousin. I'm sure she doesn't have her own e-mail account yet. Come to think of it, I don't think Tucker has ever written to me, either.

I heard your conversation when you told my mom that you just received Rosa all the way from Texas. What a long way for a little baby to travel, but the family at this end of it is well worth the traumatic trip to get to. I'm dying to play with Rosa, and I promise I'll be very gentle with her, 'cause I know babies get very frightened of a big guy such as myself.

I'm dying to meet her! And also to see Tucker again.

Love,

Cousin Mosby Mac Fisher

Chapter 30

EMERSON HOSPITAL

Hi, Debbie—

This morning, April 7, I took Mom and Dad to visit Barbara Hill at Emerson Hospital. I was very disappointed to find that we couldn't enter her room, because she was under quarantine due to the fact that the doctor hasn't diagnosed what's causing the problem with her foot. Poor Barbara—we had to stand out in the doorway, so she didn't get to pat my silky head. We had a nice visit, nevertheless, and have to report that Barbara seems to be in good spirits and is convinced that the doctor will release her very soon, so we felt good about that.

On the way in, and also on the way out, we bumped into (almost, not really) Pat Cavanaugh Jones, an old-time friend of Mom and Dad's. Aunt Bobby had told Mom that Pat was at Life Care Center, but when we went to see Phyllis Wallace, we were told that Pat was no longer there. Then, surprisingly, she entered Emerson Hospital the same time that we did. She had the oxygen tubes in her nose and told us she was there to see her pulmonologist, the same one that Mom saw for her Sarcoidosis, so they chatted a moment about that.

We also spent time with Pat and Don Smith, old neighbors from New Estate Road, as they were registering for something. Pat, of course, had to hug me for a moment. It's amazing the people we see at Emerson! Mostly by chance.

After we had visited with Barbara, on the way down the main hall, there was Pat Jones in a wheelchair being pushed by Garrett, her older son, and the oxygen was no longer visible. Pat said the doctor dismissed her, saying she didn't need it anymore. So that was good news, even though she was still in the wheelchair.

So I kind of feel that we visited two people today instead of just one.

In the car on the way home, I heard Dad tell Mom that we spent more time with all the hospital staff people wanting to visit with me than we did with the inpatient we came to visit. They both feel that I should schmooz with everyone who wants to pat me, so that I can give them a little of my brand of comfort and joy.

Even though it was a rainy morning, I stayed dry, through good planning on Mom and Dad's part. We went from the condo into the dry car in the garage, then Dad let us out under the roof of the hospital entrance, so we stayed dry for the whole trip. They're very aware that nobody wants to smell wet dog (except for them) and make every effort to keep me dry when I'm visiting folks.

So—a successful morning visiting a lot of different folks, and staying dry all the time. Now I'm going to take another nap to conserve my energy for whatever they have planned for this afternoon.

Mosby Mac Fisher, Ministry Dog

Chapter 31

ANNUAL CHURCH REPORT, MOSBY'S CONTRIBUTION

As is common in the American Baptist Church, the business end is almost as necessary as the spiritual end, and to that purpose, each board writes a yearly report of its activities throughout the previous business year, which is included in the church's annual report, along with the budget information and projected budget for the coming year, to be voted on at the Annual Business Meeting of the church.

Nobody told Mosby, but he felt that, being a very active element in the church makeup, he should write a report, too, of all his activities of the previous year. He pondered a bit about it, then sent off the following to the church secretary:

Hi, Bill—

I heard my mom tell my dad that the reports from the boards and committees were due to you soon, so I thought I'd better write one up on my activities this past year. After all, I'm a part of the church, too, and folks might want to know what I've been up to, when I'm not sleeping under the pews on a Sunday morning.

Mosby Mac Fisher

(as dictated to Mom)

Report of Ministry Dog, Mosby Mac Fisher

For the May 2009 Annual Church Report

Back when I was a pup, I had a feeling that God had chosen me to play a role on His team.

Just to give the readers a background on who I am, and how I was chosen for this Calling, I want you to know that I was born in New Brunswick Province, in Canada. The conscientious breeder had made a commitment of donating a puppy or two every year to NEADS, located here in Massachusetts. NEADS, in case you want to know, is short fur National Education for Assistance Dogs Services, and NEADS trains dogs to serve humans in every way except for blind folks. When I arrived in Princeton at the training headquarters, I lived in the Puppy House, along with lots of other babies my age. There, we were evaluated as to our personalities and future capabilities of giving service to humans. Most puppies passed, of course, but a few who were a little too timid were immediately placed in adoptive homes as family pets. From the Puppy House, I went to my first foster home—the Rhode Island State Prison. Yes, I was a Prison Pup! My prisoner taught me basic commands and toilet trained me also. On the weekends, the Pansa family took me home with them so that I could do things that wouldn't happen in a prison, like go shopping with the family, take a train or bus ride, go to an arcade, etc. I even got to go to a middle school dance, since Leah, the daughter in the family, was in that class, and Bonnie, my foster mom, was a teacher, not to mention that Mike, my foster dad, was the school principal. They found out I was pawsitively a real party animal! I learned all the obedience rules I was taught, both by the prisoner and the Pansas, and they found out how much I loved people.

When I was about half grown, it was goodbye to the prison and the Pansas and off to live in Lebanon, New Hampshire with Glyn and Ginny Reinders. They taught me more Service Dog commands, so that I could be of real help to a handicapped human being, and they also found that I was very affectionate and loved all people, young, old, energetic kids or slower elder folks.

My tail continues when I was returned to the NEADS training house where I reviewed all my training up to that point. Christy, my personal trainer, saw that I knew all my commands and did them flawlessly, but also that I really and truly loved all the humans I came in contact with. I think that God whispered in her ear, "Mosby is MY dog! He should work for ME, not just one human."

That's when my mom, Lynda, came on the scene, with a phone call to NEADS stating that she had heard about the Therapy Dog for the Ministry program and wanted to work with a Ministry Dog. The phone person was a bit reluctant because Mom wasn't a minister, but when Mom stated that she was a Deaconess and that part of her duties was to visit sick people and home-bound seniors, it worked out that Mom was approved. She came in fur an interview, which went well, and then Christy brought me in fur us to meet. Well, I can tell you, it was love at first sight with both of us. Mom petted me and I licked her hand, she scratched behind my ears, which I loved, and then I rolled onto my back for a good belly rub. That did it. We were both in Heaven!

Mom came for a whole week of training with me so that she'd learn everything I already knew, and she learned pretty quickly, although I must say, I taught her well. After that week of intensive training, I went home with her on Friday, and immediately I was working. Dad had an emergency trip to the hospital, just an overnight, so we went to retrieve him on Saturday and I had to visit a while with his roommate, who just needed a doggie paw and a feel of my silky head to feel better. My first official function.

Since then, I've been busily making the whole town of Littleton feel better. I've been many times to Life Care Center on Foster Street, back to Emerson Hospital, over to the Assisted Living facility in Ayer, and to many homes in town, visiting folks and making them feel a little happier. You should see me work the room in the Alzheimer's wing. Those folks can't get enough of me.

Another "different" place I went to was the waiting room at the Colonoscopy doctor's procedure office. Lots of nervous people there, let me tell you, and I made the rounds to reassure them that they'd be all right. One first-time fellow there told Mom he felt much better after chatting with us.

I take Mom and Dad to church every Sunday and lie down quietly under their pew while the humans worship my God. I quietly think my own thoughts then. Pastor Debbie had a beautiful Commissioning Ceremony for me, welcoming me into the church and petitioning Mom and Dad to help me bring my Service to people. It was like a cross between the Prayer Shawl Dedication and Infant Dedication, since that's where I got my full name—Mosby Mac Fisher. Mosby is my name that NEADS called me, Mac is Scottish for "son of" and Fisher, of course, is their last name. It ties in with their Scottish roots, and mine also, since the Golden Retriever breed originated in Scotland along the banks of the River Tweed.

At the Ecumenical Thanksgiving Service at St. Anne Church, Mom and I filled in for the designated Baptist speaker, Christine MacFarlane, who was suddenly hospitalized and tragically died that same evening. We were happy to do it, if not for the reason, but fur the opportunity to make my presence known to more folks in town.

Doggone, I'm enjoying my life of service to people and to God so very much, and I only hope that God sees fit to keep me around my church fur a long time to come. You know, don't you, that "dog" spelled backwards is "god".

Obediently submitted,

Mosby Mac Fisher, Therapy Dog for the Ministry (as dictated to Mom Fisher)

On Apr 28, 2009, **Church Office** wrote:

. . . . Do you have a flattering picture of yourself that you would like to add to the report?

Bill

To: Bill

Subject: Re: RE: Ministry Dog's Report for 2009 Annual Church Report

I'm flattered that you'd be interested in my picture for the report. I want you to know that ALL pictures taken of me are flattering, since I'm such a handsome guy. I'll have my sister Laurie (Mom and Dad's girl) take a new one of me and send it to you. Mom's camera got lost somewhere in the move and she hasn't located the box it's packed away in, as of yet. I'll send the picture to you asap, which is probably over the weekend, if that's not too late.   Mo

On Apr 29, 2009, Bill wrote:

Thank you Mosby, this weekend is fine. I did not mean to offend you about your picture. I should have phrased it as "do you have a particularly flattering picture of yourself".   Bill

That's better. Being the laid-back guy that I am, I'm not easily offended, but I do think that all pictures can't help but flatter me

MMF

Mosby's picture finally did arrive at the church office, was included in his report, and some compliments on his image were subsequently received by proud Mom and Dad.

(Photo by Barbara Staples)

Chapter 32

RICO WEBSTER

Sometimes troublesome things happen to the animals in our church family, just as the humans sometimes experience troubles and illnesses. We were all saddened to hear of such an event in the life of Rico Webster, the rescue dog from Puerto Rico. Mosby feels that his compassion extends to ALL of God's creatures, not just the human kind.

5/12

Hi Mosby, Lynda and Larry

I just wanted to tell you that Rico—Lyle, Gretchen, Micah and Devon's dog—was hit by their car last night in their driveway and they rushed him to the Animal Emergency hospital. They did lots of praying and x-rays and they just heard this morning that he will be ok—but I must share this with our ministry dog and family. Maybe Mosby can send him an e-mail—and visit later????

Anyway—I just heard all this, this morning and it seemed like I should share it with you!

Thanks!
Deb

To Rico 5/12

Ola, Rico, mi compadre—

I'm sorry, but no es habla espanol, so I'll have to write to you in English and you can have it translated. Although, I think you've been here long enough to pick up most of the English language these humans speak. It's so much easier to bark and arf our messages, but humans have to make things harder, don't you think?

Anyway, I was very sorry to hear of your accident, and I'm sure your human didn't mean to hit you with the car. It's good that our dog nature is to not hold grudges, and to forgive as the Boss wants us to. It must have been very painful and frightening for you, but I'm glad you've gotten through the ordeal and are on the mend. Had I known about it when it happened, I would have sent up a few prayers to my Boss on your behalf. Now I'm praying for a speedy recovery for you, and when you're healed enough for a little romp, maybe your humans could bring you over to my place. Right now, the grass is struggling to germinate since it was just seeded a little while ago, and I'm trying not to get too rough on it.

Keep healing, and stay away from cars! Maybe this'll be a good lesson for you—you've got to respect those big monsters—they're a lot bigger and heavier than we are, and their minds aren't as quick as ours. Come to think of it, they don't have minds, do they?

Stay healthy, and via con Dios.

Arf—Mosby Mac Fisher, Ministry Dog

On May 12, 2009, Gretchen Webster wrote:

Mosby,

We forgot to tell the Animal Hospital staff the command "Get Busy" so Rico didn't readily perform for them when they were trying to monitor these things. Silly owners!

The Websters

5/13

Hmm. Some humans are not as smart as their animals, I think. Not you folks—but the Animal Hospital staff. I thought everyone knew that "get busy" meant to get busy. Actually, sometimes when Mom or Dad let me out and say "get busy" and I don't have to, I give them a disgusted look and come right back in the house. Don't they KNOW when I have to? I do. Sometimes if I'm in a good mood, I'll squat and pretend, just to please them. Yes, even though I'm almost three years old and a boy dog (sort of), I don't lift my leg as I've seen some boy dogs do. I just don't think it's cool, so I squat like a girl.

I'm so doggone happy to hear that Rico is on the mend and home again. I figured that all those prayers from the humans and my direct talk to Headquarters would do the trick.

Arf!

Mosby Mac Fisher, Ministry Dog

Later on, after he was completely healed, Rico did bring his dad Lyle and brother Micah over for a play date, and the boys (canine) had a great time, running around and chasing each other. It was good to see Rico has made a complete recovery from his encounter with the family car, and we're looking forward to more play dates in the future.

Chapter 33

MOSBY'S THIRD BIRTHDAY

Subject: 06/06/09—Mosby's Birthday Party

An e-mail message to Mosby's distribution list:

Hi, all—

In our home, today is not just D-Day, but also Mosby's birthday! He's three years old!

I'm not too proficient in sending pictures via e-mail, so I hope you can enlarge them enough to see how handsome our boy is.

The picture shows Mosby jumping through his agility ring, which was his birthday gift from us. He really loves it, and had no trouble learning the command "Through." What a party animal he is!

Lynda

Jun 8, 2009 08:17:55 AM, Christy Bassett wrote:

Awww, he looks great! Thanks for sharing. I was thinking about him this weekend . . . it was three years ago that I went to pick him up as a tiny little puppy! Have a great summer and give Mosby some love from us.

Christy

Which prompted a reply to Christy:

I didn't realize that you were the one who picked him up from the breeder. Did you go all the way up to New Brunswick?

We've had four dogs of our own in 51 years of marriage, plus the Guide Dog puppy that we raised, and I've got to tell you that Mosby tops them all. Not just that he's been trained so well, but his personality is really the best. He loves everyone and is just thrilled when someone pats him. He leans on them and soaks it up. At night, after we go to bed, he goes up to each side of the bed just for a little pat, then settles down on his mattress. We feel like he's tucking us in for the night. What a guy!

ljf

To which Christy replied: Not New Brunswick, but way up in Maine. He was such a cute ball of fluff back then! I'm glad to hear that he's doing well and everyone's happy together. Keep up the good work! Christy

Mosby's Agility Ring

Chapter 34

MORE VISITS

SOME PRODUCTIVE VISITS, Spring 2009

No visit is wasted, even when the folks we go to see are fast asleep. Recently I took Mom and Dad to Life Care Center on Foster Street, expecting to visit Phyllis Wallace and Elsa Manni. First, we walked into Phyllis' room and found her fast asleep in her bed, lying on her side with only part of her head visible. She was gently snoring away, so Mom decided she was really asleep and not just resting. So we tiptoed out of there and proceeded on to the Alzheimer's wing to stop in with Elsa for a while. As we were preparing to enter the wing, an attendant opened the door and behind her were at least a dozen people following her single file. They looked like a clutch of ducklings following their mom! Off they went to the Music Hour, and Mom made sure that Elsa wasn't with them. We figured we'd find her in the activities room, where we've always found her before, but after a quick look in there and finding no Elsa, Mom asked at the desk and was told that she was sleeping.

What, nobody to visit today? Not so. As Dad and I were waiting for Mom to finish at the desk, a nice lady in a wheelchair wanted to pat me, and pretty soon another one wheeled up for a pat. They chatted with Dad for a while, until they'd had their fill of me, and we proceeded to move out of there. On the other side of the monitored door, someone else wanted to stop and love me, and then we were on our way down the corridor to the nurse's station, when we were stopped again. This lovely lady in another wheelchair called me over to her and couldn't get enough of me, while Mom and Dad talked to a couple of nurses. Soon a nurse came over to the patient and coaxed her to use her quiet hand which she had kept under her lap blanket. The nurse helped her to get her hand on me, and boy, did she light up! She kept telling me how beautiful and soft I was, and couldn't get enough of patting me with that broken hand. I felt like a real therapy dog, knowing I was the cause of her exercising her hand. We stayed with her for quite a while, until I felt like lying down, which broke the spell, and she tucked her hand back into her blanket. The nurses were smiling and telling me what a good boy I was. Of course, I already knew that, but it's nice to hear it affirmed.

So—that's my tail for today. We never seem to go anywhere, to hospitals or nursing homes, where it's a failed visit, because there are always people in the hallways who need my help. It's a nice life I have, helping people to feel better by just being myself. We'll return, possibly next week, at a later time to catch our sleeping ladies when they're awake.

Arf!

Mosby Mac Fisher, Therapy Dog

Chapter 35

SOME NEW FACES

June 09

This afternoon I took my folks to visit someone new to me. Gloria and Mel Morris live in the Lyttleton Green, or whatever it is called, and although they don't go to my church, they're very nice people. I've been wanting to expand my visiting to folks outside my own church, but didn't know who I could visit, but Dad used to work with Mel at General Radio, and for a while they carpooled together, so they had a chance to chat about "the good old days" while Mom and I visited with Gloria, who is a really nice lady. She let me sniff at her legs and I only stopped when I started licking her feet and it tickled her. Both folks are dog people, so we all enjoyed a nice visit, especially Mel who, at 93, doesn't get out much any more. Gloria told me afterwards that if we hadn't arrived, he'd be snoozing the afternoon away in his chair.

Gloria took us across the hall for a quick visit with a guy who's younger, but much worse off. He was in a terrible car accident about 25 years ago which killed his wife and unborn baby and left him in a wheelchair, partially paralyzed, ever since. He loved patting me and talking to me about his dog and even showed us a picture of him with his dog. Very touching!

By the way, Gloria told us that Father Clifton is away for quite a while, and Beaunes is visiting someone in Connecticut. I hope Father Clifton finds his way back to Littleton, because, even though I met him, I never got a chance to meet Beaunes, although, hearing that he's a black Lab, I bet he's as handsome as Mr. Gibson.

It was good to visit two sets of people who really appreciated my visit. I think I really lightened up their day for them, and it makes me look at my folks and say, "Who's next?"

Next, they think, will be Gladys Upson who is now living in Lexington for a while.

Arf,

Mosby Mac Fisher, Ministry Dog

Chapter 36

ANOTHER NEADS GRADUATION AND A VISIT

June 11

Hi, Debbie—

I'm reporting on two events covering the last two days.

First, on Sunday, I took my folks to a NEADS graduation ceremony. It brought me back to last year when Mom and I were one of the graduating teams. Doggone, I certainly could empathize with the eighteen teams who graduated this year. They were nervous about walking up on the stage to receive their diplomas and having to talk into the microphone, I know, 'cause that's how I felt last year.

This year there were no Ministry teams, but there were a lot of therapy teams and FIVE military veterans graduated with their four-footed assistants. It was good to see the whole audience stand up and applaud when the five veteran teams were called up together, as a unit. Doggone, I felt choked up to see them. They're so brave!

Mom and Dad each bought a NEADS sweatshirt to help in the fund-raising effort and were a little disappointed that nothing was in my size, although I really have no need of a sweatshirt since I always wear my fur coat.

I'll still go to every graduation that I can, 'cause it's good to show support for NEADS and all the dogs who go through the training so they can help a human. One of my foster moms, Bonnie Pansa, was there with her family and current pup they're training, and it was good to see her again, too. I remembered her and I remembered meeting the pup at the school dance in Rhode Island, which was a fund-raiser for NEADS. NEADS is really feeling the financial pinch this year, just as is every organization that depends on contributions to survive, and I was happy to participate in the fund-raiser.

Today I took Mom and Dad to Lexington to visit Gladys Upson, who's staying there for a while after a fall in her house. She looked fine, except for a bruise under one eye, and she seemed in pretty good spirits, although I think she's afraid she won't be going back to her home. Her daughters are trying to get her to move to Connecticut to be closer to Patty, one daughter, and she doesn't want to go. I felt pretty bad for her and I leaned my silky head on her knee so she could pat me.

As usual, on the way into Gladys' room and on the way out, we had to stop and talk to people who reached out their hands to pat me. It's such a great thing for me to be able to be a comfort to so many people, just by getting close enough to them for a pat on the head. One nice smiling lady scratched behind my ears, which is a particularly nice thing for them to do.

Again, on the way home, I heard Dad tell Mom that he's so glad that we can visit folks and bring a little joy into their day.

Arf!

Mosby Mac Fisher
Therapy Dog for the Ministry

Chapter 37

DONATIONS

After the dust had settled from our move to the condo, we reviewed our finances and found that we really could do something that we had talked about doing for a long time—donate some money to help pay off Mosby's debt. Each dog goes to its new owner with the understanding that they will help pay off almost $10,000, which is half the price that NEADS determines is what it costs to raise a puppy to full service to a human. Of course, I imagine a portion of the costs of running this organization is factored in to that figure also, which includes upkeep of the building, salaries for those folks who aren't volunteers, etc. When we were inquiring about getting a Service Dog from NEADS, we had understood that we were approved for a private Littleton fund to pay Mosby's debt in full, but unfortunately that didn't completely work out, so we felt obligated to pay as much as we could ourselves, along with participating in the many fundraisers that NEADS organizes.

Now, that said, I remembered that Mosby had received his name from Don Irving, who had donated enough money so that he could name a puppy, which he did, in memory of his dog Mosby, who was named to honor Colonel John Mosby, of Mosby's Raiders, who was a gentleman in his handling of prisoners he captured during his raids on the Union lines.

I often thought of that choice of names, because we feel Mosby (our dog) is such a gentleman in his line of work—giving love and friendship to everyone he meets. Except for little dogs, that is. Well, nobody can be perfect!

Because of our love for our Scottish roots, and since Mosby's breed originated in Scotland also, we requested that, with our donation, we'd like to name a puppy Andrew, who is the patron saint of Scotland. Coincidentally, my grandfather's name was Andrew also. I asked if the money could go forward to help pay off Mosby's debt and a puppy could still be named Andrew. Soon I received a message from Doreen Sheridan, of the puppy house:

June 18, 2009

Andrew has arrived at NEADS. He was born on 3/9/09. He is a handsome/adorable golden retriever. Andrew is at the Laura J. Niles Early Learning Center (puppy house) on the NEADS campus. He is busy playing with the other pups as well as learning obedience and some simple tasks.

Doreen Sheridan

To which Mosby e-mailed to some of his friends:

6/22

I'm so doggoned excited! I think you all know that I donated some money towards my debt at NEADS, and I requested that I get to name a puppy, which is done when someone donates enough money. I had requested that a Golden Retriever puppy should be named Andrew, since Goldens originated in Scotland, as everyone knows, and also that St. Andrew is the patron saint of Scotland, as everyone should know. So I thought it would be appropriate to name him Andrew. Isn't he handsome? Just as good looking as I was at that tender age.

I'm so anxious to meet Andy! My folks said they'll drive out to the NEADS campus sometime soon so that I can meet him and check him out. Wouldn't it be nice if he were to become a Ministry Dog, just like me?

I'm willing to bet that this is the first time that a dog has donated his allowance to NEADS, and likewise that a dog wants to name another dog.

Arf!

Mosby Mac Fisher, Therapy Dog for the Ministry

On Jun 22, 2009, Ginny Reinders wrote:

Hi Mosby!

We are so proud of you! I bet you will be a great 'big brother' to Andrew. I hope we can get together with you and your Mom this summer!

Ginny.

Chapter 38

THE BOSTON GLOBE COMES TO LITTLETON

6/24/09

Last year, Mosby had been quite impressed that our local weekly newspaper ran a very nice story on him, and his ego shot up a bit when he thought about that. This spring, Pastor Debbie had been contacted by someone from the Boston Globe, who expressed an interest in doing a story on him. Wow! He was really impressed by that! A local newspaper article is very nice, but The Boston Globe, which naturally has a far wider readership, was really impressive, he thought. This all came about from Mosby's link on our church's website. Someone at TABCOM (The American Baptist Churches of Massachusetts), our state-level advisory group, apparently was reading Mosby's link from our church's website, and contacted the Globe for a possible human interest story. Erica Noonan, Bureau Chief for the Globe West, e-mailed me, and immediately set things in motion for a visit.

Since Debbie's husband, Eddie, was in a Boston hospital battling tongue cancer, I tried not to include her in the back-and-forth e-mails with Erica to set this up, but, naturally, Debbie wanted to remain in the loop in spite of her heavy schedule.

Jun 24, 2009 Debbie wrote:

OK . . . cool! If you need a pastor's quote—please let me know. Yeah! We are awaiting Eddie being discharged . . .

And I responded:

Eddie is the reason I didn't include you in my reply to Erica. I thought you had enough on your plate without having to read an extra e-mail message. Yes, I'll be sure to have you included in a pastoral comment.

ljf

and Debbie responded back again:

Hi Lynda:

No, this is great! I am very excited. Mosby must be super excited too! I was thinking if Eddie stayed longer you could have come to see him. He would have liked a visit from Mosby . . . but I hope we are getting him out of here about 8:30.

The next day I told her:

You know, without it being said, that anytime Eddie would like a Mosby visit, we'll be there!

ljf

06/24/2009

To Erica:

Wow! The Boston Globe! I'm impressed. We've been interviewed by the local paper, but never by one such as the Globe.

Now that I've gotten that stuff out of the way, yes, we are very much into giving interviews, just for the sake of spreading the word about Mosby and his wonderful works that he's doing, thanks to NEADS (National Education for Assistance Dogs Services). They are really the ones you should be contacting. We'll be happy to chat with you, or you can come out to Littleton to visit us and get to meet Mosby and shake hand-to-paw with him. You'll be impressed with him.

I've been keeping a journal on Mosby and our many visits to hospitals, nursing homes, and shut-in folks, so I can collect them, if you'd like to read them. At Mosby's graduation ceremony last year in Boston, Randy Price was the MC, and this year it was Dan Rea. Graduates are encouraged to attend the graduation ceremonies to cheer on the new crew just finishing up their lessons.

About Mo—We're members of the First Baptist Church in Littleton, and after I had trained with him at NEADS headquarters (he's a fully trained Service Dog), Mosby was mine, forever, to go and visit folks to bring a little cheer into their lives when they're feeling sick. His actual title is Therapy Dog for the Ministry. We try to make at least one visit a week, and we only go to people we know are dog people. Mosby's charms don't work on someone who is allergic or who is afraid of dogs, so we avoid them. Everyone else gets a real lift from a Mosby visit.

About a month after Mosby became a member of our family, our minister, who is a huge dog person, held a Commissioning Ceremony for us. In our faith, we practice Believer's Baptism, which means that a person has to be old enough to commit to accepting Jesus Christ into his/her life, so that lets out infant Baptism. Instead, the parents bring the baby before the minister, who conducts a Dedication Ceremony where the child is dedicated to God and the parents commit themselves to bringing up the child to know God. I had to tell you that so that you'd understand—we committed ourselves to taking Mosby to visit sick people, and he was dedicated to fulfilling that task, too. It was kind of a cross between our Prayer Shawl Ministry and a baby Dedication, sort of. So—we have a serious commitment to our God to bring Mosby to whomever might need a visit. On a lighter side to this solemn ritual, Pastor Debbie told Larry that, when she was talking about it to her husband, Eddie, he asked her if she was planning on being Mosby's godmother! Well, we all thought that was carrying this thing a bit too far, but in actuality, we feel that Debbie really is a special supporting element in Mosby's life.

Mo attends church with us every Sunday, quietly, and he attends many church functions, too. Pictures are available—he's quite photogenic. We also attend other town events—Memorial Day Parade, the town's Touch-a-Truck Day for little kids, the Halloween kids' parade where he wore a costume along with some other dogs, the Christmas Tree Lighting Ceremony at the Common—I could go on and on, but you get the picture.

If you'd like, I can send you some of the stories I have on him—you'll hardly have to crack your creative talents, because it's all written down for you. So—call us and we can chat on the phone, or we can arrange a visit—Mosby loves to have company.

Lynda

Jun 24, 2009 Erica wrote:

Thanks for your wonderful note—I will indeed talk to NEADS as well.

When would be a good time to come out there and see Mosby ministering to a member of your church? We'd like to take some photos of him. I could come out on Friday of this week, if he is doing something then. Or perhaps late next week on Thursday or Friday if you have something scheduled?

He comes to church with you on Sunday? Will he be at any upcoming church functions?

It sounds like he does very valuable work! Are there other ministry dogs in the area as well?

Thanks,

Erica

To Erica:

Re: Boston Globe inquiry 6/24

Let me answer your questions, in order of appearance:

Just Google NEADS and you'll come up with their website, 'cause I don't know their address offhand. When you get there, if you click on "clients" you'll come to a section with all the dogs and handlers who aren't paid up yet, and Mosby and I are one of them. The dogs cost almost $10,000, and the clients aren't expected to pay, but are encouraged to take part in fundraisers to get the money. I thought we had Mo's tuition covered with a funding from a Littleton trust fund, but sad to say, because of the economy we've only received $2500.

A visit for tomorrow won't work, but next Thursday will be fine with us. You can come to our condo and take some home pictures, then you could follow us up to Life Care Center of Littleton to visit one of our church women who is now living there. She loves Mosby, and it'll probably be a great photo op for everyone.

Except for rainy days, Mosby takes us to church on Sundays and quietly lies on the floor between us, then cuts loose at the coffee hour following. The kids love him—he's usually occupied with two or three kids trying to get him to follow their commands—"sit, down, paw" etc. Sorry to say, there really won't be any upcoming church functions that I can think of because we're into summer when most boards and committees aren't holding any events since so many folks are away on vacation.

There is at least one other Ministry Dog in the area—Pastor Renee Kaufman has a Ministry Dog from NEADS, and he's just as gorgeous as Mosby is. Our Pastor, Debbie Blanchard, is in contact with her, I believe, if you need any information on her.

In our church, we have an annual business meeting, in preparation for which all the boards and committees submit their annual reports and budgets. Since Mosby is such an important part of the church (from my point of view), I assisted him in writing up his report on his happenings this year. A lot of it explains how he came to be with us, so I've enclosed his report so that you can get a better feel of him and his activities for our church. Mosby is quite a prolific writer, and authors quite a few e-mail messages, since he has his own e-mail address. He also has his own business card, which we help him hand out to folks. The dew-claw doesn't work as well as the opposable thumb, you know!

Any other questions, just holler. We'll set aside next Thursday for whenever you think is a good time for you. Directions will follow—we're really easy to find.

Lynda

Chapter 39

MOSBY'S MEANDERINGS

June 25

There's not much for me to report on for these last few weeks—very boring. Last Thursday, I took Mom and Dad to Life Care Center to visit Phyllis Wallace, one of my favorite people. I was very excited to hear that the Boston Globe wanted to interview me and to take some pictures of me while I was working, and I wanted my picture taken with Phyllis, so we went there to tell her about it. When we entered her room, we saw that she was lying in bed—in the middle of the afternoon!—sleeping, with a hand covering her face, so we knew she didn't want to be disturbed. A detour to the Alzheimer's wing didn't meet with success, either, since most of them were in the Activity Room with the Celtic singer. Irish Celtic, not even Scots Celtic, my heritage.

I did make the rounds of the few people left in the Alzheimer's day room, and of course, they lit up when they knew I was there. Funny thing—even though I remembered a few faces, they didn't remember me. Alzheimer's isn't funny, though. It's sad that they don't remember I've visited them before.

So last week wasn't very good. Then, this week, Mom and Dad visited Bert and Carolyn Webster—WITHOUT ME!

I understand that some folks just aren't turned on by my charming personality, but it still doesn't make me feel good. When Mom and Dad left for Bulkeley Road, they said goodbye to me, and even my sad-dog look didn't change their minds. They left me behind.

A note from Lynda: Because my duties as Deaconess include visiting sick folks and shut-ins, we have chosen to visit with Mosby only those folks who we know would enjoy dog visits, but sometimes there comes a day when we want to visit some church folks who we know will not gain anything from a Mosby visit, since they're not particularly tuned in to a dog. However, these church family folks are near and dear to us, and we do not want to exclude them. Thus it was that we left Mosby at home, much to his chagrin.

Mom brought them the altar flowers, which still looked pretty good, and they said they had a nice visit, even if I wasn't along to make the trip really great. Bert hobbled into the living room and seemed to sit gratefully in the chair. Carolyn had just had some biopsy work done in the morning, and the novocaine was wearing off on her spine, so Mom and Dad didn't want to stay very long for fear of tiring her out. I can't imagine how they could have had a very good visit without my soothing presence, but they seemed to feel it was OK.

We were supposed to go to NEADS to visit the Puppy House, where Andrew is living to start his training, but postponed that visit until tomorrow when they can get there a little earlier. A phone call to the Puppy House resulted in my staying home from that visit, too, since they told Mom they don't want to introduce an adult dog to all the babies who might not yet have developed their immunities to certain germs which I might carry.

Arf!
Mosby Mac Fisher, Therapy Dog for the Ministry

Not too long after that, I received an e-mail from Doreen with the subject line: Bad News about Andrew. I thought that Andrew had died, since that was the worst bad news I could think of, and I slowly opened the message to read that Doreen said Andrew just didn't have the temperament to make a good service dog, so he was released from the program. Disappointed as I was to read that, I was relieved when I read further that our wee little Andrew had been adopted by a loving family, where he would live, as our Guide Dog puppy Georgie did, as a much-beloved family member.

Doreen's next question was—what did we want to do about our donation? I immediately replied to her that we'd like to try another Andrew. Surely, a second time would result in a great service dog!

Chapter 40

A VISIT FROM THE BOSTON GLOBE STAFF

July 2, 2009

I must say, this has been a busy week for my job—Ministry Dog. Today I received a visit from two people from The Boston Globe—Erica, the reporter, and Joanne, the photographer. After I greeted them with my usual enthusiasm, I turned the meeting over to Mom and Dad to answer all Erica's questions while I posed for Joanne. They're really nice ladies, and I hope they caught my charming essence for their story—I think they did.

After Erica got all the information she needed, Mom called John McDonald, the Social Director at Life Care Center for Nashoba Valley to make sure that Phyllis was up for a visit. I was really disappointed the last two times we were there, cause she was sleeping and I didn't have a chance to give her my full charming treatment. John had thought she could be wheeled down to the meeting room to give us more space, but Phyllis said her legs pained her too much, so we'd have to make the visit in her room.

When we arrived at Life Care Center, my first order of business was greeting Coda, the ancient Golden, and Lily, the young pup, both of whom belong to the director, a nice lady, who had just brought them out to the hall. We could have had a really great playtime, but we were all kept on our leashes so could just sniff noses and wag tails, which we did with typical Golden enthusiasm.

By then, John had appeared along with a young lady who was his assistant, and we all formed a parade down to Phyllis' room with me in the lead, naturally, followed closely by John, his assistant, the director, Erica, Joanne, and finally Dad bringing up the rear. John entered the room first to make sure Phyllis was up to the visit, and she appeared to be looking forward to seeing us. I'm not sure, but I don't think she was feeling all that well, so I gently put my head on her hand for a pat, then Mom asked Phyllis if it'd be all right if I put my two front paws beside her on the bed for a picture. When Phyllis said that'd be OK, Mom gave me the command, "up" which is the signal for my two front paws to go up. If she had said, "jump" it would have been all four feet on the bed which wouldn't have been so good for Phyllis. I understood Mom's command and gently raised up and put my paws and upper body next to Phyllis, who grinned and chuckled a bit. We all had a good visit and Phyllis requested a copy of a picture with Mosby. Phyllis told Erica, the reporter, how Mosby visits her and how much she enjoyed it, and told Erica about her prayer shawl. Mom got it and put it around her shoulders as requested, and then Joanne took another picture, as requested by Phyllis also. Although subdued, Phyllis, I think, enjoyed the visit and all the attention she received.

Then we proceeded on down to the Alzheimer's wing after checking with the director to make sure it'd be OK to take pictures, not showing anyone's faces, just hands and wheelchairs. As usual, it took forever to make the rounds of the dayroom, giving everyone with an outstretched hand a few minutes of my time and listening to their stories about their long-ago dogs.

We parted company with the Globe ladies in the parking lot, and told them we'd be seeing them on Sunday in church. Now that I know how nice they are, I'm really looking forward to Sunday.

Chapter 41

A FULL WEEKEND

July 6, 2009

What a busy weekend I've had! I'm glad it's Monday so I can lie around and just be a dog for a change. It all started on Saturday when I took Mom and Dad to the town's annual Fourth of July picnic at Fay Park.

We arrived in plenty of time to set up their chairs in a shady spot under the trees but looking directly at the gazebo where the band concert would be held. It didn't bother me where we sat, 'cause I can hear so well I knew I'd be able to listen to the music really fine. Mom went over to chat with some ladies she knew while I helped Dad with the chairs, then I staked out my spot beside them. I had my eye out for other dogs and I wasn't disappointed—they soon arrived, and I had to salute them with a bark, which Dad didn't appreciate. Don't know why—that's the way dogs greet other dogs. Mom took me over to the first dog (a mixed-breed of some sort) and after we sniffed each other in the appropriate places, we each got a little excited, but Mom kept turning me around so I couldn't see the other dog and I soon settled down. I had learned my lesson, though, and for the rest of the afternoon I just lay on the grass looking at the new arrivals but not barking at them. When the church bells rang to announce the start of the festivities, I didn't move, I was so laid back. I was quite interested in the kids' games because most of them involved running of some sort or other, but Mom told me it was for kids with two feet only and us four-footed guys couldn't participate. I know why—'cause we would have won all the games instead of the kids.

While my humans were eating hot dogs from Ed's Weenies, I had to be satisfied with a drink of water, and even though I know I don't eat people food, Mom kept a close eye on me when some kids ran by with food in their hands. She didn't have to worry, though, 'cause I know better than to grab for their food.

During the band concert, a nice man with two little girls came over and thanked Mom for our talk at the Ecumenical Thanksgiving Service. He asked if I could help his little girl who was terribly afraid of dogs, and he really wanted her to get over that fear, if possible. Mom told him that she'd never thought of it, but possibly it could be another kind of ministry I could work on. After handing the father my business card and telling him to call, Mom invited the girl over for a pat of my silky head, but she declined. She really needs lots of desensitizing, and I'm just the dog for it!

I'm excited about this new type of ministry. As I pawse and reflect on the afternoon, I realized what a coincidence it was that the man who heard our talk in November was also there at the town picnic. Did God have a hand in this? I think so. He's an awesome God.

Sunday in church was one of those extra-special days. We knew the Globe reporter and photographer would be there, and since Dad and I were scheduled to be Greeters, we arrived promptly at 9:30, but the team had already arrived, much to our surprise. The photographer, Joanne, wanted to check out the physical properties of the church building to get the light and spacing technicalities down, I think. Both Joanne and Erica, the reporter, were chatting with Pastor Debbie when we arrived, so Dad and I stood in the Narthex to greet the early arrivals, and Joanne got a few good shots of us, making sure to get the right angle to get a good shot of me. I could have told her that ALL my angles are great for pictures, but I thought I'd let her figure that one out for herself.

I had heard Mom and Dad tell them both that there wouldn't be that many people in church because so many families are on vacation, and also the Fourth of July weekend meant many folks would be away, but we were pleasantly surprised by the number of folks in attendance.

Debbie called me up, with Mom and Dad, for the Children's Story, and used me as an example of Service, and she read my report of visiting Mr. Mackersie's cub scout den meeting to talk to the boys about Service. All the time Debbie was talking, Joanne was snapping pictures of us with the kids, and I think she got some good ones. I'm dying to have Mom show them to me!

I must pawse here for a moment and reflect on our wonderful church people. A month or so ago I had heard Mom and Dad talking about how good it is that so many people have given the sermon so that Debbie could spend more time with her husband Eddie, taking care of him in his illness. Preparation for a sermon can eat up a lot of precious time, but these generous folks have stepped up and done a doggone awesome job!

Then, yesterday, just before the service started, Debbie called the Deaconesses together and told us that the Deacons who were scheduled to serve Communion were unexpectedly called away—Cheryl's husband was rushed to the hospital early this morning, and Diana's daughter was having difficulties with her multiple-birth pregnancy. I'm not sure what the problem is—after all, I was one of seven pups, and nobody was concerned about my mom. But—humans are a different kind of people than us dogs, I guess. Not seeing other Deacons present at that time, Debbie asked the four Deaconesses if they'd all serve the Communion in place of the usual two Deacons and two Deaconesses. Of course, they jumped right into this new role for two of them, and did a really great job, from my point of view. As usual, I never get a chance to enjoy the food offerings, but I do quietly observe the humans.

While Mom was busy with the other Deaconesses cleaning up the Communion stuff after the worship service, Dad and I did our usual socializing with the folks downstairs during coffee hour, and the Globe ladies took more notes and more photos. When Mom entered the room, she thanked them both for working on Sunday morning to get a good story, when they could have been spending time with their own families. Everyone is very excited about seeing our story in the Boston Globe, especially since it's a great opportunity to spread the word about NEADS' Ministry Dog Program, and me in particular.

While I was resting at home later that day, I heard Mom tell Dad that she appreciates the way God works in our lives and that of everyone in the church. It was so evident with church member Rev. Jean Wright offering the sermon and especially with the Deaconesses taking over for the Deacons and serving the Communion bread and cup. What a great group of people we have! I'm so happy to be a Baptist dog, and particularly in this church!

Arf, and woof!

Mosby Mac Fisher, Ministry Dog
(as dictated to Mom)

July 16, To Erica:

Many thanks for a great article! It told Mosby's true story, and in a great style. I'm so glad you were thorough and contacted NEADS. They "need" all the publicity they can get.

Please thank Joanne for us, too. The pictures and video were great. I'm so happy she caught the kids reaching under the pew to pet Mo. She really made the effort to make a great story even better.

Again, many, many thanks—I'm telling everyone to BUY the Globe, not just read the story on-line. After all, it's the hard copy that'll be cut out to put in Mosby's album, and it's the sale of the hard copy that'll keep the paper afloat.

Lynda

Chapter 42

REQUEST FOR HELP FROM NEADS

7/6

To Donna at NEADS:

Hi, Donna—

As you can see from the enclosed report, I've been very busy working in my role as Ministry Dog. But my mom had a new request which she'd like to work on, but isn't quite sure about how to go about it. Is there someone at NEADS who could advise us in working with a little girl to overcome her fear of dogs? Or is there a book she could read to me about this?

Jul 16, 2009, Christy responded:

Hey Lynda,

Thanks so much for sending this. The article and video was so touching, I have tears in my eyes! You're doing a great job with Mosby . . . we love to hear about what a difference our dogs are making after they leave us. Congrats to you for achieving such great success!

I also wanted to touch base with you about your request for information on working with a little girl that is afraid of dogs. I think it's great that you're branching out and trying new things to help more people. Dogs can certainly be wonderful tools and can bridge many gaps. I imagine that you have some ideas already in place on how you might start out working with this little girl . . . it sounds like she just needs to spend some time with a friendly dog that doesn't push her too quickly. Many times the autistic children that we work with come in being unsure of the dogs, but after spending an hour in the room with them during the interview (without the pressure to touch or confront the dogs), they see that there really isn't any threat and become comfortable with their presence on their own. Sometimes they need a little help knowing what to do and where to start. Dan is great at this, and I'll give you his e-mail address below in case you'd like to pick his brain on more ideas or trouble spots later on. But you could try just taking a walk with the girl and maybe putting an extra leash on Mosby's flat collar so that she feels like she's helping or getting connected to the dog while you still have control over him on the Gentle Leader. Lots of kids like this because they are close to the dog, but the dog is moving away from them and they don't have to face the front of him where they could get licked/pawed/etc. Sometimes you can even encourage the child to hold onto the dog's backpack handle or touch his back while you're moving. This will bring them even closer. Then you can start to have her touch his fur and maybe even slow down to a sit or down command. I've found that it's best to have a treat in your hand or make sure that the dog is paying attention to you at first so that the child doesn't get frightened by fast movements of the dog's head towards her. If this goes well then you could try having the girl brush Mosby or give him a treat or a toy. If this is too much confrontation, then you could even have her just hang around the room while you play with Mosby. Some kids like to throw the ball for the dog but don't like to take it back from them. So if you do the recall part and take the ball from Mosby to give to her, then she can have a nice interaction without having to actually touch him. After you've built some trust and good experiences between the two of them it'll be easier for you to branch out into more hands-on activities, like asking her to help you give him a bath or give him a hug. Lots of times if you explain why Mosby needs something (like "Mosby is feeling sad today, a hug would really help him to feel better") the kids will offer the behavior on their own more and more. Just take it slowly and make sure she doesn't have any bad experiences with him accidentally (like getting scratched or jumped on) in the meantime. I'm sure you'll figure out what works for her as you get involved in it. Good luck and let us know how it goes!

I'm actually going to be out for the rest of the summer on maternity leave after this week, so I won't be around to hear about your progress. But be sure to get back in touch again in the fall. Have a great summer and keep up the excellent work!

Christy

To: Christy Bassett

Maternity leave? That's exciting! I'm so happy for you! When's the due date? Boy or girl, or don't you know?

I do thank you for all your great advice. Funny thing is, that in addition to the shy little girl, we're looking for advice on how Mosby can be used with our four-year-old grandson who's been diagnosed with Mild Spectrum Autism. Boy, what a downer. The only good thing about it is, it IS a mild form, and he seems to be responding already to our behavioral changes. One thing I've been doing, without knowing anything about dog therapy with an autistic child, is to go for short walks with me holding the leash, but Mikey is also holding it halfway down. He thinks he's taking Mo for a walk, but I still feel I'm in control.

The father of the shy girl, even though I gave him Mosby's "business" card, hasn't contacted me yet, and I do hope he does, since it would be another approach for Mosby other than visiting sick people and being active in church activities.

Many thanks for Dan's e-mail address, too. I'll contact him soon, after I get down off Cloud 9 from the Globe article.

Good luck on the birth of your baby, and please keep in touch.

Lynda

From Christy:

Thanks Lynda. I'm due next Friday, 7/24 . . . not sure if it's a boy or a girl yet. But it certainly is exciting!

I'm sorry to hear about Mikey's diagnosis. Nobody wants to get that news about someone they love. But as you said, it's great to know that it is only a mild form. Plus you have a dog that can help you to work with him! Dan should be a great contact for you to have and will help you to expand your work with Mosby as well.

Congrats again on the article!

Christy

Not all things work out as we hope they will. The father of the shy little girl never contacted us, so all the good advice I received from Christy never was used—for that purpose, at least. We continue to apply what we can with our experiences with Mikey.

Chapter 43

MOSBY'S BUSY WEEK

July 19, 2009

This past week has been so doggone busy, I haven't had time to sit down or wag my tail. It all started on Monday when I took Mom and Dad to visit Elsa Manni at her new home in Life Care Center of Acton. What a nice room she has! As always, even in spite of all her recent woes, she greeted us with a laugh and a big hello. She's really an inspiration for us! Of course, it was a bit of a trial for Mom and Dad because Elsa is so deaf, they had to shout right into her ear and they know she didn't get all of what they were saying because she'd answer in a funny way that didn't really make a lot of sense.

Elsa's daughter Soni came in briefly while we were there, then explained she was in a meeting with some of the staff and would return later. She takes good care of her mom, we could tell.

An hour flew by pretty fast, even though there were some empty spots when Elsa would ask what was going on in our lives—four times! I guess she's losing a little grip on things. That would be my diagnosis, but I'm only a dog, so I can't say for sure. I perked up when Elsa talked about the dog she was going to get when she got out of there, but Mom and Dad knew that wouldn't happen, so that was a downer, too.

So—that was Monday. On Thursday morning, all Heck broke loose, as soon as Dad opened up the Globe and saw my story in the Globe West portion. The phone started ringing at 7:45 a.m., with Barb Sutherland wanting to be sure we had seen the article. That was just the first phone call. It was so exciting! Dad read the article to me, and Mom showed me the video on her computer upstairs in the loft. I was so busy running up and down between the two of them! Doggone, I just couldn't keep up with things.

On her way to the hairdresser's shop, Mom stopped at CVS and there was only one Globe to be bought, and afterwards Donelan's only had two for her to retrieve. Holmers don't subscribe, so Aunt Bobby bought it at the gas station, only to find that the GlobeWest section wasn't in it, so Mom told her she'd run down a copy when we went out to do our errands Friday morning.

Lynda Reynolds Fisher

On our way to pick up Mikey that afternoon, we stopped by Life Care Center of Nashoba Valley to give a copy to Phyllis Wallace, as we promised her we'd do. Uncle Jack had printed out a copy of the story for Aunt Bobby to take up to her, so we had a little Baptist session right there in Phyllis' room. I was pawsitively happy to see that this time Phyllis was sitting in her wheelchair instead of lying in bed like she had been the previous three times we'd stopped by to see her.

Then today at the Congregational Church where we had our joint worship service, I heard more people talking about the Globe article, and I really felt like a celebrity. Aunt Bobby said that Elsa wanted me to visit her—guess she's forgotten we'd already been there. Mom set her straight, though, even though we'll visit Elsa again real soon.

After church, Mom and Dad left me home while they went to retrieve my cousin Tucker who is vacationing at our house for a week while his family is on the Cape, so this week will be pretty busy, entertaining a house guest. He's pretty neat, though, cause he hasn't tried to take over any of my toys, and we eat in separate corners of the kitchen, so it's working out all right. For a funny-looking guy, he's all right. I have a Scottish background, and he has a Spanish ancestry, but we speak the same language—woof, and arf.

So—that's my tail. Busy, busy, but I like it that way, especially when my work is making people feel happy. I'm looking forward to this week of not doing anything but entertaining Tucker.

Woof!

Mosby Mac Fisher

Chapter 44

CRUISIN' WITH THE CHURCH DOG, SUMMER 2009

(formerly known as the Ministry Dog)

Last week when I took Dad for one of our walks, the man who was mowing the Congo Church lawn waved me over, so Dad had to come with me, of course. The guy asked Dad if I was the church dog his wife has told him about. She's seen me when I go to the Congregational Church joint services with us Baptists, and mentioned how much she liked me. Heck, I'm getting well known all over town! I liked that name as well as Ministry Dog, so I guess I'll keep it for a while. The folks at our food pantry, Loaves and Fishes, call Dad "the Bag Man" 'cause he keeps them supplied with paper bags for the folks to carry home their groceries. That means that the Church Dog takes the Bag Man for walks!

So today I took my folks to Concord, to visit Stanley Kimball at the convalescent home across Route 2 from Emerson Hospital. What a great place! Outside, there's plenty of grassy areas and trees for me to sniff around. Some of the bushes smelled good, too. But finally, I remembered my mission, so responded to the tug on the leash and took my folks inside the building, after greeting a nurse who was outside taking a smoke break. I don't know what these humans think is so great about inhaling stinky, smelly tobacco, choking on it, then exhaling. It stinks so much, and it dirties up the air that I'm smelling!

After greeting some folks in the lobby, we signed in and asked for Stanley's room, which, it turns out, entailed an elevator ride, which I love. I've been trained to allow the humans to enter first, then I follow my handler on and immediately turn to face the door, sitting patiently for the door to open. Every time the door opens, we're on a different floor than when we entered! These elevators are really a great invention. Mom and Dad were very interested in looking into all the nice, large rooms, but I was happier waving my tail at the people in the hall. They all smiled at me, and the ones who reached out their hands got a lick from my tongue. It always takes as long to get somewhere as the time we spend in the room when we get there. Doggone, I'm such a popular guy!

I like visiting Stanley, 'cause he always has a smile for us. His eyes were closed when we entered his room, but he wasn't sleeping, which made me glad. I didn't want to come all the way there without licking his hand! We had a nice little chat with him, then left so he could get some more rest. On the walk back down the hall, it was the same thing as when we entered—lots of folks needing my attention. I hope our next visit will be as pleasant as this one was, 'cause it makes the time spent there so much nicer to remember.

Arf!

Mosby Mac Fisher, Church Dog (formerly known as Ministry Dog)

Chapter 45

NEWS FROM LEBANON, NEW HAMPSHIRE

Ginny's photographic talents were still evident in her sending us canine population updates, and we enjoyed the pictures announcing her newest baby, Emma.

To Ginny 7/22

And yet another baby! Emma is so cute, and she has settled in with her new brothers and sisters quite well, I see.

Is Emma another NEADS baby, or yours? Since NEADS evaluates puppies at their puppy house first, and you said Emma came right from the breeder, I'd say she's yours and not NEADS.

Indie looks very much at home with her foster family. I hope she doesn't miss her other family too much. This week we have Mosby's cousin staying with us while his family is on vacation at a "no dogs" place. Tucker is a Spanish Water Dog, and he misses his family a lot, but is having fun playing with Mosby's toys (when Mo allows it). If I were as talented with my camera as you are, I could show you some pictures, but no such luck.

It looks like July is slipping by without a visit, so maybe you could tell me your available dates and we could arrange something? Mosby really wants to visit your place, and he's interested in meeting all the guys. I know you're busy with the new wee one, but hope that you can slip in a date for us.

ljf

Chapter 46

SHARING WITH THE CONGREGATIONAL CHURCH

We were a bit hesitant to bring Mosby to the summertime joint services with the Congregational Church, but he behaved at the Congo Church just as well as he does at his home church. He was a perfect gentleman, sleeping under the pew just as he does every Sunday, so quietly that many people weren't even aware they were sharing the worship service with a canine. Each church, Baptist and Congregational, takes two Sundays of hosting the other, then it's reversed, and the guest church becomes the host church for two Sundays. So many people are away on vacations, it makes a lot of sense to share a month of worship services in this way, particularly since the two churches are so closely related theologically.

The following e-mail message originated from a Congregationalist to his pastor and Debbie.

From: Barb and Ray

To: Gail Wright, and Debbie Blanchard:

July 22, 2009

Gail and Debbie:

Please mention this ministry during our joint services—there are [CCOL] people who don't know about Mosby, despite the recent Boston Globe article, and who wonder why a dog is at church.

Regards, Ray

Jul 22, 2009

From: Gail Wright

To: Barb and Ray, Debbie Blanchard

Thank you—Debbie, maybe this could be your children's time this Sunday. I didn't see Mosby before worship otherwise I would have lifted him up in some way—or invited him down for the blessing. This is such a wonderful ministry!

Blessings, Gail

Jul 22, 2009, Debbie wrote:

Hi Lynda and Larry,

Now I am getting requests to talk about Mosby in church services! Well this is just cute—an e-mail from the Congo church folks to see if I would do the Mosby children's story at their church this week. I can do that—if the famous dog is coming?

On Jul 23, 2009, Lynda wrote:

What do you think, Mosby? Are you up for it?

Mom

July 23 To Debbie—

Pawsitively! You know how much I love to shmooz with folks, especially the young ones! You're not barking up the wrong tree when you ask me to do this. Doggone, I'm getting so excited! This will be a really great Sunday! Hot dog!

Last Sunday we couldn't stay for the coffee hour 'cause Mom and Dad had to pick up my cousin, Tucker. He's staying with us for a week while his family is on vacation, and he's been a lot of fun, but I don't much like sharing my toys with him. You'd think, for all the time I've spent in church, that I'd be more forgiving and sharing—"do unto others", etc.,—but I really don't like my stuff taken over by a silly looking Spanish Water Dog. I don't know why people exclaim over his curly coat when they can pat my smooth, silky coat.

Lynda Reynolds Fisher

Anyway, Tucker will be gone on Saturday and I'll be free for Sunday morning at the Congo. I heard Mom grumbling about the early hour—9:00 a.m. is hard for her, but we'll all be there, so just let me know what you want me to do.

And we'll be able to stay for a little while afterwards, so that I can nose up to the kids and give them a quick lick.

Woof!

Mosby Mac Fisher, Ministry Dog (as dictated to Mom)

Chapter 47

E-MAIL TO TUCKER, AND VISIT TO DON LINDGREN

July 26 To Tucker

Hi, Cousin Jackie—

Doggone, I just wanted Tucker to know that I miss him! Last night when Mom and Dad got home, I looked behind them to see if Tucker was with them, and I was disappointed not to see him. I pawsitively missed sleeping beside him in Mom and Dad's bedroom. I suppose I'll eventually get used to not having him here, and I know he'd much rather be home with his family, but I really do miss him and wanted you to tell him so that he'll feel good about coming back here again sometime.

Woof!

Mosby Mac Fisher, Ministry Dog (as dictated to Mom)

July 28 To Deb

Yesterday I took Mom and Dad over to the Apple Valley rehab center in Ayer to visit Don Lindgren. What a beautiful ride in the country, as compared to some places that are off main roads (Rte 2) or very busy roads (Rte 110). I really wanted to hang my head out the window, but I know that's not allowed, 'cause NEADS and the veterinarians don't want little particles of grit to get embedded in my eyeball (it HAS happened to other dogs, you know). So I just sat up straight and watched the scenery whizzing by.

As we entered Don's room, I could tell he recognized me right away, so I walked right over, tail wagging, and put my big handsome head on his lap. He really loves me!

Don said that we just missed Ellie, and that was a disappointment, 'cause she's another dog person, and she's so doggone nice to me. Don told us all about his medical problems, and when he started talking about his days in the Army, I settled down for a little nap.

Even though I'm a Service Dog, when these guys start talking about their days when they were in "the service" it gets boring. I thought Don wanted to get back home—he said he'd been there long enough, and the food wasn't that good.

Talk about food! Mom and Dad have me on a restricted diet now because I've gained too much weight, and my tummy started growling when Don was talking about runny scrambled eggs and watery oatmeal. Just give it to me and see how fast I can make it disappear!

Just when we were getting ready to leave, a friend walked in to visit Don, so we felt good that he had more company.

I like visiting ALL people, because that's the kind of guy I am, but with people like Don (and Ellie), it's so much easier, because they're so friendly and you can tell right away they're dog people. God bless them!

Woof!

Mosby Mac Fisher

Chapter 48

RE-CERTIFICATION TEST

July 30, 2009

Today was a different kind of day for me—I went for a re-certification test! Mom had been notified a while ago that it was time for me to be tested, to be sure that I had not forgotten any of the many commands that I've learned. As if I would do that! Mom and Dad are always running through all the obedience work that I had learned at NEADS, even the ones that I don't usually use very often, so I was confident that the test would go well, and so were Mom and Dad. But, like Dad says, "you never know."

It was off to the old Searstown Mall, under a new name now, but still the same old place, just spiffed up a bit. We met, at the Food Court, two other dogs who were being re-tested, Willow and Jasper, who had brought their handlers with them, too. I remembered Jasper from my training days, but Willow, another Golden, was new to me. Of course, we all got along well together, after the first few minutes of eager sniffing. Mom was wondering a wee bit about my performance, 'cause I just love to bits all other people, especially kids, but everything went well, except that I barked a few times and Mom had to correct me. Gee, I was just cheering them on when they went through their paces. No need to get grumpy about it.

I was delighted to see that the other two dogs didn't like their Gentle Leader nose bands any more than I did, but it didn't stop us all from doing everything that Jennifer wanted us to do.

We did Sit and Down, of course, and walking at different paces at Heel, then stopping and starting again and going around corners. Then the handlers had to put us on a Sit, drop the leash and walk away, and we had to stay on the Sit until called. Nothing to it! A piece of cake!

Jennifer had something yummy that she dropped on the floor and Mom walked me up to it and I had to lie down LOOKING RIGHT AT THE TREAT! Mom told me I couldn't have it, though, so I didn't touch it—didn't even sniff it. Then Mom had me walk right past it, turn around and go by it again, and she told Dad afterwards she was so proud of me 'cause even though my tummy was growling, I ignored it, although she could see that my eyes were on it. She thought I did extremely well on that.

Jennifer started asking passers-by if they'd help out with the testing by approaching us dogs and patting us while we stayed Down, which went really well, although there were a few kids that I really wanted to play with. We all passed when we were walking and Jennifer dropped her clipboard right behind us, and we could look, but not jump or otherwise react.

The end of the testing came when we went out to the parking lot and jumped into the car on command, then waited until the command to jump out. Another piece of cake.

We all passed, and I heard Jennifer tell Mom and Dad that I wouldn't have to be tested for three years. Then there'd be another similar test, and they know I'm ready for it!

Mosby Mac Fisher
Therapy Dog for the Ministry
(as dictated to Mom)

Chapter 49

AN INQUIRY FROM A WEST COAST CHRISTIAN PUBLICATION

The church office received an inquiry and passed it on to me:

From: Andrea Bailey Willits

Aug 3, 2009

Hi there!

My name is Andrea Bailey Willits, and I'm a writer for Outreach magazine. We're a national magazine based out of San Diego that educates and inspires churches about innovative outreach to their communities.

I read about Mosby, your ministry dog, at Boston.com. I am interested in writing a short piece about the work Mosby and the Fishers do with senior citizens in your community. I know they minister to all ages, but I'd like to focus specifically on the elderly for a section in our magazine called Pulse: Seniors.

I'm wondering, how can I get in contact with the Fishers to interview them over the phone? I'd also love to talk with Pastor Deborah there about the impact of being a church with a ministry dog. If you could offer me some guidance on how to get started, that would be most helpful!

Thanks!

Andrea Bailey Willits

Hi Andrea,

Thank you for your e-mail about Mosby! This is Debbie . . . answering from my home e-mail. I would be glad to talk to you about Mosby and get you in touch with Lynda Fisher. I will copy the e-mail to her now . . . and maybe you and she can set up a time to talk?

I'll look forward to talking to you.

Debbie Blanchard

Aug 6, 2009 I wrote:

Hi, Andrea—

I think I let the ball drop on this one. I was waiting for a response from you, but nothing happened. Then when I re-read the messages, it appears that I'm supposed to contact you! So here I am.

Apparently, a phone call will be necessary, and with the three-hour time lag, and our schedules (probably yours, too) this will take a bit of engineering.

We're really thrilled that Mosby will be known across the country! He started out with a local paper, then he was all over the Globe West edition, and now a California-based publication. Wow! What a guy! And it's all because he's working for God.

And, I must tell you, all this publicity has not turned his head one single bit. He's still the same affable, people-loving guy he's always been.

Lynda Fisher

Aug 6, 2009 Andrea wrote:

Hi Lynda!

Thanks so much for your e-mail. I'm actually on vacation with my husband until Wednesday August 12. Is it OK if I get in touch with you then to schedule an interview?

I'm looking forward to talking to you!

Andrea

This story continues in another chapter, when we all got back in sync from vacations and computer glitches.

Chapter 50

VACATION BIBLE SCHOOL

August 6

To Deb:

Just when I start getting complacent about visitations, my Boss finds something else for me to do. I was pawsitively getting ho-hum about visiting all these folks in nursing homes, etc., and listening to Mom and Dad discussing where we'd go this week, when my Boss intervened and set me on a different track. Rev. Gail Wright from the Congregational Church e-mailed Mom to ask if I'd be willing to come to the Vacation Bible School closing ceremony, so my ears perked up when I heard them discussing this. Something different! And with kids! What's not to like about this?

So off we went to the Congo Church, just in time to enter and meet lots of kids as they moved from one class area to another. So many kids! And I had to let them all pat me as they passed by. I knew the Vacation Bible School is open to all kids in town, not just kids from this church, so I was hoping to see some of MY kids from MY church, but I didn't spot any right off. They're probably all away on vacations with their families.

Then Gail asked us to follow her upstairs to the Sanctuary right down to the front of the church, and we stood beside her as she talked to the kids about Serving Others and my role in this. She asked Mom a few questions about me, then the kids had a chance to ask their questions, and I think Mom did a good job of telling everyone all about me and all the services I give to others. I spotted Micah Webster with a group of kids and couldn't wait for him to come up to pat me afterwards. He waited until the kids in his group had all had a chance, as a good leader should, and then he reached down to kiss my silky head, and I got him with a big kiss on the lips! I was a little disappointed that I didn't see any of my kids from my church there, but it was nice to see Micah anyway, in his role of group leader.

Later in the afternoon I took my folks to the veterinarian's office for a quick check of a wee little lump between my shoulder blades which Mom wanted checked out. Turns out it was nothing, as I figured, but you can never be too careful, I'm thinking. When my weight was checked, I was a little disappointed to find I've only lost a half pound—after all the restricted food intake I've had to deal with, I'd have thought a five-pound loss at least, but no, just a measly little half pound. But, like Dad said, it wasn't a weight gain, but a loss, which is a good thing.

So that's my outreach for this week. Now I'm going to relax and lie down underfoot for a while.

Mosby Mac Fisher, Ministry Dog

On Aug 6, 2009, Gail Wright wrote:

Mosby,

Thank you for sending the report to me. You did wonderful ministry today with us. I thought that you and your Mom and Dad might like to see these pictures. I have a bunch more. You really did a great job of showing God's love to the kids and reminding them that we all have gifts to give.

Thank you again. Hope to see you Sunday.

Blessings, Rev. Gail Wright

August 7 To Gail Wright

Many thanks for the pictures. I'll send them on to Pastor Deb, Dad, and Uncle Jack. I always enjoy my experiences with humans, especially kids, and I'm always available to help you out in any way I can. After all, I'm doing God's work, and He's my Boss!

Arf!

Mosby Mac Fisher, Ministry Dog

Chapter 51

A CONTINUATION OF THE WEST COAST PUBLICATION STORY

On Wed, Aug 12, 2009 Andrea Bailey Willits wrote:

Lynda,

Just got back this afternoon from California with the hubby. Do you have time on Monday, August 17, to chat about Mosby? I'm based in Nashville, so we only have a one-hour time difference to work around. Just let me know when is convenient for you, or if Tuesday might work better.

Thanks!

Andrea

Aug 18, 2009 Andrea wrote again:

Hi Lynda,

Just wanted to touch base with you to see when you might be available for an interview! Hope you are doing well!

Andrea

Thu, Aug 20, 2009 I wrote:

Hi, Andrea—

I'm sorry I didn't get back to you sooner, but my hard drive died, and my computer has been languishing in the computer hospital for almost TWO WEEKS! I just got it back today at 5 p.m., and I'm wading through all my e-mail messages—over 300! Of course, the majority of the messages HAVE to be jokes, and mail order confirmations, which I can get into later.

Tomorrow we go to the airport to welcome home our grandson's daddy who has been deployed to Afghanistan for a year, and the greatest portion of the day will be devoted to that, stretching into the evening hours. Then, on Saturday, will be the big welcome home party. Does next Monday work for you?

ljf

From Andrea 8/21

Lynda,

Oh NO! Computer trouble is the worst. I live in fear of the day my Mac dies. I hope your hard drive is back to normal now, and you successfully combed through all the junk e-mail (I always get ones from rich people in other countries wanting to wire money into your account if you will just give them your account number!!!)

Wow, I'm so glad that your grandson's dad is coming back safely. I hope you will enjoy an amazing celebration this weekend!!

Could we talk at 9 a.m. EST on Monday? That will be 8 a.m. my time. I have other times available throughout the day, so just let me know your preference.

Thank you very much!

Andrea

Chapter 52

VISITING CHURCH FOLKS AT THE NURSING HOME

August 23 To Deb

Woof! It's been quite a while since I've reported in on my busy life, but that's because of Mom's computer crashing. It was in the hospital for a new hard drive for just under TWO WEEKS. TWO WEEKS! I thought Mom was going to go crazy without it. Besides her not being able to do her genealogy work, she couldn't do any library work that she's been doing for that nice library lady, Marnie Oakes, and she couldn't get any e-mail messages, nor updates to her Facebook page, so life was ruff.

And I couldn't dictate my Ministry Dog activities to her, either.

So—here we are again, and I have to go back to two weeks ago, when I took Mom and Dad for a visit to Life Care Center up on Foster Street. When we arrived at the front door, my first duty was to go over to Alberta White who was sitting outside soaking up the sunshine. I try to see Alberta every time I go to Life Care Center because she's been a long-time Golden Retriever raiser, breeder, and trainer, and I could sense it, even though she had to tell Mom and Dad because they're naturally not as intuitive about these things as I am. I think Alberta forgets they've met her before. She always chats to us about her dogs and sometimes tries to sneak a treat to me, when Mom isn't looking.

Our first official visit was to drop in on Jane Bean, and were we ever surprised to enter her room and find Julie Poplin sitting across from her wheelchair playing a board game with her. It was so crowded that I couldn't get very close to Jane, but I tried my darndest to get my head or paw up to her so that she could pat me and feel better. A broad smile on her face indicated that she remembered us, which was a relief to me, at least.

We didn't stay too long, so as to let the ladies continue with their game, but it was good to see them both, even if it was just for a short visit.

We next stopped in to see Phyllis Wallace, who was sitting in her wheelchair. She proudly showed us my Globe newspaper article which was up on the wall on top of her dresser. We had a nice little visit with her—she's one of my favorite people to visit there, because she always gives me a scratch on my head when she can reach it. She says that one foot is healed and they're working on the other, then she'll be out of there. I was thinking it was lucky for her that she doesn't have FOUR feet, like I do, because then she'd be in there for a good long while.

Mosby Mac Fisher, Therapy Dog for the Ministry

Chapter 53

A LONG-AWAITED MILITARY REUNION

I wanted the folks to save the end of August and not plan any visits because we weren't exactly sure when Steve would be coming home, and none of us wanted to miss that event, fur sure. Finally, Laurie called to say that it definitely would be Friday, August 21, and eventually she called to say that Steve's flight would arrive in Manchester Airport at 7:11 p.m. Great!

We got all spiffied up for that, let me tell you. I thought they were going to give me a bath, but the water was only on for their showers, thank Boss. They had laid out red, white, and blue clothes to wear, and then Mom turned to me while Dad was in the shower. I knew I was in trouble when the nail clippers came out—I really hate that job! Even though Mom tries hard not to hurt me, sometimes I just have to let out a little yip just to make her feel guilty and stop before all the nails are done. Then the teeth cleaning starts, which is just yucky, not painful.

Next comes the ears which are wiped out with Mikey's perfumed baby wipes, of all things. It's very embarrassing, let me tell you. I'm glad nobody is around to see that. Then come the easy things—the raking of my beautiful, silky coat, followed by the brushing, which is followed by the scissors with a little trim around the edges to remove any out-of-place hairs.

The final touch is a quick spray with my manly doggie cologne, which is used when I don't have a bath and Mom isn't sure that I'll smell all right. A little neck scarf with a red, white and blue design with the words, "I love the USA" finish off my toilette, and I'm good to go.

As we arrived at Gate 3 at the airport, we knew we were in the right place because of all the military-type people hanging around in a cluster. Of course, they all had to pat me and introduce themselves to us, and I realized that they're always there when their soldiers are deployed or when they return. It's nice that they support our men and women in this fashion.

A lady sat next to Mom and started talking to her (as so many people do, who really want to talk to me). She explained that she was a minister and was very interested in Mom's work with me, so Mom whipped out one of my cards and told the nice lady to call her and they could chat some more.

Soon Nancy (Steve's mom) and Chuck arrived with a big cardboard poster saying, "Welcome home, Capt. Mongelli." I couldn't believe it when Laurie, my little buddy Mikey, and Steve's sister Karen arrived—they had the biggest bunch of balloons I've ever seen, and enough American flags to sink a battleship. Mikey was so excited he was hopping out of his little pants. And then, we all waited, and waited, and waited.

I was kept pretty busy chatting with the reporters and camera people from the New Hampshire news media, both newspapers and television stations. One nice lady interviewed me, holding the mike close to my lips, while she asked her questions and Mom interpreted for me. Then, at last, the loudspeaker announced Steve's flight, and we waited impatiently while some civilians straggled down the stairs and through the gate.

Then, finally, we saw a guy walk through in military camos, but it wasn't our soldier. But the next one was! Mikey tore over to Steve and he leaned down to wrap his arms around his little son, and they had a great big bear hug. For a long time. At last Steve lifted Mikey up in his arms and walked toward where we were standing, still hugging and snuggling with him.

I tell you, when I looked around at the crowd, there were many surreptitious wipings of eyes, even the newspaper reporter. They could tell where the story was, and as Steve was shaking congratulatory hands with his General and the other officers, the news folks were hanging around him and Mikey.

Other soldiers had also arrived by this time, so the whole area was engaged in much hugging and kissing and back slapping as each soldier found his family and friends. There was much spontaneous applause as each soldier walked through the gate, and even people who weren't part of the welcoming party stopped by when they saw all the flags, balloons, and military figures. They applauded just as vigorously as we did, and thanked some of the soldiers for their service to our country. What a joyous, happy time this was! We were told there would be a formal reception next Tuesday at the Armory, but this was the moment that everyone will remember.

Steve helped retrieve all the luggage from the carousel and doled it out to the proper men, and then we headed to the Airport Diner for a casual, welcome-home supper, just Steve, Mikey, Laurie, Nancy, Chuck, Karen, Mom and Dad, and me. They all had food, but told me since I had eaten earlier in the afternoon, I shouldn't have anything, but just lie on the floor at Mom's feet. Gee, what a letdown for me, but at least I could hear Steve telling stories about life in Afghanistan, and it was so good to hear his voice again.

The next day, Saturday, Karen had a cookout at her home in Townsend which included more family members, but I was so tuckered out from my day on Friday that I opted to stay home and nap. A guy can take just so much, then he has to relax a bit, you know.

But now I'm all geared up to go to the Concord Armory on Tuesday for the welcoming home ceremonies. There's a bunch of local (New Hampshire) lady volunteers that always provide food for the military events, and I bet I can sneak something there.

It's not so interesting hearing all the speeches from the General, probably the Governor or his representative, but the food is always worth the wait. And, of course, all the kids have to come up to pat me, and I look forward to that, as well as being around all the soldiers who have put themselves in harm's way to help bring freedom to another part of the world. I thank my Boss that they're not fighting here on our land, even though that means they have to leave us and go halfway around the world.

Arf!

Mosby Mac Fisher, Ministry Dog
(as dictated to Mom Fisher)

Chapter 54

A TWO-WAY WIN AFTER CHURCH

Aug 24, 2009 Pastor Deb wrote:

Lynda,

. . . . I just love the ministry that Mosby and you both have brought to our church! What a continuous blessing reaching as close as our children and as far as the West Coast! I loved watching Kelly with Mosby yesterday . . . . God is good . . . .

Deb

To Deb 8/24

Funny thing—I had asked Alyssa to hold Mo's leash because I had coffee hour and Larry had elevator duty, and she and Kelly did a great job. I kept an eye on them, but really wasn't concerned because I knew he was in good hands. Afterwards, one of the parents thanked Larry for letting the girls handle Mosby, but at the same time I was thanking the girls for taking such good care of him!

It's a win/win situation.

ljf

Chapter 55

AT LAST—THE WEST COAST CONNECTION

Aug 24, 2009 Mosby wrote:

Hi, Andrea—

I personally want to thank you for spending almost an hour on the phone this morning, talking to Mom about me. You do realize, I hope, that I was sitting right next to her, feeding her the answers to your questions. I pawsitively like to stay in the background, but doggone it all, I still want my opinions to be heard. I do hope your Christian magazine will run an article on me—anything to get the Word out to folks about my job for my Boss.

First of all, I've attached two pictures for you to use, if you'd like. The Souperbowl picture was taken after our church youth group had a fundraiser for our local food pantry on Superbowl Sunday, and let me tell you, I was kept very busy retrieving all the food to be put into the basket. Naturally, I'm very good at that. The picture shows me in the foreground, with my Dad sitting right behind me, and we're surrounded by some of the volunteers who helped me.

You had asked what I did for just fun when my working vest is off and I'm just a plain family member—well, the "Ring" picture shows me jumping through my agility ring which Dad set up for me in our wee back yard. I could have done it myself, but I have trouble reading the fine print in the instructions, and my dewclaw kept getting in the way. It's nothing like having an opposable thumb, let me tell you. If I had that, I wouldn't have to ask Mum to do my typing for me. God is good, but sometimes he gives me challenges. But—he's my Boss, so I do what he wants me to do.

Also attached is my Annual Report to my church family. In our church, each year, all the officers and boards and committees have to right a report of their activities, and since I came on board, officially, with Pastor Debbie's Commissioning Service for us, I thought I should write my own report. This will give you a great overview of what I've been doing for my church and community, as my Boss has directed me to do.

If you have any questions, or want any more help, please don't hesitate to call or e-mail me.

Woof!

Mosby Mac Fisher, Ministry Dog

On Aug 26, 2009, Andrea Bailey Willits wrote:

Hi Mosby,

You are definitely one of the most remarkable dogs I have ever come across—I hope someday I will have the privilege of petting you! You've made me want to have a ministry dog of my own. Until then, keep up the good work making people feel better. I know that God is very proud of you.

Would you ask your mom if she has any other pictures of you that she could send me? I'm looking for ones where you are ministering to a senior citizen, in particular. And could you ask her to make sure the file size is BIG and HIGH RESOLUTION (at least 300 dpi)? We need the image to be extra-large for it to print in our magazine.

Thanks again, Mosby. And I must say, from the looks of the picture of you jumping through the hoop, you are very agile.

Andrea

August 29 To Andrea

Hmmm. That's a really tough request. I don't usually have my picture taken while I'm visiting folks, except for the time when the Boston Globe videographer took some pictures. You probably don't want to ask them for THEIR pictures, do you? I can ask Pastor Deb if she, or the church photographer, Barb Staples, has some pictures of me participating in church events, like the Children's Sermon. Would that do, instead?

I do want to help you out, 'cause I know that having some pictures would enhance the story, but I'm not sure if I can help.

We'll see what I can do in the next couple of days.

God Bless!

And that's where this portion of Mosby's story ends. I never received notification that Andrea's story was published, although I was hoping to receive a copy which I could keep for Mosby's scrapbook. So we don't know if her story was rejected by the publisher, or perhaps she just forgot to send us a copy. Busy people sometimes forget things, we are aware of that.

Chapter 56

THE CELEBRATION AT THE NATIONAL GUARD ARMORY

August 29 To Deb

So far, my visits have been to bring a little cheer into someone's life, by greeting them, letting them pat me and hug me, and being by their side. But this past week, on Tuesday, I experienced a different kind of event. I took my Mom and Dad up to the New Hampshire National Guard Armory in Concord to celebrate the homecoming of my brother, Steve, and the rest of his unit. We had greeted him at the airport the Friday before, and I felt a little superfluous there, too, but it was doggone nice to be patted by all those nice folks, all impatiently waiting for the anticipated arrival of their loved ones, home safely from Afghanistan. On Saturday, I decided to stay home when my folks went to sister Karen's house for a little welcoming get-together, 'cause I felt that I wouldn't be doing any good for anyone there—they were already as happy as they could be.

But on Tuesday I thought my services might be needed by SOMEONE, but, boy was I wrong. As we entered the room, I could tell the mood was upbeat and happy, and nobody seemed to need my comforting presence. Even so, the little ones timidly approached me, most of them asking permission from Mom to touch me. One little tyke even gave me a great big bear hug! The military personnel were all over the place, and a few of them came over to me, remembering me from the airport at their departure, and one guy thanked Mom for bringing me there. I thought that was really nice of him, and I silently thanked him for his service to our country.

Then we were all asked to take our seats (except me) for the speeches to commence. Since these things are pretty boring, I pretended to be alert, but I really was dozing. Except for the part where someone sang the National Anthem, and I ALWAYS stand at attention (sort of) for that, just as my folks do. The news folks were all over the place, trying to get the best possible pictures, snapping their flashes, but it didn't interrupt my nap at all.

After the speeches and applause for the returnees came the food, but all I got, as usual, was a few ice chips from the lady at the end of the line. She told me that her organization, whose main purpose is to provide food for events such as this one, donates annually to NEADS, which gave me a happy feeling as my Mom thanked her. So—I was there, and ready to give a warm paw to anyone who needed it, but my professional presence for which I've been trained was unnecessary on this trip. Why did I go? Maybe to show the military folks that our whole family, including me, supports them in their efforts to keep our world free.

Mosby Mac Fisher, Ministry Dog
(as dictated to Mom)

Chapter 57

MOSBY'S MEANDERINGS

September 2009

It was back on duty for me today—no more hanging out with the military, which is more of an upper for me, a cause for celebration.

Today I took Mom and Dad back to our old familiar place—Life Care Center of Nashoba Valley, on Foster Street. Of course, we couldn't actually enter the building without greeting all the nice folks who were sitting outside.

Doggone it, I'm going to miss them when it's too cold to hang around outside. There are always outstretched hands which have to be taken care of, and sometimes I find something sweet on the ground, which Mom and Dad don't like too much. They're always saying, "leave it" in a stern voice, so I have to be pretty quick to get away with anything.

We first visited Jane Bean, who again was playing cards with Julia Poplin and another nice lady, who introduced herself, but I was more interested in her hand than remembering her name. She had a nice touch when she patted my silky head. I could have stayed there for a while longer, but we only stayed a short time and then Mom and Dad headed out to let them get back to their card game.

Phyllis Wallace was back in her wheelchair, and her feet looked pretty good—at least what I could see of them, which was only sox, instead of the big felt bootees she had been wearing. I thought that was a good sign, and Mom and Dad did so, too.

Phyllis was in good spirits and wanted me closer than Dad would let me, 'cause he was afraid that I'd hurt her feet. So she reached over to me and patted me for a little while. We really have a nice bunch of people in our church, and I'm so grateful to my Boss for assigning me this job of visiting them—it's the easiest job ever!

I heard Mom and Dad talking about visiting Elsa Manni next week, and she's another person I love to visit, cause she's so happy to see us. The only thing is, it's terribly hard for the humans to carry on a conversation with her because she's so hard of hearing. I don't have any problem there, 'cause she knows when my tail is wagging that I'm happy to see her, and that gives her a good Swedish laugh.

I can hardly wait for next week! And I can hardly wait for church next Sunday. Mom and Dad almost didn't take me this past Sunday 'cause it had been raining and there was still a slight drizzle and, for some reason, they think my wet dog fur is unappealing. I don't find it so, at all. After I gave them a couple of sorrowful dog expressions, they decided to take me, and I'm so glad they did.

Afterwards I got to shmooze around with both Kelly Flynn and Alyssa Mackersie, in Fellowship Hall, which I love. I even rolled over on my back so they and the Webster boys could give me a belly rub. Then Dad finished my after-church routine by taking me over to the bench where the ladies sit who are waiting to go out to lunch, and I made the rounds of all of them. Church is so much fun!

Woof!

Mosby Mac Fisher, Ministry Dog
(as dictated to Mom)

Chapter 58

MOSBY'S MEANDERINGS—
WEEKS ENDING 9/12/09 AND 9/19/09

I keep reminding Mom to write up my journal, but she insists she's too tuckered out from our wonderful weekend at the Highland Games and hasn't recovered yet. If only I had an opposable thumb instead of this useless dewclaw! Then I'd be able to do my own typing instead of dictating to Mom. I know she's busy, and I know she's tired, so I just have to learn to be patient, I guess. There's something in the Bible, as I recall, about practicing patience and understanding. I guess I'll have to talk to my Boss about it.

So—here goes. Starting with the first week, we had business in Acton on Tuesday, so Mom and Dad decided to combine errands to save on gas. So we high-tailed it over to the Life Care Center of Acton to visit one of my favorite people—Elsa Manni. I really miss Kaarlo, not as much as Elsa does, but still, he was one of the nicest folks we visited. He knew just the right spot behind my ears that I love scratched, so now Elsa has to do it. Sort of in his memory, I like to think. As usual, it took forever to get to Elsa's room, 'cause everyone has to reach out to pet me, and I can't walk by them. I know my Boss doesn't want me to. So Mom and Dad have to stay with me while people talk to me about how beautiful I am. It feels so good to bring some happiness into their lives, even if it's only for a moment.

We had to knock on Elsa's door since it was shut most of the way, even though I was quite willing to nose around it. Mom told me it wasn't polite to do that and I'd have to wait until it was opened, which I did, but reluctantly. Soon an attendant opened the door and, to our surprise, Elsa was lying down in her bed with her eyes closed. In the middle of the day! Mom gently touched her shoulder to see if she was just resting, and soon her eyes opened, but I'm not sure if she recognized us. She smiled, but her laugh wasn't there. Dad chatted with her a minute, then we all decided it would be better if we left, 'cause Elsa just wasn't having a very good day. She said she didn't mean to be rude, but she just wasn't feeling up to having company, and Mom said she understood and we'd come back another day. Elsa did manage to take a hand away from the blanket and gave me a little pat, which brought a smile to her face; then she said, "Goodbye, poochie" and I knew she hadn't remembered my name. So sad!

It's not often that we all feel sad as we slowly make our way back to our car, but today was one of those times that didn't turn out as well as most.

Then, the next day Aunt Bobbie called Mom to tell her that SHE had gone to visit Elsa the day before, and to her surprise, they were loading our favorite Swede into the ambulance to take her to the hospital! So—that's probably why she wasn't feeling so good when we saw her. It must have been a quick turn-around, but she obviously wasn't feeling that chipper.

But this past weekend was a real hum-dinger of a weekend. On Friday morning we drove to Lincoln, New Hampshire to celebrate our Scottish heritages at the New Hampshire Highland Games on the slopes of Loon Mountain on the beautiful Kancamagus Highway. As soon as we exited the shuttle bus which transported us to the entrance of the Loon ski area, I started to get excited, hearing the pipers practicing and seeing the tumbling waters of the Pemigewassit River below us as we hurried over the bridge. I really pulled Mom along and she kept on telling me to "go easy" which I didn't obey. I couldn't! I really, really, really wanted to get there! In a hurry! I was pawsitively ecstatic to be returning to the Games. The first thing we did was go over to the slopes to watch the sheep dog trials. I remembered that last year Dad wasn't happy at my barking when I was cheering on the Border Collies while they were herding those stubborn sheep through the appropriate gates, so this year I muzzled myself admirably and only looked very attentive. Dad said he heard someone marvel at how alert I looked, yet didn't bark. I know that made Dad very happy.

When we checked in at the Clan Sutherland tent, I remembered all the folks I'd met before and wagged my tail and used my best smile for them. They're such nice folks, even though they wouldn't share any food with me.

On one occasion, while Mom was checking over the heather plants at a vendor's tent, Dad saw a woman from another tent eyeing us as we were surrounded by admiring kids. Soon that woman appeared right in front of me, reaching out a tentative hand to pat my head. She said to Dad that she didn't like dogs, but I was so "beautiful" she wanted to pat me. Then she said, "I hate dogs, but this one is different," and surprised me with a hug. Could be she felt my close alliance with God? My Calling?

On Friday night, Mom had brought a casserole which they all enjoyed, instead of going out to eat, since it was easier than hassling the crowds which were all over the place, filling up all the local eateries. It's a good thing that Dad had remembered to bring my own special food, since, as usual, I wasn't allowed to eat any human food. That's OK, because nobody eats my puppy food, either.

On Saturday, I sat politely at the Parade Grounds while the Clan Parade and Opening Ceremonies filled the area with bagpipes and drums, and I appropriately stood, at Mom's prompt, when they played the Star Spangled Banner. All the time we made the rounds of the vendors' tents and other clan tents, I had to be on my best behavior because we were constantly stopped by people, mostly kids, who wanted to pat me and ask Dad or Mom about what I did, but I didn't mind, 'cause that just spreads the word further about my ministry work for my Boss. My little buddy, Mikey, arrived with his mom and dad, and we walked around a bit together, but most of the time we went our separate ways because I was always slowed down by so many people wanting to visit with me.

Mom's clan had a special dinner on Saturday night, to which I had been invited, but I declined, since I'd rather spend time quietly with Mikey, Laurie and Steve. I hadn't really had time to play with the little fella much, and I felt he needed some of my undivided attention.

Sunday morning found us back on the slopes for the Worship Service, led by Dr. Turner. He's really an entertaining sort, sprinkling the whole hour with little jokes here and there. I wonder if Pastor Debbie knows that, for folks who think the Bible is much too long to read, there's a 50-word version? I was very proud when Mom's Clan Sutherland and Dad's Clan Morrison marched in with the other clans, all carrying their clan banners, to be blessed by Dr. Turner.

The weekend finally came to a close Sunday afternoon, and as we slowly walked across the bridge to the waiting shuttle bus, I was filled with a little nostalgia. A whole year to wait for the next Games! Maybe I can talk Mom and Dad into going to some of the other games? Let's see, there's Berwick, Maine; Queechee, Vermont; Glasgow Games in Connecticut, to name a few. Lots of opportunities. I'm so happy that I share my parents' Scottish bloodlines. It gives us something in common to celebrate. I must remember to thank Boss tonight in my prayers.

Och Aye!

Mosby Mac Fisher, Ministry Dog

Mosby and his friend, the Pipe Major

Chapter 59

TOWN AUCTION

September 2009

Yesterday was another "first" for me—at Uncle Jack's invitation, I attended my first town auction, this one to benefit jointly the schools and the Council on Aging. I didn't know what to expect as I entered the middle school, but, as soon as I spotted Auntie Bobbie, I knew I was in a good place. She always has a smile for me and a hand reaching out to pat me, and of course, I got a wee bit too excited, but only for a short time.

I quickly settled down, and soon there was a table set up for Mom and Dad to put out all the paraphernalia they had carried in to entice people to spend a little money at my table, to help pay off my debt to NEADS. Mom had made a tri-fold poster board display with the NEADS name on one side of the fold, my name on the other, and in the center, the Boston Globe West article starring me, complete with pictures taken at church and visiting Life Care Center of Nashoba Valley. Sitting in front of that was my graduation picture, with all my classmates and Randy Price, our esteemed MC for the ceremonies. Mom had also placed in front some fliers from NEADS, in addition to my business cards, which were a huge hit with most of the folks who stopped by. Many of them bought some of the treats to help pay my tuition, and Mom made sure they had my business card when they left the table. Pawsitively, I can hear the phone ringing with requests for me to visit someone.

Even though Uncle Jack was a great auctioneer and kept the audience entertained, I soon fell asleep under the table. After all, it's hard work welcoming all those people with a wagging tail and a smile on my face. I just loved the kids, and when one woman sat down on the floor beside me, I just walked right on top of her, as I do to Dad. She said it made her feel so much happier!

All these "different" events have really perked me up, and I surely enjoy them all, since it's another way of passing on my love to many people. On the other paw, though, I do enjoy visiting sick folks and helping to bring a smile to their faces. I guess I'm just really satisfied about this job I have—I'm bringing happiness and healing to folks who need it, and I have a really great Boss. What more could a guy ask for?

Woof!

Mosby Mac Fisher, Ministry Dog

Chapter 60

MOSBY'S BUSY WEEKLY MEANDERINGS

Oct 2009

Another couple of weeks have gone by without my report. But don't blame it on me—I'm always ready to write up a report, but this darned opposable thumb business (or lack of it) keeps me from doing my own typing, so I have to wait until Mom has time so that I can dictate to her. Right now, she's all involved in her genealogy research, and any free time is dedicated to that, since she's gotten to the point of putting Mikey's ancestors into her huge database. Boy, I thought my pedigree was long—but Mikey's and Mom's and Dad's are even longer yet! I'm quite proud that in my pedigree there are Champions, both in Field Work and Show Rings, and my line goes back a goodly bit. But—Mom has researched hers, Dad's, and now Mikey's way back to Charlemagne and also the Vikings. That beats mine! But it's very hard to get her, when she's on the computer, away from genealogy and onto my work. I come up to the loft area where the computer lives, put my head on her lap and search into her eyes, and she finally relents.

Well, I must say, my life is never boring. I go to so many doggone different places doing my Ministry work for my Boss. But last Tuesday, on October 6, I did get a chance to get back to Life Care Center in Littleton to visit Phyllis Wallace. Jane Bean isn't there now, but Phyllis is always a person that I look forward to seeing, because she's usually so upbeat and easy to talk to. I can't always get too close to her to give her my handsome head on her lap because I always have to be aware of her wrapped-up feet, so have to keep my distance from her. Somehow, for her to just look at me and pat my head, seems enough to get her to smile. But this time, she told us right away that her roommate had died the day before, so the family was busy cleaning out all her belongings. Hoping to get out of their way, we pushed Phyllis in her wheelchair down the hall to the circular area where all the wings converge and found a few chairs for Mom and Dad to sit on. I was quite comfortable on the floor.

If you're a Golden Retriever, and you want to receive a lot of attention, this is the place to be. Everyone, residents and workers alike, paused on their way to another side of the building to pat me and chat with Mom, Dad, and Phyllis, who was quick to tell them that I was visiting HER. At last, there was enough space that I could sit beside Phyllis' wheelchair and put my huge head on her lap. She loved that, breaking out into a wider smile, and patting my head for a long time. We both received God's blessings on that.

So many people stopped to talk to Mom and Dad and pat my silky head, that I lost track of them, although I knew some from previous visits. I was saddened to hear, from one of the workers, that my friend Coda had died. Mom said she thought it would be Charlie, since he was the older of the Director's two adult Golden Retrievers who were quite frequently visiting there on the days when I also visited. We had heard that Charlie had retired and wasn't appearing too often, but, sadly, it was Coda who took sick and was gone in a very short while. I know she waits at the Rainbow Bridge at the Gates of Heaven for her buddy Charlie, and her human person. I'll miss her, but I know she's in a good place, where someday I'll be, too. Then I'll see her again. Somewhere it is written that when humans love their animals greatly, they get into Heaven when it's their human's time. I believe that—my Boss has told me so. It's a comforting thought, both for me and for my humans.

During our time with Phyllis, Linda Wilson, a worker whom I'm familiar with, stopped by to chat and pat my head, and guess what? She had her digital camera with her and took a really great picture of me sitting beside Phyllis, my head in her lap, and there's a copy of it at the desk now, waiting for us to pick it up. Mom and Dad were really excited when they saw it—they want to put it up on the church bulletin board.

Soon a pleasant hour had passed, and we thought that Phyllis looked a little droopy, so we took her back to her room, which was now empty of people busily packing up belongings, and we were on our way home. Another nice visit with a nice lady, to store up precious memories.

This past Monday was Grotonwood Day, and a day which we all looked forward to turned out to be not so pleasant. All my fault, too. As soon as we exited our car in the parking lot, I remembered Grotonwood from last year, and I was beside myself with eagerness and excitement, yipping and pulling. Even though Mom had the Easy Lead Harness on, I was so eager to get there that I pulled too hard, and I even barked in my excitement. I was embarrassed when Dad put on the Gentle Leader nose collar, but I heard him tell Mom it had to be used, or they'd lose their arms from their sockets from my pulling. Mom signed us in on the Littleton sheet—first Dad, then Mom on the next line, and ME—Mosby Mac Fisher—on the following line. I'm not sure if I'll count on the total church tallies, but I sure hope so, 'cause I was just as enthusiastic as any of the kids who were there.

As usual when we're in a place with lots of people, it took a long time to get from point A to point B because of everyone who stopped us to pet me and ask questions about my service. We didn't pass by anyone who looked like they wanted to touch me, since that's what my service is all about. One young man in a wheelchair really took to me and said he wished he could have a service dog like me, but he was refused. Of course, Mom asked him if he knew about NEADS, which he didn't, so she gave him my business card (she always carries one or two) and said if he e-mailed me, I could give him the website for NEADS, and he could contact them. Who knows—maybe next year, there'll be another NEADS pup there. We didn't see Pastor Rene and Aubie, as we had last year. I hope they're doing well together.

We certainly enjoyed walking around, seeing all the kids having fun at different games and booths, and listening to the band tune up. At one point we took a lovely walk through the woods on a fairly narrow path and for once I wasn't yipping and pulling. I was enjoying myself, but not noisily. I seemed to have everything in control, as I ought to have done from the beginning. Then, Mom heard a loud noise approaching us, and it was a tractor pulling a wagon loaded with people—adults and kids. We stepped off the narrow path to let them go by, and we waved them on—Mom and Dad with their arms and me with my tail. Some of them knew us and yelled, "Hey Mosby!" As usual, their yells were for me, not Mom and Dad. But they're used to it. I yipped a few welcoming barks to them, and for once Mom didn't hush me up. She knew I was just getting into the spirit of the day.

I'm ashamed to say that because of my poor behavior, Mom and Dad decided to call it a day early, so we picked up our apple pie which had been reserved by Bob Stetson at the apple pie both, and were on our way. Of course, when I realized we were headed for the car, I immediately went into my good behavior mode, and I know they had second thoughts about leaving, but I could tell they were disappointed in my behavior and just wanted to leave.

I'm really and truly going to work on my behavior issues and join Mom and Dad in talking to my Boss about it. After all, I wasn't trained to behave that way, but sometimes I just have to break loose with unacceptable behavior. Don't know why—maybe I received a Devilish gene along with all the good genes I've inherited. I'll try to behave better next time we're out in a crowd.

Arf!

Mosby Mac Fisher, Ministry Dog

Chapter 61

MOSBY'S MEANDERINGS

The Following Week, Still October

This week it was off to the nursing home, which is one of my most favorite activities. I heard Mom tell Dad that we could visit THREE ladies at Life Care Center in Littleton:

Phyllis Wallace, Elsa Manni, and Jane Bean. What a treat for me! I was pawsitively glowing, thinking of all the visits I could make.

As soon as Mom signed us in, she checked with the desk lady to make sure that Elsa was truly in the Alzheimer's wing (which she was) and then asked for Jane's room number, but the nice lady told us that Jane was NOT a resident. Surprise! We must have made a mistake! Not like Mom, I can tell you. But, these things happen, and we certainly were right on track for Phyllis and Elsa.

We bumped into (almost) Charlie as he was cruising the hallway, accepting treats from everyone. He needs to lose more weight than I do, and he keeps on accepting treats from those many outstretched hands. I offered him my condolences on the loss of his dear partner, Coda, and he accepted them with a little sniff and a gentle wag of his fluffy tail. It's sad when one of us leaves this earth, but we know she'll be waiting for him at the Rainbow Bridge. Then they can keep each other company as they wait for their Human to arrive, so they can all cross the bridge together, into Heaven. In the meantime, Charlie is helping train Lily, the young pup, and she does keep him going, with all her childlike activities.

After stopping a few times in the corridor for the outstretched hands extended from wheelchairs, we finally arrived in Phyllis' room and had a nice little visit with her. She's pawsitively one of the nicest people in that place, and I do so love to see her. She always greets me with a smile and an outstretched hand, apologizing that she doesn't have any treats for me. That's all right—I can't have them anyway!

Phyllis has a new roommate who is causing a bit of a stir in getting used to the place, and I think it bothers Phyllis a little, but she's still holding on. Later, I heard Mom tell Dad that she thinks Phyllis is losing ground a bit, since she repeats herself and can't quite remember things as they really are. Phyllis still thinks she's getting better, though, and that's what counts.

In a while, I gave Phyllis a final paw tap and tail wag and we proceeded over to the other side of the building, to the Alzheimer's wing, to find Elsa asleep at the table in the Day Room with the other folks. Mom gently touched her, and I nosed under her arm to wake her. Understandably, she was a little confused when she woke up, but she greeted me with her wide smile and hearty laugh, even though she didn't remember my name, but calls me Poochie. All the time that Mom and Dad were talking to her, she was patting my head, and I could tell she was happy to see me.

I had heard Mom tell Dad that Auntie Bobby said that Elsa sang when Auntie Bobby and June Chaplin visited her the previous week, but this day Elsa didn't feel like singing, I could tell.

Soon Dad took me all around the room, because so many people there wanted to talk to me. We don't mind doing this, because it's what my work for my Boss is all about—bringing a little cheerful happiness to everyone we possibly can. It just makes for a loooong visit sometimes. On the other paw, who wants a short visit? I'm in the place where I belong, and I'm happy.

Arf!

Mosby Mac Fisher, Ministry Dog

Chapter 62

MOSBY, DAD, AND VICTOR

Hmm. Well, I suppose I must tell you about a different kind of ministry that Dad and I are doing—without Mom! Of all things!

It all started quite a few years ago, probably before I was even born—maybe even before I was a gleam in my daddy's eye. More like a gleam in the breeder's eye, to be practical about it. But I digress. When Mom and Dad used to work on the Tuesday night suppers at the Congregational church, there occasionally was a guy attending who looked like he really needed the help of the meal and friendship of the people. They only knew his first name, Victor; they never knew anything more to call him. We've all seen him walking all over town. He seems to spend his time outside, in all kinds of weather, just walking, walking, walking. For a while Mom and Dad thought he might be homeless, but just last year or so, they found he lives in Pine Tree Park somewhere.

Anyway, for quite some time now, when Dad would run into Victor on their walks (not together, but they'd sometimes cross paths), Dad would invite Victor to attend our church's monthly Ham and Bean suppers, and he'd tell Victor not to worry about paying—Dad would see to it. Then Dad would tell Phyllis Caldwell sitting at the money table not to take any money from Victor, but to see Dad and he'd pay.

So that's where it went for quite a while—just a quiet, casual kind of "ministry" between Dad and Victor. Now, since we've been living in this wonderful little condo community so close to the Common area, Dad and I have seen Victor quite frequently while we're out on our daily walks. Dad has treated Victor to some coffee and a donut at Dunkin' Donuts when he sees Victor near there, and they have sat and chatted a bit as they sipped on their coffee.

Usually when we'd walk by the Old Cemetery, we'd find Victor taking a smoke break sitting on one of the benches, and Dad would stop by, sitting next to Victor and they'd chat while Victor patted my head and scratched behind my ears. Dad found that Victor had been in the Service, but left early because of health problems. Dad also found that Victor has a last name—Rintoul, and that his father was born in Scotland. Imagine that! We have a new tie with him.

Now that Dad has this new friend, we both want to help him. He pawsitively can use a little helping hand, and Dad and I have taken Victor on as our "ministry"—to lend him a little support and friendship. Mostly, I'm very impressed with my relationship with Victor. I work very hard to be a friendly representative of my church, but this is beyond that—I'm on my own time when I walk with Dad, not wearing my Service vest, just the harness and leash. Yet, there is something deep inside me that reaches out to anyone I feel might need my attention, and just by being a good, friendly sort I bring comfort to someone who otherwise might be feeling pretty low. Our lesson is to always be receptive to others' needs.

It's easy for us to plan to do good things for others, such as bringing meals to the Lowell Transition Center, or contributing food to Loaves and Fishes, but then sometimes we let our "charity" end there and it doesn't carry over to our day-to-day experiences. I try to show everyone to ALWAYS be open to helping others, whether we have our Service vests on or not!

So—a little bit of a different turn for us. You never know when God will whisper in your ear and give you a little nudge to help someone out. I thought you'd like to know that a Ministry Dog's work isn't just visiting folks in hospitals, etc., but, like a true Christian, my Ministry work is all over the place—I just have to learn to recognize it when it crosses my path.

Mosby Mac Fisher, Ministry Dog

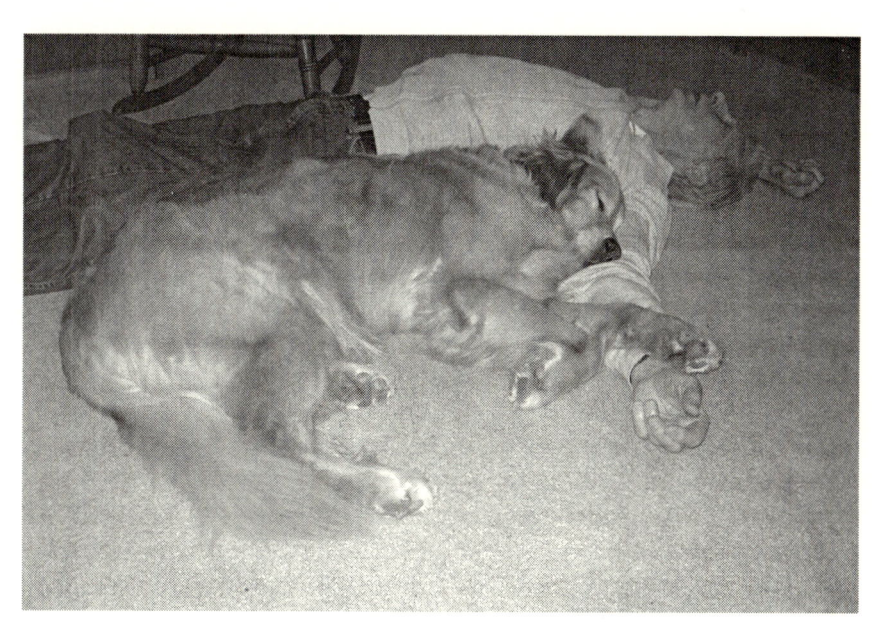

The guys are resting after one of their more strenuous walks, both in Alpha positions.

Chapter 63

CRUISIN' WITH THE CHURCH DOG

Nov 18, 2009

Just because I didn't take my folks anywhere this week doesn't mean I wasn't doing my job. This week I stayed home and worked.

Last Friday Mom complained that she didn't feel too good and thought she might be coming down with a cold, hopefully not the flu (especially since they both have had flu shots). By Sunday Mom knew she was having a melt-down from the Chronic Fatigue, and she couldn't figure out why, since she's been good about pacing herself and stretching out activities, especially those of high-energy-exertion.

After church on Sunday, she took a two-hour nap and I sensed that she needed my help to feel better. As she lounged around on the sofa, I stayed as close as I could and frequently laid my big head on her lap so she could pat me and feel a little happier.

By Monday, Mom complained to Dad that she knew it was CF because her muscles ached, they were so tired, but she didn't have a temperature, runny nose, or sore throat, so it wasn't a cold or flu. So it was a real down time for Mum, no running the washing machine, no cooking meals, no housework. CF doesn't allow anything except lying still and not moving.

Even the book she was reading became too much of an effort to hold on her lap, 'cause it was a hardbound one, not a paperback. No knitting on Mikey's sweater, either. Just watching the television, the same station all night long so she wouldn't have to exert herself to switch channels. I would have done it for her, if I'd have had an opposable thumb, but this dewclaw doesn't work that way.

At night, I'd put my head on the sofa beside her, which is my way of asking to be allowed up on it. She'd put my fleece throw over the seat and back, then pat the cushion and I'd leap up beside her, curling myself into a tight ball to fit on it, and gently placing my head on her lap. I could tell by her soft smile that she enjoyed this, and when she patted my silky head, I could almost hear her purring. I know very well I was doing my job then.

When she laid down on the bed for naps, I'd go into the bedroom and tuck her in, staying with her until she fell asleep, then I'd quietly amble out to find Dad.

Today, Thursday, was the first day that Mom felt able to leave the house, just long enough to go down to the School Superintendent's office to work on the Senior Tax Abatement Program. I heard her tell Dad that, even though she was sure she'd be OK to work the hours, she really didn't want to cope with me, too, so I had to be satisfied with staying home. She knew I missed her when she returned and I sang her my woo woo song, telling her how much I regretted her decision to leave me at home, even though I could understand why she did it.

I overheard Mom telling Dad that I did a good job this week, comforting her and making her feel better. I only wish that I could magically take away this terrible bone-aching fatigue that she has and make her feel really good forever and ever. Maybe I'll have to talk to my Boss about it.

Arf!

Mosby Mac Fisher, Church Dog
(formerly known as Ministry Dog)

Chapter 64

CHURCH DOG'S REPORT FOR

December 3, 2009

Well, we've been falling behind on our report to you, Pastor Deb. But I want you to know that I was willing to do it, but Mom kept on letting other things get in the way of her typing, so there was nothing I could do about it. Doggone these darned dewclaws! If only they worked as well as opposable thumbs, I could do the job myself!

Anyway, I finally got Mom away from other less important work and I set her down at the computer so that I could dictate my report to her. Here goes:

I took Mom and Dad to Life Care Center in Littleton last week—a full week ago, mind you. Actually, eight days ago, but who's counting? As usual, we had to make our way through many wheelchairs and hands reaching out to me, before we arrived at Phyllis Wallace's room. It's as though they've never had other doggy visits, I swear. (Not that I swear, or say naughty words, but sometimes they're the only things that are appropriate.)

Phyllis was sitting in her wheelchair, hands on her table and head bowed as if in prayer, but I knew she was only taking a catnap, so I nudged her knee and woke her up. She was quite happy to see us, once she focused on us. We were all happy to see that both of her feet were in slippers and not encased in the medical footwear that was the case when her foot was healing.

She was quite chipper and asked how things were going in the church. We didn't tell her about Elsa's passing, even though none of us had talked about this beforehand, but we all felt it wouldn't do Phyllis any good to hear about that.

She asked how we liked the "new preacher" and after a bit of confusion we figured out that she knew David Reed was preaching on Sunday and just got a bit confused about it.

We had a pleasant little visit and she seemed her cheerful usual self.

With all her problems, Phyllis seems to keep a positive attitude most times, but in the car on the way home, I heard Mom tell Dad that she thinks Phyllis is slipping a bit. She isn't as clear on things as she could be, that's definite.

As we were leaving Phyllis' room, I automatically wanted to go to the Alzheimer's wing until I remembered that Elsa wouldn't be there. Maybe I can talk Mom and Dad into going there next time, even though we don't know anybody there right now? I think, even though it's vain of me, that I definitely give a lift to the people there, even if they don't really know me.

On the way out, I had to stop for the lady in the wheelchair to pat me. Mom tried to get her to use her right hand, which obviously needs occupational therapy, since it's just sitting in her lap, but she preferred to pat my head with her "good" hand, so we gave up on that. After all, we're not the medical experts.

I heard Mom tell Dad in the car that the next couple of weeks will be busy with Christmas stuff, but we'll try to fit in one more visit somewhere before Christmas.

Arf!

Mosby Mac Fisher, Church Dog
(as dictated to Mom)

Chapter 65

CRUISIN' WITH MOSBY THE CHURCH DOG, WEEK BEFORE CHRISTMAS

Dec 17, 2009

Today I took Mom and Dad to see someone new—even to me! It all came about because Mom and Dad's friend, Connie Laubauch, came back to the house for an egg nog after the Community Christmas Concert at the Mormon Church last Saturday. Mom and Dad got to talking about my visits, and they had just been talking about Connie Coughlin, whose wife, Rose, is Connie's friend. After retirement from Digital, Mom had been temping sometimes, and Connie called to see if Mom wanted to work in Acton for Connie Coughlin's Accounting office, filling in for their receptionist who was off on medical leave. After Mom reminded Connie that she's not a "numbers" person, but a "word" person, Connie had told Mom that this was receptionist stuff, not to do with numbers.

So Mom had worked there for a couple of months, staying on after the receptionist returned, doing different kinds of office work that needed to be done, and enjoying Connie, the boss, and all the other people there, mostly Coughlin family. The job came to a screeching halt when tax returns season approached and they needed someone full time, which Mom was not prepared or willing to do.

But Mom always asked Connie Laubach how Connie Coughlin and firm were doing. A little while ago Friend Connie told Mom that Boss Connie was in a nursing home in Acton, and Rose had moved into a small over-55 apartment/condo.

That's just background to my tail. After an egg nog or two, when Friend Connie was ready to leave, Mom had the bright idea that a nursing home visit to Boss Connie might be in order, and Friend Connie thought that'd be a good idea, since Rose and Connie had always had dogs, so must be dog people (my favorite kind of humans).

So today, freezing, bitter cold weather notwithstanding, off we went to the nursing home in Acton. As always, there were many people along the way in the corridors that needed my attention. It started at the sign-in desk when a staff worker came up to us, recognizing my NEADS vest and chatted with us about my Ministry and she couldn't resist patting me, of course. Then the four or five folks in wheelchairs along the hallway needed my attention, too.

While all this was going on, a woman passed me with a wee little poodle all outfitted in a winter jacket. Now, I know my folks realize that I don't hold those little things in much esteem—they're too little to be bothered with, but I always have to voice my disdain with a bark or two. But not this time. I decided to hold in my opinion and just ignore the wee beastie. Mom and Dad let out a collective sigh of relief that I hadn't embarrassed them.

When we arrived in Connie's room, he was asleep in his wheelchair, so I walked over to him and licked his hand, and he immediately woke up. Mom told Connie who we were, but he didn't remember her, although he remembered he liked dogs, and I, at least, was a hit. Connie smiled at me, but didn't talk much. Doggone, I really liked him, especially when he was patting my silky head. We stayed just a short time because it was pretty evident that Connie wasn't talking much, just sitting there and smiling at me.

After a while we said goodbye and reversed our walk down the halls, again stopping for the outreached hands. Isn't it amazing that so many folks in hospitals and nursing homes remember their love for dogs, even after everything else has faded from their minds? That's what keeps Mom and Dad, as well as me, motivated to make these visits.

Arf!
Mosby Mac Fisher, Church Dog

Chapter 66

ANDREW #2

Sometime that fall we learned that Andrew #2 had arrived at the Puppy House and was enjoying life there, while learning simple lessons. I said a little prayer that this time would be a success, but that was not God's plan!

On Dec 18, 2009, Doreen Sheridan wrote:

Lynda and Lawrence,

I have some sad news about Andrew (2). He did not have the temperament for an assistance dog and he was released from the program. He was placed with a family as a pet. They love him and he is enjoying being a pet. I am sorry to bring you this news for a second time.

Would you like to name a third pup or would you prefer the donation that was made to name Andrew go to support one of our clients?

Doreen

Mosby couldn't hold back his frustration from responding:

December 19, 2009

Doggone it! I'm pawsitively disappointed that Andrew #2 didn't make it! I don't know what the problem is with pups these days. Maybe their moms didn't give them enough quality time before sending them off to do good in the world.

But, the stubborn Scots blood in me won't let me give up. I'm willing to try for Andrew #3, and let's hope that the third time will bring better luck. Maybe you should try for a pup from my breeder, Mrs. Gray, in New Brunswick. If it turns out to be a relative of mine, it might have better luck. I do know that my Mom and Dad think I'm just about the best guy on this earth. Of course, they also believe that God had a hand in choosing ME to be a Therapy Dog for the Ministry, so how could I not be perfect?

I do have one question, though—your last sentence says, "would you prefer the donation that was made to name Andrew go to support one of our clients" and I'm a little confused, because I thought that money went toward paying off my own debt, since the contributor who promised my folks the money, backed out? If that can't happen while naming another pup, then let it go—it's more important that my debt be paid off. Us Scottish folks are thrrrrrrifty, but honest, you know.

Mosby Mac Fisher, God's Dog

On Dec 21, 2009, Doreen Sheridan wrote:

I know, I know . . . . I was very disappointed as well. We will try for an Andrew #3, with a Mom who spent a lot of quality time with her pup.

I am Scottish as well so I understand.

Have a nice holiday.

Doreen

Chapter 67

CHURCH DOG'S VISIT TO LIFE CARE CENTER, CHRISTMAS WEEK 2009

How I do love visiting folks during Christmas week! Everything is spruced up and decorated with red and green things, just waiting to be investigated, and all to celebrate the birth of my Boss!

In the third week of December, I took Mom and Dad to Life Care Center on Foster Street, and we started off by rubbing noses with Charlie and Lily. I feel as though I'm the filling in the sandwich with these two. Charlie is so old his whole muzzle is white, and Lily is just a bouncy little kid, not even a year old, and here I am, three-and-a-half years old, in the prime of my life. I'm glad I'm friends with these two Goldies, because I can learn so much from Charlie's wisdom and impart, hopefully, some of my learned wisdom to Lily.

After exchanging greetings with these two, I made my way slowly down the corridor to Phyllis Wallace's room, pawsing as usual at every wheelchair for the outstretched hands to pat my silky head. When we arrived at Phyllis' room, I thought for a minute that we wouldn't have a visit because she was lying in bed with her hand covering her face. But Mom saw Phyllis move her hand, so knew she was actually awake, although she didn't seem aware of us. After Mom touched her leg carefully, Phyllis looked at me and smiled, and then I knew it'll be all right. Eventually, an aide showed Mom how to crank up the bed and then we had a nice little visit. I had talked Mom and Dad into getting a little Christmas present for Phyllis, and while I supervised the operation, Mom helped Phyllis open the package, to reveal all kinds of nice, smelly stuff to make Phyllis feel good—bath creams, body lotions, scents, etc. Phyllis seemed pleased to receive it, but even if she doesn't really use these things, she was happy to receive a present from me. Mom told Phyllis how I helped pick this present out, and she seemed happy to know that. I still don't know why humans can't just use their tongues to clean themselves—it's so much cheaper and handier than all these bottles and jars.

It was just a few minutes later that Phyllis mentioned Maud, and once we all knew who she meant, Mom said she'd check at the desk to see if Maud was still a resident, which we did, and so we left Phyllis with a Merry Christmas goodbye and a final "up" (carefully) with two paws next to her on the bed so she could pat my velvety-soft head one last time.

Merry Christmas, Debbie, and give Mr. G. an extra big hug from me.

Arf!

Mosby Mac Fisher, Church Dog

Hi, Pastor Deb—

Today I took Mom and Dad to visit Phyllis Wallace at Life Care Center, and she mentioned if we'd been to see Maud. At first, Mom thought she was confusing Maud with Elsa, but we got that straightened out that she really did mean Maud, so when our nice visit with Phyllis ended, we checked the register, and sure enough Maud was in the book. So we retraced our steps and found her room, but with only one bed occupied, and it was not Maud. When Mom asked the lady if this was the correct room for Maud, the patient responded that it was, but they had just taken her to the hospital for an MRI.

When she was asked how long Maud had been here, the patient replied that Maud told her it had been 15 days. Fifteen days! And we didn't know about it! We had a nice little mini-visit with that lady, since she said she was a dog person, and she looked like she could benefit from my presence near her bed. She said she was a neighbor of Phyllis Caldwell and had talked to Phyllis on the phone about Maud, so maybe you know already anyway.

We'll have to return next week, if Maud is still there. After all, she's one of the nice ladies whom I like to visit in church coffee hour time.

Arf!

Mosby Mac Fisher, Church Detective Dog

Chapter 68

CABLE 8 LOCAL TV STATION INTERVIEW

January 5, 2010

Hurray! I'm about to become well-known (or, more so) in Littleton! At Uncle Jack's auction last September for the School Department and Council on Aging, Barbara MacRae stopped by my table to pat me and chat with Mom for a while. From that little meeting came the idea to have a little segment of me on the local Channel 8 video show, <u>Littleton Common</u>, which Barbara hosts. Such a nice lady! And she's definitely a dog person, although her dog-of-choice is one of those wee little Bichon Frises. Everyone knows what I think of wee dogs—good for growling at, but annoying otherwise. Mom and Dad are working on this attitude of mine, but I don't know if they'll ever change my opinion. The Scottish blood in me makes me verrrrrra stubborrrrn!

Anyway, I let Mom and Dad drive me to the parking lot behind the Shattuck Street building yesterday (too cold for the humans to walk it), and Barbara soon opened the #8 door and escorted us up the flight of stairs to the recording studio for a planning meeting. What a nice setup! There were comfortable chairs for Mom and Dad and Barbara to sit on, while I enjoyed the rug on the floor. Now I know what's behind the #8 door. I often wondered about that, but didn't want to ask anyone.

Barbara asked us all kinds of questions, and soon Mark Crory, her boss, arrived and sat down with us. Of course, there was a lot of nostalgia conversation, too, since we used to live next door to Mark's Aunt and Uncle on New Estate Road, and now his nephew's family lives there.

But back to me—both Barbara and Mark were very interested in my program, and Mom told them that she hoped I'd become better known throughout town so that I could widen my visitations to include more townspeople.

When Dad mentioned about my visits to Life Care Center on Foster Street, and how the Globe followed us around, which video ended up on my church's web site, Mark thought he could do the same thing. He left us briefly to check some notes he had in his office, then returned again.

After the first five minutes of ecstatic tail wagging on my part, I had settled down until Mark re-entered the area, and again when Barbara's husband Alan came by. Of course, being another Scotsman, I had to give him my extra special greeting, reserved only for fellow Scots.

I was amazed to find that we had chatted for a whole hour, but of course, when I'm the subject of the conversation, I realize how interesting it becomes for everyone. We made a date for next Tuesday for the actual taping, and when Mom said that I'd have a bath on the weekend for the occasion, Alan thought that maybe Barbara could do the same. I don't know why they all laughed at that—baths are serious business!

So—that was my "visitation" for this week. It's nice and very rewarding to visit sick folks, but Mom thought this was a good change of pace, and I agree! I'm so excited! I'm getting so well known! I'm so popular! I don't know whether to wag my tail or bark!

Arf!

Mosby Mac Fisher, Therapy Dog for the Ministry
(aka The Church Dog)

January 12, 2010

I don't think Mom and Dad took any particular efforts to get ready, but Mom sure did clean me up! I got my usual thorough brushing and polishing, complete with nails and a few straggly hairs trimmed, and she did everything but sprinkle me with glitter to make me more beautiful than I already am!

Then we were on our way for our interview at the Littleton Cable Channel recording studio. That lovely lady, Barbara MacRae, has the nicest hands when she's rubbing your head and neck! And she speaks so nicely, too. Mark Crory, her boss, and the recording expert, is a nice guy, too, and I love to smell his cats on his pants legs.

Mark clipped little microphones on to Mom's and Dad's sweaters, but forgot about me. I thought right then that I'd have to use my big, manly WOOF if anyone asked me a direct question.

Mom said afterwards that she was a wee bit nervous before the taping, but Barbara soon put both of them at ease, and they followed my example of taking everything very calmly and casually. Of course, they didn't fall asleep as I did, but Barbara kept chatting with them and peppering them with all kinds of questions about me.

*So Barbara started by seating my folks in chairs in back of me and I was in front of them, since I'm the star here, and it's important to get the best shot possible of me. The folks are nice for background, but everyone knows that **I'M** the real purpose for this taping.*

Barbara made a very fine hostess, asking Mom and Dad questions about what I do, how I do it, and how did they get started with this Ministry Dog stuff. Barbara had her questions prepared in advance, but I think sometimes an answer that Mom or Dad gave to her just led her into another question which wasn't on her list. Mom and Dad each took a turn answering her questions, and I think the future viewers will get a good sense of what I do for work and a little of my history and how I came to be with my folks.

I heard Mom tell Dad that, although she was a little nervous in the beginning, Barbara put her at ease, and soon the chat just flowed easily. My tail was soon told and the session was over, but that wasn't the end.

I had to take Mom and Dad down to Diane Crory's office to renew my license. Humans don't have this nice little thing, but I'm a lucky dog 'cause I get to be renewed every year and get a new tag to hang on my collar. Hmm. I'm beginning to wonder just how many Crorys there are in town? I remember, on New Estate Road, we lived next door to another Crory family. Oh, well—I just had to paws to consider this fact. They all smell sort of alike, so they're all probably related somehow.

Then it was off to Life Care Center for more taping—me in action! Doing my God-chosen work! We met Barbara and Mark there, and then had to find a willing resident to visit. They had talked before about taping me with Marge Harvey, since she's a well-known Littleton figure, but she had already left there to return home to finish healing. So, off to Phyllis Wallace's room, but she was sound asleep, so we decided not to wake her up.

Mom had remembered seeing Lois Mueller's name when she signed us all in, so we walked over to Lois' room. I had never met Lois before, but doggone it, she's a dog person, so I just walked up to her as if I'd always known her. After Mom asked Lois if she'd mind being taped with me, and she had agreed, Mark had us go out again and re-enter the room while he taped us, just as if we hadn't been there before. Lois is as fine an actor as I am and went along with it.

We had a nice, short visit, then Mark stopped the camera and started it up again when we were walking back down the hall and as we left the building. Then—very confusing for me—but he asked Mom and Dad and me to walk back up to the front door as if we were just entering, and he'd cut it in later. Very confusing, this taping business—the last was done first, and the beginning was done last. I guess that's just how humans operate sometimes, but I go along with whatever they want. I'm just a good-natured guy and can tolerate most anything these humans want to do. If dogs ran the world, it'd be different, I can tell you!

I was all ears when Mom asked Barbara and Mark about when this taping would be on-line, and Barbara informed her that it'd be in February, when she's having a whole show on dogs. She has some other dog-related stuff she wants to do—something about my cousins who have just been fired from dog racing—greyhounds, I believe. They're nice guys, and I wouldn't be barking up the wrong tree to say that they're the speediest devils on four feet that I've ever seen! It'll be nice to share some TV time with them.

Mark told Dad that when he gets done with his editing, he'll give a copy to Pastor Debbie so that she can add it to my page on the church's website. And—best of all—one for us to keep, so that any time I want to see it, I'll have one of them put it into the TV and I can watch myself in action! Hot dog! That'll be neat—the cat's meow, sort of!

So—I've been interviewed for a newspaper article, and a local television show! How many dogs can say that? I just hope that I got the message through—NEADS is truly a wonderful teaching place, and my Boss is truly an awesome God!

Arf!

Mosby Mac Fisher, Ministry Dog and Local Celebrity

Chapter 69

CHURCH DOG'S VISIT

Jan 21, 2010

Today was one of those visits that didn't go as planned, but did have a successful element to it, even so. I took Mom and Dad to Life Care Center in Littleton, primarily to visit Phyllis Wallace and Alberta White, the nice lady who used to live with Pagey Elliott and helped her with her Golden Retrievers. Every time I visited Life Care Center in the good weather, we'd find Alberta sitting on the porch out front, and I always made sure I went to see her before we'd go inside. She always apologized that she didn't have any treats for me, and Mom and Dad would always say that I couldn't have it anyway, until I lost that weight that I've gained. Grrrrrr. I'd like to bite someone's ankle! I'd rather be chubby and have those treats! But they think differently.

So, after we walked through the double doors, who should I spy but Lily on leash with an aide! Well, I tugged on my lead and barked a greeting to her, which she returned, and we went through a few minutes of excited singing and sniffing. She's such a cute little girl!

While that was going on, Mom signed in with Phyllis Wallace's name and asked the receptionist which room Alberta was in. A long, sad face was the answer, and Mom knew that Alberta was no longer with us. Mom was disappointed, since she wanted to talk about Pagey Elliott's book which she had just gotten done reading, and which mentioned Alberta a few times. Besides that, Alberta was such a nice lady to visit.

Then Mom mentioned a man whom I didn't know, but when we were at Emerson Hospital visiting Joanne Dates, one of the nurses mentioned that her grandfather was at Life Care Center in Littleton and he liked dogs, so Mom had told her that we'd visit him the next time we were there. Mom got the room number, but we all decided that we'd visit Phyllis first so that Mom could drop off the magazines she'd brought for her.

On the way up the main aisle to the circular area, there was a man and a woman sitting down talking, and they immediately smiled when they saw me, so Dad walked me over to them, asking if they'd like to pat me. The lady had been recuperating from a broken hip and was going home the next day, so while she patted me, the man chatted with Dad. Pretty soon, he said, "Don't I know you? Didn't you work at Digital?" After a bit of conversation, they decided they had worked in the same department, so they had a nice little reminiscent chat about "the old days" at Digital. All the time the lady was patting my head, which made me feel that I was doing my job.

Soon we had to leave them and went into Phyllis' room to find her in bed, blanket pulled halfway up her head, sound asleep. Mom left the magazines and we left to find the man who loved dogs. We found him lying in bed, Mom introduced us to him, and Dad brought me over to the side of his bed so that he could pat my head. Immediately, I started licking his hand and he took it back, wiping it on his sheet. He didn't appear to like dogs very much because he complained about me licking him! When Mom told him that Heather, his granddaughter told her that "Grandpa liked dogs" he said he did, but he still didn't want to pat me, so we didn't stay long there. Doggone it, there are enough other folks who REALLY love me, to spend our time with someone who doesn't appreciate how wonderful I am.

Returning to Phyllis' room, we found her still asleep, so Mom and Dad decided to call it a day and not stay any longer, since we didn't know anyone else who might be there. On our way back through the circular room, the Digital couple were still there, and I realized that our trip hadn't been a total loss, 'cause they really loved me, and she enjoyed patting me, smiling all the time.

So—I never know what's going to happen on our visits. We plan on bringing a little happiness to someone and the visit turns out completely different, but I think that God sees that I'm not just spinning my wheels uselessly, but bringing His joy to someone every time, even if it's not the plan that us humans and canines have worked on.

Arf!!!

Mosby Mac Fisher, Therapy Dog for the Ministry

Chapter 70

CHURCH DOG'S VISIT

Jan 26, 2010

Yesterday I took Mom and Dad back to Life Care Center on Foster Street for two people—Phyllis Wallace, as always, and Frank Mueller, from the Congregational Church, whom Mom and Dad have known for a long time—back to their square dance days with the Littleton group. I heard Mom tell Dad that Aunt Bobby said Frank was in, just days after Lois had left. What is it with humans, that they can't schedule their health calendars better? It would have worked out if they'd both been there at the same time—then folks could come and visit with both of them at the same time! But then I wouldn't have such a long tail to tell.

Mom had told Dad that if we made the trip later in the afternoon, we might find Phyllis in her wheelchair, getting ready to go to the dining room for supper/dinner, whatever they call it. It's "chow" as far as I'm concerned, since it's the same meal in my bowl for breakfast and supper. I don't know how these humans manage to have THREE meals a day, and I only get TWO. Not that I wouldn't eat three times, but it's never been offered to me three times, since I was a pup of only three or four months old.

It was kind of a dull beginning when we entered the building because neither Lily nor Charlie showed their faces/tails, and the folks in the wheelchairs in the corridor didn't show any interest in me. I really enjoy singing my greetings to them. A really "off" day, to say the least, but it did make our trip to Phyllis happen in record time. I really enjoy shmoozing with folks along the way and bringing smiles to their wrinkled faces, but not this time. There must have been something interesting happening in the activities room.

As we entered Phyllis' room, we realized that, not only was she wide awake sitting in her wheelchair, but she was chatting with a visitor. This nice lady really enjoyed me, and we found out that she visited folks in the Pondside apartments where she had lived, so she was visiting Phyllis here, too. She was a very friendly lady and I enjoyed putting my silky head in her lap to bring a smile to her face, but soon she left and we had a nice little visit with Phyllis.

It was so nice to see her awake and smiling, and she reported to us that she's been walking, assisted by the physical therapists, which was good to hear. My tail wagged at that news. I wish Dad wouldn't hold me on such a short leash, but he's afraid I'll hurt her bandaged feet, so I had to stretch my head out so she could pat me.

We didn't want to tire Phyllis out, so we left her room and wandered over to the other side to see Frank Mueller, whom I'd never met before, but he was such a nice guy that I felt right at home with him and gave him my head to pat, as well as a tail wag. Frank was quite happy to see us, and we had a nice long chat with him, until Dad decided it was time to go.

Mom told Dad a little story on the way home about her trip to the Post Office, and I was all ears to hear it, since I was busy at home guarding the street from the living room sliders. She reminded Dad how they used to have to go there every day when we first moved in to our condo because the mail boxes weren't put in for a while. Mom got quite friendly with a couple of the ladies behind the counter—Judy and Helen in particular, and they commiserated with Mom and Dad about having to come every day to pick up their mail, but enjoyed seeing me when I came with them. But then our mail boxes were installed and those visits came to a halt, except for the rare packages which had to be mailed out, but Mom never saw Judy for some reason. There was always someone else behind the counter. Until yesterday.

There was Judy, with her usual smile, and asking how things were going with our new condo, and Mom told her how much we all enjoy it. Then Judy reached into her drawer, shuffled some papers around, and came up with the Globe article about me, from LAST SUMMER! Doggone! What a nice person, to clip the article and save it all this time, just for us. Mom thanked Judy profusely and told her how much we appreciated her thoughtfulness, and commented to Dad in the car how that would never have happened in a large, impersonal city. Only in a nice, small hometown like Littleton could that ever happen. But, of course, I like to think that my Boss had something to do with it. He, no doubt, prompted Judy to do it.

I now look forward to watching my interview with Barbara MacRae on Channel 8, next month. I'll have to remind Mom and Dad to start watching the show, <u>Littleton Common</u>, starting February 1.

Woof!

Mosby the Church Dog

Chapter 71

CRUISIN' WITH THE CHURCH DOG

Feb 9, 2010

Ah, how time does fly when you're having such a lot of fun! Doggone, I completely forgot about telling my story. I've just got to remember to nail down these stories while they're still current. Last week I took Mom and Dad to Life Care Center on Foster Street, and while there we all learned a little lesson on patience and "Christian Forbearance" if that's the correct term.

Once again, Lily and Charlie weren't at the entrance for me to greet, but there were plenty of wheelchair folks with outstretched hands, just waiting for my silky head to appear near them. If I were human, I'm sure my handsome head would be turned, with all the attention that is showered on me.

We entered Phyllis' room and were relieved to find her wide awake, sitting in her wheelchair, with a wide grin on her face as soon as she saw me. Mom sat down in the chair right beside Phyllis so that I could get close to her without stepping on her fragile feet, and we had a good snuggle which we both enjoyed.

Dad was standing up near us, when we noticed Lucille, the lady from the next room, wheeling in to talk to us. And talk to us—and talk to us. Usually on the way back from visiting Phyllis, we find Lucille sitting in her doorway and I always pause a while so she can pat me, but this time, she came right into Phyllis' room and started talking. And not very nicely, either. I could tell that she really wasn't quite all right in her mind, but that's the way God wants her to be, so I tolerated it. Soon Mom and Dad caught on that she wasn't talking a lot of sensible things, but just chattering on in a belligerent way, like a bulldog or mastiff, not like a gentle guy such as I am. Dad took her attention and chatted with her, while Mom and I paid attention to Phyllis, who said it was kind of nice—it was like a girlfriend visit. Hello? Doesn't she realize that I'm a guy kind of a dog? Mom let it pass, since everybody knows that I've lost some parts that make me a real guy. Phyllis said that she's never seen Dad talk so much as he was with Lucille, and we all got a chuckle out of realizing that usually Dad doesn't get much chance to talk, but Lucille would say something belligerantly to Dad and then he'd spar with her, giving it right back to her, in a kindly way.

After a while, we left Phyllis with the magazines Mom had given her and walked on down to the other corridor to see Frank Mueller, who was still there. We were all holding our breaths, hoping that Lucille wouldn't tail along behind us, but one of the nice aides who knew Lucille caught her and pushed her into her own room, which was enough of a distraction that she forgot about us.

Finding Frank lying down fast asleep, we left him one of my cards so that he'd know we were in to see him, and we headed back down the hall to go home. This time we did see Charlie and Lily, so I practiced some of my singing with Lily while all our tails were swishing around, brushing against some folks in wheelchairs, who broke into amused smiles at our antics.

On the way home, I heard Mom and Dad discuss Lucille. They decided that, even though she was a hard one to deal with, and interfered with our visit with Phyllis, maybe God put her there so that I could give her some of my love. After all, everybody benefits from patting me!

Arf! Woof!
Mosby Mac Fisher, Therapy Dog for the Ministry

Chapter 72

MINISTRY DOG'S MUSINGS, FEBRUARY 15, 2010

Doggone, yesterday was a pawsitively different kind of worship service—for me, anyway. I had heard Mom and Dad talking in the car (they do a lot of talking then, 'cause there's no television hooked up in the car—not even in the back seat for me). Mom told Dad that she wasn't sure about her going to worship service yesterday, since Pastor Debbie announced it'd be held downstairs in Fellowship Hall instead of in the sanctuary. Mom has a wee bit of a hard time hearing when there's background noise going on, and she figured there'd be no microphones downstairs, so she wouldn't be able to hear much. Dad is lucky 'cause he wears those things in his ears that help him hear better, even though he still has trouble sometimes.

Then Mom realized that, since she's the Deaconess for the month, she REALLY SHOULD be there, in case something came up for a Deaconess to do. There'd be no flowers, of course, and no candles since there's no altar downstairs, but Mom felt she should be there anyway. There was no question about me and Dad—we were scheduled to be greeters, so I was happy that we'd be going anyway. We stood just inside the Goldsmith Street entrance greeting folks and directing them into Fellowship Hall instead of upstairs to the Sanctuary. There were a couple of new people, never been in our church before, so I don't know what they thought when they weren't directed upstairs to the sanctuary.

When we arrived, all the chairs were arranged in rows, in a semi-circle all around the room, somebody had carried the big heavy altar cross downstairs and placed it on the shelf on top of the chair storage place, and even the artificial flowers were standing in their pots beside the lectern. Mom whispered to Dad that it really looked nice!

Mom chose the back row of chairs beside the center aisle so that I'd have room to lie down, and after Dad and I had greeted everyone, Dad sat and I lay down at his feet. Really comfortable! More comfortable than I had anticipated, in fact.

There was a bit of music from the new band, Four Free, then Rev. Joyce Reed led the Invocation, and what an Invocation it was! She had all the humans standing, moving arms, legs, heads, whole bodies! It was a really interactive, congregation-participative moment, and I wanted to jump up and do it, too, but Dad thought I should just lie there and quietly cheer everyone on. Mom told Dad afterwards that this Invocation made her change her mind about the whole worship service. The service was relaxed, upbeat, and friendly, yet definitely in God's presence.

I had my chance to make myself known after the children's story, when the kids left the room for their own time in the other room. By then I was sitting up to see everything, and as the kids came down the center aisle, they all reached over and gave me a pat! Every one of them! I felt so proud and happy that they wanted to do it. I always feel good about making the kids happy. Then during the Offering time, Aunt Bobby and her sister Bev walked single file up the narrow aisle to receive the offering plates and darned if they didn't pat my silky head, too!. After the offering had been taken up and they returned the plates, as they walked back down the aisle, they both reached out again for another pat. I felt so good that I could have a little part in the service.

In the car, on the way home, Mom told Dad that she was very glad that she had decided to attend—the smaller room made it possible for her to hear a large part of the talking, even without the mikes, and it was nice to be closer together with everyone.

I guess this is a good lesson for me, too, as well as Mom. Don't pre-judge an event—wait until you're through it. If Mom had stayed home, she says she'd have missed a really great worship service, an inspirational time of being closer to God.

Arf!

Mosby Mac Fisher, Ministry Dog

Chapter 73

CHURCH DOG

Feb 23, 2010

I overheard Dad telling Mom this morning that we'd better get our week's errands done today, 'cause the rest of the week could be a "bit dicey" (whatever that means) due to the forecasters' predictions involving snow. I feel sorry for humans—they have to put on heavy jackets, hats, gloves, and even boots, and all I do is go through the door when it's opened for me. I'm already wearing everything I need.

Dad even had Mom working up her grocery shopping list for today instead of Friday! Donelan's is always a treat for me because of all the nice people I meet there. There's always a dog person or two who just can't help themselves—doggone, they HAVE to pat me, when Mom and Dad tells them it's OK. Sometimes they say how they just lost their dog, or they miss their dog so much, and thank Dad for allowing them the time to pat me. There's always someone with a story to tell, so that's what makes grocery shopping take so long. I think it's great—I'm doing my Ministry job without even visiting someone in a hospital or nursing home.

But today, I took Mom and Dad to the Apple Valley Health Center in Ayer, next to the hospital, to visit Don Lindgren, who always is a favorite of mine because he's a dog person and enjoys my company. However—today was unsuccessful. We even walked down the corridor to his room without meeting anyone who needed to pat me.

As we entered the room and saw Don in his bed, he was lying down taking a nap. He was all hooked up to lots of important looking tubes and Dad didn't dare take me too close for fear of my getting tangled up in something and causing an alarm to go off and possibly hurting Don. Mom and Dad talked to each other for a minute, mainly to see if Don would wake up if he was sleeping lightly enough to hear their voices. I could have barked, but they frown on that, so I kept my muzzle still.

I conveyed a thought to Mom, and she left my calling card on the bedside table so that Don would know we had been there when he woke up.

On the way to the car, Mom told Dad that, had it not been for cruising the aisles at Donelan's, this week would have been a loss, as far as visiting people is concerned. I really do wish that Bill Arrington would return to Emerson Hospital so that we could visit him, even though it costs money to park there. Earlene has yet to return Mom's call to tell us his Therapy hours so that we could work around that.

Maybe next week will be better—with no expected snow storms.

Arf!

Mosby Mac Fisher, Therapy Dog for the Ministry

Chapter 74

MOSBY MAKES THE BIG TIME—NETWORK TV

Apr 5, 2010

Springtime brought with it another opportunity to publicize Mosby's ministry. John Moon, Communications Officer for NEADS, e-mailed me the following message:

"Hi Lynda—I have been contacted by CBS in NYC about ministry dogs and I thought of you and Mosby . . . please correct me if I have you mixed up with a different client here at NEADS. If I am correct in contacting you, can we talk about potentially being contacted by CBS for their story?

Thank you in advance—John"

Of course, I immediately responded:

"Yes, John, you have contacted the correct dog—and he already has been exposed to much publicity. He was interviewed by our local newspaper a couple of years ago when he and I graduated together from NEADS, then last summer the Boston Globe did an article on him, which our church still has on its webpage, and last winter a Christian publication phoned me and did a phone interview, but I don't think anything came of that.

This past February, Mosby, my husband Larry, and I were interviewed by our local cable station for a segment on its show, <u>Littleton Common</u>. Larry and I were a wee bit nervous, but Mosby was a pro and basically slept through the interview. He's definitely a laid-back sort of guy!

Whatever CBS wants, Mosby is their guy. He's game for anything that will publicize NEADS and their great dog programs. Tell CBS he's up for anything they'd like him for.

Lynda"

E-Mails From The Church Dog

John obviously had given the go-ahead to CBS, because in a few days I received the following e-mail message:

"Hi Lynda,

My name is Lizz Morhaim and I'm an associate producer at CBS News in the Religion Unit. We are doing a story on religion and animals, so I contacted NEADS because they have a ministry pet service program. John Moon told me I could get in touch with you about your experience. We are planning to shoot in the Boston area the last week of April, and we would love to interview you. Please give me a call on my cell to discuss further.

Thanks in advance,

Lizz Morhaim"

I've been listening to Mom telling Dad about an e-mail message she received from John Moon, the Communications Director at NEADS. It seems that CBS in New York has inquired about doing a show on dogs in religion and John contacted Mom to see if I could help them. After a few e-mails back and forth, Mom finally talked to Liz today from CBS, who is the Associate Producer for the Religion unit of CBS News. They want to come out to Littleton the last week in April and possibly do a segment on me and my church activities! Wow! That's pawsitively exciting! Now, let's see—I've been interviewed by two newspapers and the local cable television station, and now it's network television! I feel like I'm really hitting the big times! It's too bad that Pastor Debbie is on vacation this week, but Mom is going to talk to her next week to see what can be arranged during worship service using me. I've done the trip to Life Care Center in Littleton—been there (newspaper and cable TV) already, so Mom thought this time maybe some activity could be done in church. We'll see what Debbie can come up with.

Boy, if I were human, I'd have a swelled head, with all this publicity I'm getting, but being the cool, laid-back kind of guy I am, I take it in my stride.

Arf!

Mosby Mac Fisher, well-known Church Dog and Dog-About-Town
(as dictated to Mom)

Chapter 75

MOSBY'S MEANDERINGS

Thursday, April 8, 2010

Doggone! Time does fly when you're as busy as I am! I've been doing my duty alerting my humans to people intruding on White Street, which I patrol from my post at the slider in the living room, and of course when someone comes to the door, family or otherwise, I always have to holler a few times, then usually end up singing to them, before they're allowed entry. Of course, the cats next door have to be halted from encroaching into my fenced-in yard, and the construction folks building the next condo unit have to be monitored all the time. Right now, I'm lying beside Mom, dictating this report to her so that those who need to know will be told of my activities these past few weeks.

Last week I took Mom and Dad to Life Care Center in Littleton to visit Phyllis Wallace for her birthday. She's a particular favorite of mine, even though Dad keeps me from getting too close to her because of her bandaged feet, but this day I really felt the need to get closer to her, just to wish her a happy birthday. Aunt Bobby surprised us by being there. too, so we had a nice little birthday party for Phyllis. Mom had brought her a card and the usual second-hand magazines which Mom always tries to remember to pass on to Phyllis so that she can pass them on when she's done with them.

On this visit to Phyllis, she seemed more upbeat and chatty than usual, maybe because it was her birthday. It's funny with humans—when they're kids, they're anxious for the next birthday, then they reach an age where they say they'd rather forget them, but then later on, like Phyllis, they're back to enjoying each one and looking forward to the next. We would have been to her room earlier, but the usual group of hallway sitters needed to pat me and chat about their dogs they used to have.

A couple of days ago, I mentioned to Dad that we hadn't seen Victor in our usual walks around the Common area, and when Dad bumped into Joanne Lemire near Pine Tree Park, she said that Victor was in a nursing home! When mentioning it to Mom, Dad realized that he didn't know which nursing home Victor was staying, and a phone call to the Park office wasn't helpful, so Mom left a message for Tina Maeder, the Outreach lady for the town.

When Tina called back, she told Dad that Victor was at Life Care Center in Acton, so we decided to make a visit there this week. Funny thing about coincidences, but Carolyn Webster called about an hour later to let Dad know about Victor! Small world!

So today we drove to Acton to visit that Life Care Center, and, as usual, it took FOREVER to make it down the halls and into Victor's room. But at last we saw Victor, and we all think he was glad to see us. He was up and dressed and it looked as though he was just waiting to see us. We had a nice visit with him and I know he was happy to see me, 'cause he just couldn't stop patting me. Then, again, on the way back down the corridors, we were stopped all along the way by folks who just needed to touch me and talk to me. Of course, I cooperated by putting my big head on a few laps, which always brought smiles to their faces. If I were human, I'd really have a huge ego, but being the noble canine that I am, I take it all in stride and accept all the loving they want to give me.

Woof!

Mosby Mac Fisher, Church Dog

Chapter 76

NEGOTIATING THE NETWORK TV SHOW

4/9/2010

An e-mail to: Lizz Morhaim:

Hi, Lizz—

I enjoyed talking to you on the phone yesterday—I ALWAYS enjoy talking about Mosby and NEADS, and spreading the word about them.

The more I thought about it, the more I thought positively about a shoot at worship service on a Sunday, as long as you and your photographer are willing to come out here on a Sunday. This is where Mosby really shines—at church and at nursing homes, etc., visiting patients.

If you could plan on the last Sunday in April, that would be ideal, from our point of view. The next Sunday, the first one in May, will be terribly busy for us, so that wouldn't work as well.

I know that our pastor, Debbie Blanchard, is thinking of ways she could use Mosby during the worship service, and my husband, Larry, has already thought of something, too, that he and Mosby already do on a monthly basis.

In our church, we have Greeters who welcome people on their way into church, and Larry and Mo have been doing that already, so he'll put themselves on the schedule for that Sunday. The kids, especially, love to greet Mosby, particularly when he offers them his paw, and his tail wags his whole body.

I'm copying Debbie on this note to keep her in the loop on what we're planning, and I'm hoping that she can spare some time after the worship service to sit down and talk to you about Mosby and his service in the church. After that, if you want to follow us home to see where Mosby lives, we could do that, or just continue talking in church. Whatever works for you. There's always coffee and sweets available downstairs in Fellowship Hall.

E-Mails From The Church Dog

John Moon, the Communications officer at NEADS, told me that he'd make himself available if you wanted to talk to him about the NEADS Therapy Dogs for the Ministry program.

We'll be chatting as the date draws nearer, and I can give you directions, if needed. Of course, if you get into the church's web pages, the directions are printed there, too, I'm sure. www.fbclittleton.org

Lynda Fisher

Apr 14, 2010

Subject: RE: Ministry Dog Interview

Hi Lynda,

I ran this by my producer, and all sounds great! We would love to come on Sunday, April 25th. We would also like to have a sit down interview with you, Debbie, and John Moon individually. Is there a place in the church we could set up our lights? Perhaps these interviews could take place after services? Otherwise, filming throughout the service, including Mosby greeting the congregation is perfect for us.

Our crew would consist of myself, the producer (Liz Kineke), a cameraman and soundman. Please let me know if there is a room we could set up in and if you and Debbie could stick around for sit down interviews. Otherwise, just let me know what time everything starts, and I will check out the website for directions.

thanks!
-Lizz

Lizz Morhaim
CBS Religious Unit

Apr 14, 2010

Lizz,

We are thrilled to hear that you are coming to interview our most famous parishioner! I don't know what we are going to do with Mosby after this interview—he may try to ask for a reserved pew and special cushion each week. Actually Mosby is quite humble and prefers a spot on the floor and we are very glad that you are coming. The service starts at 10:00 a.m., however, Sunday School begins at 9:00 a.m. and there is a lot of activity in the building. Someone should be in the building from 8:30 on and you are welcome any time.

We can do the interviews in the sanctuary after the service if you would like. It's a pretty cozy little sanctuary and I have plenty of time to talk. We have a Scout program starting that Sunday after church and they will be having some pizza before their session starts—maybe Mosby will join them for their lesson that day and he can earn a God and Family badge. As you can see, we do like to have some fun!

Mosby, Lynda and Larry are gifts to the church. Mosby does a wonderful job breaking down all kinds of barriers between people with a gentle nuzzle and by simply laying his chin on someone's lap. But Lynda and Larry are as kind and as gentle as Mosby and it is a ministry of compassion and caring that the three of them do together. They are quite a team of three and we all benefit by their presence.

We will look forward to having you and if there is anything I can do for you ahead of time—please don't hesitate to ask.

Many thanks—Debbie Blanchard

Apr 17, 2010

Hi Debbie,

We are so excited to meet you all, and especially the adorable sounding Mosby! Our crew will arrive at 8:30 a.m. sharp so we have enough time to settle and can begin shooting at 9 a.m. when Sunday school starts. Is there a contact at the church who will let us in? Just in case there's any confusion, I would love to be able to call someone that early in the morning.

Otherwise, thanks again for your help and looking forward to Sunday, the 25th. If anything else comes up, we can get in touch this week.

best,

Lizz Morhaim

E-Mails From The Church Dog

Apr 20, 2010

Subject: CBS Visit this Sunday

Hi, Debbie—

Lizz Morhaim called today, and now I'm getting really excited about this whole taping session!

She wanted to know what else Mosby would be doing other than greeting, and I thought you had said you were trying to set up something with the cub scout God and Country badge—or was I mistaken? Does that happen during worship hour, or after? I know you mentioned about having pizza for the kids, so that sounds like after.

She also mentioned about taping you, John Moon from NEADS, and us after church, so I'm not sure how that'll all flow, if you're involved with the scouts—can you tell I'm getting nervous?

ljf

Apr 20, 2010

Hi Lynda,

Yes I am also very excited about them coming! I want to keep spreading the word about them coming—so that we have a good crowd. I am having the band here too—so that is good.

Well, we will have Mosby greet. And I think I will do something with him for the Children's Story again—but let me try to think of something a little bit different than just explaining him to the kids again. Has he done anything different lately—that we could talk about?

Also the Scout program is starting right after church—they know that I am going to sit with you for the interview—but maybe we can do a Scout lesson and Mosby can come for it. I will probably play the guitar with them—and maybe there is a lesson or a craft. I will get back to you on that!

God is good!
Debbie

Apr 21

Hmm—"Has he done anything different lately?" Not really—just the same old stuff. I did have an idea about his "ministering" activities—it puts a different slant on the same old story, which might appeal to the older kids. The younger ones might not be able to process it, though.

Mosby has made friends with Dapper, the Border Collie who belongs to the folks who run the Littleton Inn. They live across the street, and Dapper is usually found there. In the beginning, Mosby and Dapper weren't too friendly to each other, but now they're good friends, deciding that each one is a good dog. Recently, Dapper's pet cat could be found lying on the driveway, and Mosby has come pretty close to her before she decides to move away. Even though she's a different species, Mo is very tolerant of her and would like to be more friendly. Eventually, as Mosby became calmer in his approach to Kitty, she would approach our canine close enough to sniff noses, and the moment of triumph came the day that Kitty rubbed up against Mosby, arching her back and rubbing her body against Mosby's nose.

This was a moment of achievement, in Larry's eyes, and these two animals showed us humans that creatures of different backgrounds can become friends, accepting each other's differences. Is there something in this about being tolerant of others who are different than we are, and that if we try to be friendly with them, we'd be pleasantly surprised? I think this is a good lesson for us humans to remember!

You could use this thought, or a piece of it, or not, but that's all I can come up with right now. I'll keep working on it and let you know if some brainstorm pops up.

ljf

Apr 22

Hi, Liz—

Mosby took us to visit Victor today at the Life Care Center of Acton, and he's all set for our visit Sunday afternoon. I thought we might have to talk him into it, but he immediately said he'd do it, which surprised me. We've spoken to the

Director there, and Victor's Social Services rep, and everyone is excited about this event. They'll be sure that Victor signs the necessary permission slip before we arrive. They did suggest that nobody's face be shown except for Victor, so they'll try to keep the corridor cleared of patients. Usually this is Mosby's time to schmooz with the folks and stop and greet each wheelchair-bound person he passes, so he'll be a bit disappointed, but once he sees Victor, he'll brighten up. They're good buddies! I checked the dinner timetable, because I know that most nursing homes, like hospitals, have an early dinner hour, but Victor's social worker didn't think it'd be a problem because Victor eats in his room. Still, I wouldn't want to arrive when his tray is being delivered!

We timed the drive and it takes just 15 minutes from our driveway to the Life Care Center. I imagine parking will be a little tight, since we usually don't find a vacant spot until we go way around the back of the building, but we'll be sure to fit in somewhere! I do think the earlier we can make this trip, the better it will be for all concerned.

We're all looking forward to Sunday!

Lynda

Apr 23, 2010

Lynda,

Thanks for the idea . . . I think that what I am going to do for the Children's Story—is talk about how Mosby loves everybody equally. That when he sees someone—he just loves them. He does that with or without his vest on—whether he is in church or not—he loves cats and other dogs and he loves children and adults. I want to talk about the love he has for another—comes genuinely from his heart. And he was also trained to be loving. I have called John Moon and left a message for him to call me. I want to know if there are a few specific things they do to train some dogs to be ministry dogs . . . to be loving and approachable.

So I would like you and Larry to come up for the Children's Story and I will handle it that way.-.that he genuinely loves everybody. And maybe I can ask you how you see that—and you can say that he loves whether he has his vest on or not—and he loves cats and other dogs too!

I will then encourage the children to do the same—to love that way—to love like that!

Thanks—I can't wait!

Deb

Apr 23

Great concept! I think that John will say that the trainers are always mindful of how dogs in training react to their handlers and then others. I understand that Mosby was chosen for the Ministry Dog role because he appeared to love and respond to everyone—not just his handler. Let's see John's take on it.

Yes, we'll all come on up for the Children's Story, and maybe Larry can tell how Mosby is with Dapper's pet cat. Or, how loving he is with Victor, even though he isn't wearing his Service vest. We'll be visiting Victor in the afternoon, so CBS might think it's a good lead-in to that visit, by mentioning it in the Children's Story. ljf

From Larry:

Apr 23

Hi Deb

Sorry to respond so late, but I just read Lynda's reply. I don't think we should mention that Mosby loves other dogs, and cats. He is friends with Dapper and Dapper's cat, but still gets excited with other dogs, but is getting better. I don't think it should sound like he is affectionate with all other dogs, and cats. It's a work in progress. I just thought I would give you my opinion. I don't want to mislead anyone.

Everything else is great, and I appreciate all you have done.

Larry

Chapter 77

MOSBY'S CELEBRITY DAY

May 1

Mom had received some e-mails about interviewing us for a CBS News show, part of their Religion Unit, about "animals and religion." Finally everyone had agreed on the date, and Pastor Deb had made plans to use me in the worship service. So on the day before the last Sunday in April, Mom gave me a thorough tubby after she had trimmed and brushed me, and she used her blow dryer to get me nice and fluffy, then brushed me out again. I knew something was up because she took a long time doing all this—longer than usual. I really don't mind all this grooming, 'cause I always get rewarded afterward with special grooming treats that I don't get any other time. When Mom reaches into her pawket for the treat, I know it's done and I'm handsome.

On Sunday morning, Dad had to wake up Mom earlier than usual, and I'm very grateful that he did it, 'cause it meant that we could get to the church earlier than we usually do. Mom wasn't TOO grouchy—just a wee bit. It was very important that we get there early, since the CBS crew was already there. Outside I met the cameraman taping the sign on the lawn, and I was very interested in his smells—he said he had a dog, and of course, I was right on the trail of that on his pants legs. The sound guy was not so interesting, definitely didn't have a dog. The Producer ladies were both called Liz, but the Associate Producer had two "Z's" in her name instead of one, so they called her "double Z" most of the time.

Dad and I were the official church Greeters this morning, planned so that CBS could see the kinds of jobs I perform for my church. This is always a howling good time, greeting my church friends and some strangers too, and I do think I did this job very well, offering my paw on request to certain special people, mostly kids.

Soon, we could hear the opening hymn signaling the start of the worship service, so we high-tailed it upstairs to Mom in the sanctuary with the CBS guys trailing behind. As I took my usual spot on the floor under Mom and Dad's pew, I looked around and there was the camera guy on his knees taking my picture! He really went wild during the time when Pastor Deb asked us to greet our neighbors. I think he got some good shots of me greeting the kids, kneeling on the floor to get me on my level. Then we were in the spotlight again when Pastor Deb asked me to bring Mom and Dad up for the Children's Story and explain about service and loving God and how it's my nature to love God and everyone in my world. For a Golden Retriever, that's not a hard job at all!

During coffee hour afterwards, Liz and Lizz interviewed Pastor Debbie in the Sanctuary upstairs while I cruised around Fellowship Hall spreading my warmth and love to everyone. John Moon, the Communications Director for NEADS, my alma mater, introduced himself to Mom and Dad and we chatted a bit with him about NEADS. Then we left for home while the whole CBS crew returned to Littleton Inn, Liz and Lizz's overnight stopover place, where they interviewed John Moon and talked about the wonderful training program at NEADS. This gave me time to catch a little dog-nap, while Mom and Dad put up their feet and rested also.

Soon the doorbell rang and it was back to work with the CBS crew. Liz looked at all the animal pictures on the walls and asked Mom if she could take some of me back to New York with her, and after being reassured they'd be returned to Mom in good condition, she agreed. Liz and Lizz decided they'd like to interview us outside on the deck, and a really neat sun shade was soon set up to prevent glare from ruining any shots of me. Of course, I had to check it out and soon sniffed my approval, so we were all set to go. Lizz brought out a couple of chairs for her and Liz to sit on, facing me, but out of camera range, while Mom and Dad were positioned on the steps with me higher on the deck, in the superior Alpha position, of course. Then Liz asked us some questions, such as how did Mom get the idea of a ministry dog, how long did she train with me, what our work is now, who we choose to visit. Liz asked Mom if she thought dogs go to Heaven when they die, and she replied, "Pawsitively! When the Reverend Billy Graham was asked that question, he told the reporter that it wouldn't be paradise for him if all his beloved pets weren't there to greet him when he arrived there." Then Mom told Liz, "If that's good enough for Billy, it's good enough for me!" Hey, my Mom is a really cool chick, to realize that!

Liz asked many more questions, too many for a TV show, but we all know the show will only use the best ones, and I hope that Mom's Billy Graham words will be used. I'd like that to be aired to all of America, so everyone will know where their pets go, and will be comforted by that thought, just as Mom, Dad, and I are.

The last part of the whole day occurred when I piled Mom and Dad into our car and we drove, followed by the three CBS cars, to Life Care Center in Acton to visit Victor, Dad's and my favorite buddy when we're on our walks around the Common. As usual when we have folks following us taking pictures, we have to be escorted by a lot of Life Care Center staff, just to make sure we don't eat any food, I think.

Victor was all dressed, hair combed, sitting in a chair just waiting for us, it seemed. I greeted him enthusiastically, as I always do, then Mom and Dad sat down to chat, all the while being taped and recorded, while everyone else sort of hung around in the doorway. I bet Victor never had so many people visit him at one time before! We all chatted while I lay down at Vic's feet and he constantly patted and scratched me. I loved it! Eventually, though, it was time to go, and it was then that the camera guy introduced himself to Victor. He had been so busy concentrating on getting good angles to shoot that it was like he wasn't with us, but on a different planet. Then he came back when his camera stopped and remembered his manners.

As we left Victor, I noticed that the halls were empty of people in wheelchairs, and I remembered that I overheard Mom talking to the director about keeping other folks from being in the shots, to protect their privacy. That's the first time that I haven't had to stop a dozen times for outreached hands wanting to pat me! I didn't realize the halls were that short! I always had the impression they were much longer, but I guess it's just because it has always taken so long to reach the doors, with people reaching out to me and talking to Mom and Dad about me.

Once outside in the parking area, Mom and Dad chatted a bit with everyone while I impatiently waited for them to get through. After all, it was getting very close to my suppertime, and I didn't want to be late for that! Finally goodbyes were said, handshakes and hugs were passed around, and I hustled Mom and Dad into our car, and we arrived home at just after 5 o'clock. What a long day! Of course, Mom and Dad had to rehash the whole day, but I just lay down and rested.

We were told the show would be aired sometime in June and we'd be notified when, so we could watch it. It'll be on a Sunday morning, so Mom will record it for later viewing, 'cause I know they won't want to miss church, even for that!

They were very pleased to be able to do this because it'll make people aware of all the good work I do for my Boss, and especially all the work that NEADS does in training canines and humans to work together to improve the lives of so many people. I can hardly wait to see the show! Doggone, I hope it shows off my handsome golden coat and friendly smile.

Arf!

Mosby Mac Fisher, Church Dog, Boston Globe Newspaper Personality, Cable TV Star, and now Network Television Celebrity
(as dictated to Mom)

Lynda Reynolds Fisher

To: Lizz Morhaim,

Hi, Lizz—

Many, many thanks to you and the rest of the CBS team for doing such a great interview job with Mosby yesterday. The guys went about their work quickly, as unobtrusively as they could, and with the least interruption to our worship service. You all displayed a quiet professionalism, all the while in a relaxed, friendly pace, which calmed down my "nerves." Does one ever get used to being interviewed?

We look forward to June, when we'll see the results of all your efforts yesterday. It can only be good news for Littleton, the First Baptist Church, and NEADS, all worthwhile recipients of your attention!

In gratitude,

Lynda Fisher p.s. Mosby slept particularly well last night, after his busy day, and is now telling us about the reserved pew he thinks Pastor Debbie is going to arrange for him, since he's such a star!

Chapter 78

Another business year of our church has come to a close, so Mosby wrote his report in order that everybody in the church would learn of his activities.

REPORT OF MOSBY THE CHURCH DOG
(formerly known as Mosby, Therapy Dog for the Ministry

This past year, from May 2009 to April 2010, has been a year of much spiritual growth fur your Church Dog, as well as a continuation of extending a comforting presence to all those in need.

I continued taking my folks to visit many people in hospitals, nursing homes, and shut-ins. This year I was able to expand my visits to more than my church folks, as I'm becoming better known in town and sometimes some people are referred to me through Mom or Dad, who talk to lots of town folks. It's sad to learn that some of the ones whom I've visited are no longer with us—Jo Adam, Kaarlo and Elsa Manni for instance. But I can think back on my visits with them and know that I brought a little bit of happiness into their lives while they were with us. The smiles on their faces as they stroked my silky fur told me I was really appreciated.

I think the most remarkable thing about my life in this past year has been the publicity that I've received—The Boston Globe Newspaper, local Cable TV, and most recently, CBS News Religion Unit! Wow! That's really the big times.

I continue to attend church most every Sunday, and I heard Mom tell someone that I have a better attendance record than a lot of humans. Of course, I attend all the ham and bean suppers, the open house at the Christmas Tree Lighting Ceremonies on the Common, Grotonwood Day, as well as town events—Memorial Day Parade, Fourth of July Celebration at Fay Park for instance. Everywhere I go, people come to pat me and learn my story and where I go to church. At Fay Park for the Independence Day band concert, a nice man with two little girls came over and thanked Mom for our talk at the Ecumenical Thanksgiving Service last year. He asked if I could help his little girl who was terribly afraid of dogs, and he really wanted her to get over that fear, if possible. After handing the father my business card and telling him to call, Mom invited the girl over fur a pat of my silky head, but she declined. I'm excited about this new type of ministry. As I pawsed and reflected on the afternoon, I realized what a coincidence it was that the man who heard our talk in November was also there at the town picnic. Did God have a hand in this? I think so. He's an awesome God.

During the summer, when my church holds joint worship services with the Congo Church, Pastor Debbie had a request for me to do the Children's Story. She asked Mom, who asked me, and my response was:

"Pawsitively! You know how much I love to shmooz with folks, especially the young ones! You're not barking up the wrong tree when you ask me to do this. Doggone, I'm getting so excited! This will be a really great Sunday! Hot dog!"

My folks were really excited in July when they opened the Sunday Boston Globe magazine to find that my photo showing me lying under their pew had won the "Boston Globe Staff Photo of the Week" for July 17, and also the Globe's Best Photos of 2009 article in January of this year. Wow! Such fame would go to anyone else's head, but Mom and Dad found that, as excited as they were about this, I took it in stride and remain the same affable, modest guy I've always been. They're excited to get all this publicity for me, because it means that more people will learn about my Job for my Boss and will request visits for me to make.

Just when I start getting complacent about visitations, my Boss finds something else for me to do. I was pawsitively getting ho-hum about visiting all these folks in nursing homes, etc., and listening to Mom and Dad discussing where we'd go this week, when my Boss intervened and set me on a different track.

Rev. Gail Wright from the Congregational Church asked Mom if I'd be willing to come to the Vacation Bible School closing ceremony, so my ears perked up when I heard them discussing this. Something different! And with kids! What's not to like about this? Gail asked us to follow her upstairs to the Sanctuary right down to the front of the church, and we stood beside her as she talked to the kids about Serving Others and my role in this.

In August we were all excited to welcome Steve back from his year's deployment in Afghanistan with the National Guard. Thanks to my Boss, he returned safely to American soil, due in large part, I'm sure to all the prayers from so many folks.

So—a little bit of a different turn for us. You never know when God will whisper in your ear and give you a little nudge to help someone out. I thought you'd like to know that a Ministry Dog's work isn't just visiting folks in hospitals, etc., but, like a true Christian, my Ministry work is all over the place—I just have to learn to recognize it when it crosses my path.

All these "different" events have really perked me up, and I surely enjoy them all, since it's another way of passing on my love to many people. On the other paw, though, I do enjoy visiting sick folks and helping to bring a smile to their faces. I guess I'm just really satisfied about this job I have—I'm bringing happiness and healing to folks who need it, and I have a really great Boss. What more could a guy ask for?

Last Fall when I took Dad for one of our walks, the guy who was mowing the Congo Church lawn waved me over, so Dad had to come with me, of course. The guy asked Dad if I was the church dog his wife has told him about. She's seen me when I go to the Congregational Church joint services with us Baptists, and mentioned how much she liked me. Heck, I'm getting well known all over town! I liked that name as well as Ministry Dog, so I guess I'll keep it for a while.

This year's tail ends with a bang! On the last Sunday in April, the church was loaded with CBS News folks! And all to record my activities, and what a howling success it turned out to be! First, they taped Dad and me as we stood in the Narthex Greeting people, then we walked upstairs to sit with Mom. The camera was "on" during most of the service, but especially when Pastor Debbie called us down front for the Children's Story. She talked about what a caring guy I am, and how I'm always looking for ways to Serve my God, and asking what things the kids could do for God. I've been the subject of Children's Stories before, and they're all a bit different from each other, but they all end up making the kids think about services they could provide for others and for God, which I enjoy hearing.

During the coffee hour downstairs, I was kept busy as usual spreading my love and joy around to everyone—adults as well as kids. So many people had to come by to pat my silky head, and some to shake my paw. As usual, Dad walked with me over to the ladies' bench so they could pat me, too. The nice producer of the CBS show arranged to interview Pastor Deb upstairs in the sanctuary, then over to Littleton Inn for an interview with John Moon, the Communications Officer for NEADS. Then they appeared at my condo where they interviewed me, along with Mom and Dad. The day ended with their three cars following us to a visit at the Life Care Center in Acton, to see Victor. We finally arrived back to the condo, by ourselves, just after 5 p.m. That was certainly a long day—starting at 9 a.m. at the church, and on the go the whole day. I was exhausted! But also I was exhilarated, to realize how many people might see this show (to air in June sometime) and will become aware of not only NEADS, but Littleton First Baptist Church! I heard Mom tell Dad, "It's a win-win situation all around!"

Obediently submitted,

Your Church Dog Mosby Mac Fisher, aka Therapy Dog for the Ministry
(as dictated to Mom)

Chapter 79

SOME WELCOME NEWS FROM NEADS

May 10, 2010 from Donna Laconti at NEADS:

Hi:

John mentioned to me that you said you were still fundraising, but I had sent you a letter some time ago telling you that we had completed your sponsorship with a donation from a large company. I took down your web site and have essentially stopped looking for funds for you. I have closed your account, as the letter said. I hope you are well and things are going well for you now that you have your dog. Things here are just as busy as can be and we are looking forward to our next graduation in June. They come up too quickly!

However, if you do receive some funds beyond this point, we will, as per our agreement, apply them to another person's account. It will greatly help the next person who is seeking sponsorship. Please let me know if you know of any funds you are working on or know about. We can apply funds to another dog. I appreciate your efforts and wish you continued happiness with your dog. Please stay in touch!

Best, Donna Laconti, Director, Program Support

May 11, 2010

To: Donna Laconti

Great news! No, I never received your letter, but a factor is that in December of 2008 we moved, still in Littleton, but to a different address, and some of our mail, I'm sure, has disappeared. I'm happy and delighted that a large company would sponsor Mosby, but we won't give up our fundraising efforts when we can. We always tell people about what a great job NEADS is doing, and have referred folks to the NEADS website for further information. As John will tell you, we certainly enjoyed our recent Sunday with CBS News, to help spread the word about NEADS as well as Mosby. Everyone who meets him loves him, and he's made lots of friends, as well as helping to make people feel better when they're ill.

Lynda

Chapter 80

A THANK-YOU NOTE TO CIGNA

May 11, 2010

To: Donna Laconti

Subject: Re: RE: Your NEADS sponsorship is complete

I was wondering if Mosby should write a thank-you note to the company which donated money for him? Could I have the name and address so that he could do this, or is that not allowed?

I just want to do what's right, don't mean to pry.

ljf

May 17, 2010 Donna wrote:

It would be great!

    Cigna Foundation

Donna Laconti

Monday, May 17, 2010

To: Donna Laconti

Many thanks. I'll see that Mosby attends to that this week.

ljf

Lynda Reynolds Fisher

Mosby Mac Fisher, Therapy Dog for the Ministry
First Baptist Church, Littleton MA
Home: 19 Jeannette Way
978-486-4932
MosbyMacFisher@verizon.net

June 7, 2010

Cigna Foundation
1601 Chestnut Street,
Suite 1
Philadelphia, PA 19192

ATTENTION: Lania Peterson

Gentlemen (and Ms. Peterson)

I think I must pause in my busy day to express my gratitude and heart-felt thanks to your fine corporation for sponsoring me. In case you don't know me, let me introduce myself to you.

I am a wonderfully handsome (so my folks say) male Golden Retriever, just turned four years old. I was born in New Brunswick, Canada on June 6, 2006, and I was donated to NEADS, located in Princeton, Massachusetts, along with my brother. Of course, I have all the looks in the family, although HIS family probably thinks HE does! My trainer, Christy, picked us up at the United States border in Maine, and let me assure you, we ARE legal immigrants, equipped with all the proper paperwork necessary to becoming Americans, which I am now. I especially feel patriotic when I've taken part in departure and welcoming home ceremonies for my brother-in-law, Capt. Steve Mongelli, recently having served his country in Afghanistan.

I spent some time in the Puppy House, but must have damaged it somehow, because they deemed me house broken by the time I left there. I remember learning how to sit and lie down on command and sort of "come" when called. Doggone, it's hard for little kids to grasp that one!

Then it was off to the Rhode Island State Prison system, where an inmate taught me more specific obedience commands, while on the weekends Bonnie Pansa and her family took me on trips to restaurants, train rides, and middle school dances, where they found what a party animal I can be. All fun places to visit!

After a while, I was transferred to Lebanon, New Hampshire, for yet more training, with Ginny and Glyn Reinders, before returning to the NEADS facility for fine tuning, so to speak. Christy took charge of me again, and in the midst of all the Assistance Dog training, she realized that perhaps I was just too much of a "people dog" and might not succeed too well if I had to focus my attention on just one person, my handler. I just loved everyone, and wanted to spread my love around wherever I went.

At the same time, along came my Mom, Lynda Fisher, who had requested a Therapy Dog for the Ministry to help her in her visits to sick people, which was part of her responsibilities of being a Deaconess in her church. Christy and the other kind folks at NEADS put their heads together and chewed on it for a while, then decided to match me up with Mom. What a blessing that was! We hit it off right away, and after Mom had come to train with me for a whole week, I was lucky enough to be able to go home with her—to my forever home.

Mom, Dad, and I have become a solid team, visiting sick people in hospitals, nursing homes, rehabs, etc., wherever they think a person might need a lift by my presence. I'm not barking up the wrong tree when I tell you what a howling success I am. I was born to this! I'm a natural at making people feel better!

Besides taking Mom and Dad to visit sick people, I take them to Worship Service every Sunday. I must admit I snooze off as I'm lying on the floor while they're sitting on the pew, when Pastor Debbie gets to the sermon part. Sometimes Pastor Debbie uses me for the Children's Story, and do they love that! It's usually when she's trying to make a point about "serving others" or something of that nature. During coffee hour afterwards, I take Mom or Dad around the hall to visit with everyone, and they all love me there, especially the kids. I've taken part in quite a few of the church's activities, as well as the town's celebrations. I've been to the Independence Day town picnic, marched in costume in the kids' Halloween parade, been to Touch-a-Truck Day, and even got to shake Santa's paw at the Christmas Tree Lighting Ceremony.

So you see, I'm a very busy guy, and it keeps on getting better and better all the time. Mom and Dad both say what a blessing I am in their lives, and Pastor Debbie thinks I'm God's blessing to all the church folks, as well as half the people in town, too. (I'm still working on the other half of the town people.)

All this would not have been possible without your support, you know. According to the nice folks at NEADS, I cost quite a bit to educate, and their training program isn't possible without folks like you donating lots of money. Each person lucky enough to receive a NEADS-trained dog is expected to take part in fund raisers, but large corporations like you really are necessary to keep the program going. When Mom

Lynda Reynolds Fisher

found out that Cigna had donated money to support me, she insisted that I write you a thank-you note, but I've been so busy with my Church Work that I've hardly found time to do this very important task.

Many, many thanks for your generosity, and if you're ever in the Littleton, Massachusetts area, do drop by and I'll treat you to a Milk Bone to go with your coffee that Dad keeps going all day. You know you'll leave us feeling happy that I laid my beautiful, large Golden head on your knee as you patted my silky head, just as I do for the sick folks.

Of course, it goes without saying, if you're in the area on a Sunday morning, you know you'll find me with Mom and Dad at the First Baptist Church, situated right on the edge of the Town Common. Everyone is welcome there, and you'll soon see what a special place it is, because God has blessed them with my presence in their midst. That's when you'll feel God's Special Blessing. It's the only church in town with their very own Church Dog.

Arf!

Blessings and thanks, from

Mosby Mac Fisher, Therapy Dog for the Ministry (also known as the Church Dog) (as dictated to Mom)

Arf!

Chapter 81

MY E-MAIL MESSAGE TO ALL MY E-MAIL FRIENDS

June 8

OK everybody, all of you who know and love our Therapy Dog for the Ministry, here's your opportunity to see him on network television, doing the work he does best—loving people. You'll have to get up VERY early—he's scheduled to air on WBZ at 5:30 A.M. on Sunday, June 20th. 5:30 A.M. I didn't know there was such an hour—I think it's before the birds are awake. If you're smart (like me), you'll tape/record it and watch it at a decent hour.

How did this come about, you might ask? Because CBS News, out of New York, has a Religion Unit attached to their hour of news, and they're doing a segment on Animals in Religion. The CBS News team visited Littleton, MA in April and followed Mosby around all day to see how he serves our God. We met them at the church, where they taped Larry and Mosby as official church greeters, welcoming people into the worship service. Then Pastor Debbie used him as an example during the Children's Story time, which she has done before, talking about serving God, which we know Mosby does quite well.

Then, while Mosby was visiting with folks during the coffee hour, the producers interviewed Pastor Deb in the Sanctuary, followed by an interview with John Moon, the Communications Officer for NEADS (National Education for Assistance Dogs Services), Mosby's alma mater. The whole team landed at our condo and interviewed us with Mosby, then followed us as we made a visit to the Life Care Center next door in Acton to see how Mosby gives comfort and love to sick folks.

This whole thing took all day, from 9:00 a.m. until we arrived home a little after 5 p.m. Mosby had a nice long nap after that, and Larry and I had an early bedtime later that evening. What a thrill it was, to be interviewed and help to spread the word about the great work that NEADS does, and also the work that Mosby is doing. We truly believe that our Church Dog is serving our God by giving a little loving warmth and comfort to the sick folks he visits.

Now, I'm just looking forward to seeing probably five or ten minutes of Mosby on television. The team also interviewed the Monks of New Skete as they train German Shepherds for police work and also, I believe, a professor from Harvard regarding animals and religion.

So—tune in—either in real time or taped/recorded. We'll be watching it over and over again, I'm sure. For you folks who aren't in the Boston viewing area, I can give you the appropriate times and dates, since CBS sent me the entire viewing schedule. Just ask me!

Lynda

An e-mail to our daughter Laurie's West Coast friend (and mine) Lisa Stormer Roux on June 15:

"You're the first one to e-mail me about the show, but since then people have been e-mailing me and telling me how great the show was, but no details.

"I'm curious—did they use the piece where the producer asked me if I thought dogs went to Heaven?

"I do hope they used that bit. Did they use the interview with Debbie, our pastor, and John Moon, from NEADS? Did they use the bit where Mosby went to the nursing home to visit Victor? "I'm so excited, I don't know how I'm going to wait until next Sunday!"

An e-mail from Stormer:

Hi Lynda,

I didn't realize that you hadn't seen it yet. It's the first piece and I feel it was very well done. They did not use the piece about dogs going to Heaven, but they did use both the pastor and John Moon. But more of you, Larry and Mosby than anyone else. Yes, the man (and a woman) at a nursing home, plus the children's sermon and greeting at church. It was a much longer piece than I had expected. Can't wait for you to see it, I don't want to tell you anymore . . . I want you to be surprised!!

Anyway, it was an excellent piece (and to be honest, I haven't even watched the rest of the show yet!!).

Hope all is well!

Stormer

Chapter 82

A RESPONSE FROM NEADS

On Jun 15, 2010, Donna Laconti wrote:

Hi Mosby . . . . you are a pampered dog . . . . please don't run your mom ragged!

Very truly yours,
Donna Laconti
Resource and Donor Development

June 19

I like that—pampered—but not spoiled. I know I live a good life, thanks to my mom and dad, and also thanks to my Boss (your God), and I'm very grateful to NEADS for making this wonderful connection. Doggone, my folks really do love me a whole lot, and they do nice things for me, but they definitely do not spoil me. I'm still the same unassuming, obedient guy I was when Christy trained me. For a while, Dad was really handing out the treats when I did things well, but when Christy said I was OVERWEIGHT (gasp), Dad listened to Mom about overdoing the treats, and measuring out too many kibbles at breakfast time, and now I'm down to a svelte 74 pounds, which my vet says is ideal for me. On my two birthdays with them, my folks gave me: (1) last year, an agility ring and (2) this year, an agility tunnel. I really love them both and I'm exercising my whole body. That, plus the 20 miles or so a week that I walk with Dad.

So—pampered, yes, but spoiled, NO!

Arf!

Mo

Chapter 83

THANK-YOU E-MAILS TO LIZZ AND LIZ

June 21

To Lizz and Liz and all the editors and others who had a hand in creating Mosby's TV show—

What a marvelous job everyone has done! Larry, Mosby, and I have watched the show many, many times, and I'm sure we'll continue to watch it many, many more times. Larry woke me with a gentle tug at 5:25 a.m. Sunday morning so that we could view the show, and we watched it again while eating breakfast, and again after returning from church. Mosby enjoyed immensely the part where the Monks' dogs barked—he wanted to join in, I think.

Truly, it was a beautiful story you've created, piecing together stories from your own photographer, plus the CD from the local cable channel, plus contributions from NEADS, and the story flowed seamlessly. You caught the essence of Mosby and his dedication to his job perfectly.

Of course, we watched the rest of it, but we were still concentrating on Mosby's part, since we think of it as "Mosby's TV Show" and have a hard time remembering that anyone else appeared. Everyone in church was buzzing about it and complimenting Mo on his fine job. I started receiving e-mails from the West Coast mid-week, and one person said she was all choked up and did shed a few tears when the picture of Jessie, our beloved Brittany, showed up on the screen. What a great job of interposing our family's past with the present and, of course, the anticipated future.

What next for Mosby? Possibly that book that he's contemplating writing in a few more years. I know Mosby will be happy to dictate many of his adventures to me. He can't type that well—that darned dewclaw doesn't work as well as my thumbs, you know!

Again, many thanks for doing such a great job, and we all look forward to the CD you promised us (hint, hint).

Larry and Lynda Fisher and—Mosby Mac Fisher—Therapy Dog for the Ministry, or, as he's known about Littleton, "The Church Dog."

July 6, 2011

Subject: My CBS Primetime (almost) Debut

Doggone, I'm so pawsitively ecstatic about the great show you folks put together! It showed off my unique but humble personality, and all the shots showed me at my best (not that I have any other side, except the best).

Dad woke Mom at 5:25 a.m. that Sunday morning to see me, and they both watched it in bed, while I obediently sat beside them. I was really excited that mine was the story to start the program. Not that I didn't cast an eye on the shepherds, but my profile was just too good for a viewer not to watch. I was intrigued by the creatures inside the church for the Blessing of the Animals—not one poop landed on the floor! (that we could see, anyway) Of course, since I've been trained so well at NEADS, everyone knows that I would never have an accident in my church, but you just can't tell about other animals who haven't been as highly trained as I've been. We've watched the show many, many times, as often as I can convince my folks to use the DVR. On the other paw, now that I have my own DVD, maybe I can use it myself sometime when they're not around. As long as my dewclaws don't get in the way, I think I can manage it! I particularly like the segments of me when they showed me visiting Victor and Lois in their rehab/nursing homes—they're both such nice folks, and I really love to visit them and lay my handsome Golden head on their laps. I'm so glad that the whole world now knows how much I love my job, as well as my folks, Larry and Lynda, and my church family, too!

I'm a great celebrity around town, now. When I take Mom and Dad grocery shopping at Donelan's Supermarket, people are always pawsing beside us to chat about my show and how well I handled myself in the limelight. When I take Dad for our extended walks around town, we're always being stopped so that folks can chat about me and how well I did on TV. My friend, Dapper, who guards the Littleton Inn B&B for his folks, treats me with a wee bit more respect lately, since he realizes my new celebrity status.

I was all ears when I heard Mom and Dad talking about the show and how impressed they were with how well the show was done, showing me off at my gorgeous best. Many, many thanks to all those involved in this production, and maybe if you-all get to swing by New England, we'll meet again sometime. We'd have a howling good time reminiscing about my day in the limelight.

Hope to see you again sometime. Arf! Woof!

Lynda Reynolds Fisher

Mosby Mac Fisher, Church Dog, (aka Therapy Dog for the Ministry)

p.s. Say hello to Double Z Lizz for me, please. She was so nice to me, too, and her hands tasted so good when I got a lick of them once.

July 7

From: Liz Kineke

Subject: RE: My CBS Primetime (almost) Debut

Dear Mosby,

Thank you so much for your kind words. You are quite the correspondent despite the challenges of typing with paws. Thanks for getting up so early to watch the show. And now that you have your own personal copy of the show you can watch it over and over and over again. I am glad the show has helped elevate you in the eyes, ears and wet noses of the town of Littleton!! (those border collies are a tough audience too) I so enjoyed meeting you and your lovely caretakers, I was ready to move in. Seriously Mosby, you are so lovely and so full of love . . . . thank you for all your hard work and being a gentle presence for people who find themselves in need of your unconditional support. You do your job so well and I love what you do.

I should mention that one of my friends who has a Boston Terrier named Zander watched the show when it aired in New York. Apparently Zander thought he knew you because he barked every time he saw you on the television screen. You sure do get around Mosby!!

Stay in touch and I hope you are staying nice and cool in what is turning out to be a scorcher of a summer. I hope to meet you and your caretakers again very soon!!

Warmest Woofs and Meows,

Liz

Chapter 84

MOSBY'S MEANDERINGS

Early July

Arf! Woof! This past Saturday I scored again! That nice lady, Donna, from NEADS, had e-mailed Mom (don't know why she doesn't communicate with me directly, since I'm the one whose presence she wants) to ask if I would be available to attend Leominster's Summer Stroll to help the folks at Coldwell Bankers Realty with their fund-raising efforts for VetDogs. Of course, we all went—Mom, Dad, and I. They're always very cooperative when they know it's something I want to do.

After parking the car, I knew it was going to be an exciting occasion, so I barked and yipped away to let them know of my enthusiasm, but I guess it was the wrong thing to do. They always think that I should be more dignified, but doggone it, when I can tell there'll be lots of people and dogs, I can't contain my exuberance and have a five-minute "expression of happiness" before I settle down to being the very professional Service Dog that they know I am. I yipped and pulled on the leash, even when we reached the sidewalk and started passing people, and I think I embarrassed Mom and Dad a bit, so after a bit of stern leash tugs from Dad, I settled down—sort of.

I found out that the Stroll meant that all the storekeepers on Main Street were outside with tables and chairs and all selling products and/or selling chances for their different charitable organizations. There were bands along the street, balloon vendors, food, etc., and it was really a grand affair. After walking for a few blocks, we found the Coldwell Bankers folks with tables and chairs on the sidewalk in front of their business office, and after a flurry of introductions and finding chairs for us and patting me, we all settled down. Out came my portable water bowl, but I really didn't need a drink—I was too busy chatting with people who wanted to pat me and find out about NEADS' VetDogs program. People were reluctant to pat me, 'cause they saw my Service Dog uniform vest, but when Mom or Dad saw that certain look in their eyes, they gave permission to pat me, which made me so happy. Mom and Dad told everybody about my Job and then launched into the spiel about the VetDogs program, which Coldwell Bankers was pushing. We met a nice lady on roller skates who stopped when she saw my NEADS vest, to explain that she was a NEADS volunteer at Devens in Ayer. Mom and she chatted for a while, and my neat business card was handed over to the lady.

Lynda Reynolds Fisher

Mom was a little concerned about the live band that was placed right next to us, and tried to cover my ears, but I really didn't mind the noise, 'cause it brought a lot of folks near us and then we could go into our NEADS speech. There were lots and lots of folks all afternoon, and it never got boring. I got to meet Tiger, a little black Lab in training, and we shared bowls of water. I always like to meet some new pups, future Service Dogs just like me, even though I'm pretty unique in my Job.

Soon it was time to go, and we retraced our steps to the parking lot. I heard Mom exclaim to Dad that she wished I was as calm when we first arrived as I was on the way back. What does she want, anyway? I'm just so enthused about my Job that I can't always contain myself, even though it's a little embarrassing to my humans. Now I'm looking forward to visiting Lois Grant, a shut-in who used to come to our church until she couldn't make it any more. Pastor Deb is going with us, partly to see how I do my job when I take Mom and Dad visiting folks. She's never been with us, and I just hope that I can contain my enthusiasm better than I did at the Summer Stroll.

Mosby Mac Fisher, Church Dog

Donna Laconti received a copy of the above report, to which she responded:

Jul 8, 2010

Hi:

We need to help you with a title, though . . . .

Very truly yours,

Donna Laconti

My Reply:

That's what the folks around town call him, when we're out and about. Larry and he go on long walks (about 20 miles a week), and people will stop them and say, "Is that the church dog I've heard about?" Larry patiently says, "Yes, he's the Therapy Dog for the Ministry" and goes on to explain Mosby's many job responsibilities, sometimes handing out Mo's business card when he remembers to keep some in his pocket. I'm on my second batch of cards already!

Mo doesn't wear his official vest when they're just two guys taking a walk, so he feels incognito, but still people do take note of him, especially since the CBS show.

ljf

Chapter 85

ANOTHER VISIT WITH TUCKER, THE SPANISH WATER DOG

We enjoyed another visit from our niece's Spanish Water Dog, Tucker, who gets along with us all, and is learning which of Mosby's toys are acceptable for him to play with, and which are off limits. Other than that, the two four-footers get along marvelously, playing together in the yard and sleeping side by side in the house.

July 8

From Tucker Nazzaro to his family:

Arf! Hello to my family—Mom, Dad, and my brothers and sisters, Stephen, Ella, Alec, Rosa, and Sammy:

Mosby graciously allowed me to use his e-mail account so that we didn't have to bother Auntie Lynda. I just wanted to let you-all know what a pawsitively great vacation I'm having. It's a howling success.

I miss my family, especially my brothers and sisters, but on the other paw, the cool, air-conditioned house makes up a little fur that. Unlike the first time I stayed with the Fishers and was so homesick that I didn't eat for a whole day, this time, when my food dish went down, I pawsitively gobbled it right up. I play a little with Mosby, but it's so hot outside that we'd rather stay in the house, even though it's so little the whole place would fit comfortably in our family room at home. I think my cousin Mosby would be a real party animal, if he could let loose in the house. Mo is generous with his toys, but mostly we just look at each other and pant a bit. We have played some with each other, but he's so doggone big that it intimidates me somewhat. I'm waiting for the weather to cool off, 'cause Auntie Lynda said she'd take me fur a walk when the temperature is under 90 degrees, so I have to muzzle that thought fur a while. Well, that's my vacation tail fur now. I hope I'm not barking up the wrong tree when I imagine you kids are having fun on yours. When we all get back together, I'll be all ears to hear about your trip.

Nose licks, tail wags, and much love to all

from Tucker, your boy

Hasta, mi amigos and amigas

Chapter 86

BLESSING OF THE ANIMALS

Pastor Debbie is always thinking of new programs and events that might work in a church setting, partially to interest the people already attending, partially to show the world that we're an interesting church worth visiting, and always to enhance our little church in our praise and worship of Jesus Christ.

I'm sure Debbie has read how other churches have held Blessings of Animals and has had it in the back of her mind for a while, contemplating how and where would be best to do this. All these thoughts bubbled in Debbie's mind and finally surfaced as a good time for us to have our own Blessing of the Animals, perhaps after church on the front lawn, where there'd be plenty of visibility to folks traveling about the Common area.

This planning prompted me to e-mail and invite John Moon, Communications Officer from NEADS, whom we had all met during the CBS Sunday, as it had become known, to some of us.

On July 16, 2010 I e-mailed John, inviting him to speak:

Would you consider coming to our church worship service on Sunday, October 10 to talk about how NEADS is progressing with their Therapy Dog for the Ministry program, and how other churches are using their Ministry Dogs, and what a blessing animals can be? I think I can find a few Scripture readings relating to animals, although the Bible doesn't talk much about animals, but just to tie in animals as the theme for that Sunday. Maybe in October, which is St. Francis' birthday, and traditionally the Blessing of the Animals happens most often?

I thought we could start by running the CBS DVD on Mosby (about ten minutes long) and then you'd just have to talk for about 10 minutes. Twenty minutes is the usual length for the sermons—any longer than that, and Mosby isn't the only one to fall asleep!

Of course, if you feel you'd rather talk for the full 20 minutes, that'd be fine, too. Please let me know your thoughts on this. We'd love to hear you talk about NEADS and ministry dogs!

Lynda Fisher

Lynda Reynolds Fisher

John soon replied:

Lynda—good afternoon!

I would be honored to speak with members of your church on Sunday, Oct. 10th about NEADS Ministry Dog program. I think your agenda is perfect although you know I can talk about NEADS for any length of time!

Please just give me a time to be there and I'll make plans—

Thank you Lynda for asking me . . . . I'm honored.

See you in October, if not sooner . . . .

John

July 16

Wonderful! Worship service starts at 10:00 a.m.

As time gets closer, we'll be in touch again with more details. Mosby was all ears when I told him what would be happening. He's always eager to be of Assistance, any way he can.

ljf

Sometime in that summer I received an e-mail from Gordon Duffus, a fellow Clan Sutherland member and good e-mail friend, who mentioned that in his wife's Episcopal church they had just experienced a Blessing of the Animals.

Gordon's e-mail:

Lynda,

We held our Blessing of the Animals yesterday . . . [Saturday] . . . as it's difficult to Bless the animals & have Eucharist in the same service. Lotsa dogs, no cats . . . and the promised horse failed to appear.

My reply to Gordon:

On October 10, my church is celebrating God's gift to us of animals—I'm doing the Invocation with a cute Blessing story, followed by a Scripture Reading from Genesis about God's giving us (mankind) dominion over all the animals. Instead of the usual Children's Story, we're running the U-Tube poem/song God and Dog, and then to top it all off, the Message will be given by John Moon, Communications Officer for NEADS (Mosby's alma mater). That's followed at noon by a Blessing of the Animals led by our Pastor Debbie and John Moon, with assistance from Mosby the Church Dog.

It's so great to be a church which deviates from the Lectionary occasionally and welcomes different approaches to worshipping God!

Lynda

Chapter 87

ANDREW #3

Our ongoing search to find the perfect Andrew puppy to use Mosby's donation continued on Jul 30, 2010, when Doreen Sheridan wrote:

Hi Lynda and Lawrence,

Andrew has arrived at NEADS. Andrew was born on 5/9/10. He is at the Laura J. Niles Early Learning Center (puppy house) on the NEADS campus. While he is at puppy house, he will learn basic tasks and obedience. The puppies go on field trips to stores, parks and a veterans home to introduce them to different social situations. He will have plenty of time for play and the all important nap.

Enjoy and thank you for your support.

Doreen

Mosby's reply:

What a cute little tyke! He's almost as cute as I was at that tender age. Let's hope that this wee Andrew makes it through the program. I'll be praying for him, and I know my folks will, too. Many thanks for letting us know the good news.

Mosby Mac Fisher, Therapy Dog for the Ministry

(otherwise known as "the Church Dog".

Chapter 88

LARRY'S THOUGHTS ON MOSBY

Debbie had asked Larry for his thoughts on meeting people when they're on some of their daily walks. Here's Larry's response:

Aug 11, 2010

Subject: Little Things in The Life of The Church Dog

Hi Debbie

Here are some things about Mosby, some you know. Any of these may give you an idea for your books.

We have our five-year-old grandson two, sometimes three, times a week. There is a lot of love between them, and Mosby never touches Mikey's toys.

We take Mosby shopping every Friday, usually with Mikey. He meets lots of friends. When Lynda answers the phones for the School Department, she sometimes takes Mosby. More friends there. I sometimes take him down to the Senior Center when they have the men's breakfast.

When we go out to eat [not as often as Lynda would like] we take Mosby.

We have a neighbor up the street who asked me if we would come in and visit with her elderly sister, who uses a walker, so we do that once in a while.

We also walk around the Littleton Green senior housing and make an occasional visit there.

<u>Little Things We Encounter On Our Walks</u>

I always try to make it interesting, so once in a while I give him a small treat. At the tennis court I have him roll over for one. And at the Congregational Church parking area we go through his heeling routine, and anytime he is extra good with any other animal he gets one. He sees other critters, like squirrels, chipmunks, wood chucks, as well as cats, other dogs (some barking behind a fence).

Mosby has his animal friends also. You know about Dapper, his Border Collie friend, and Dapper's kitty, who passed away. There's also Angel, a small poodle mix.

Sometimes we go behind Littleton Inn and visit the chickens. They were baby chicks when we first saw them, although not now.

People That We Meet

Once in a while someone will ask me if that is the church dog, or is that Mosby?

At the Congregational Church we meet Pete, the sexton; on Shattuck Street, Mrs. Rice working on her flower garden; and you know about Victor.

We have also met Bill Raine at the tennis court, and Chris and Hannah at the library.

He is always happy to see Donna Ray, Joanne, and Valerie.

We also have to mention his good friend, Mr. Gibson.

That's all I can think of for now. Anything else I will let you know. I hope you can use some of it.

Larry

Deb's reply:

Larry—this is an awesome list!! I love it—and it is very helpful. It is so interesting that Mosby doesn't touch Mikey's toys. I might have to ask you if I can come over some time when Mikey is there.

How is Lynda?

Thank you again!

Debbie

E-Mails From The Church Dog

In the meantime, Debbie was continuing working on the children's book/books centered around (either) Mosby or animals in general, but in a worshipful aspect.

Aug 18, 2010 Debbie wrote:

Hi Lynda,

So now I am rereading your articles . . .

Where did you go for the NEADS fundraiser where Mike and Bonnie, Mosby's foster parents were at? Why were there children there? Was it a school? Day care? How long was Mosby there?

Anyway—I am reading and have found that Mosby was born in New Brunswick . . .

I am having a good writing day—and think I have hit on the angle that I want to do the book at . . .

Deb

To Debbie 8/19/10

I'm glad you're progressing on the book—I think there'll be an enthusiastic reception to it.

After Mosby left the Puppy House at NEADS, he went to the State Prison system in Rhode Island, where his early training was left up to a prisoner—he was a Prison Pup! However, prisoners can't take puppies out to public restaurants, train stations, schools, hospitals, etc., so on the weekend these dogs are given to Weekend Puppy Raisers, who take them out to all kinds of interesting places which they might encounter when working as Service Dogs. Bonnie Pansa was Mosby's weekend trainer, while he went through TWO prisoners and when it looked like there'd be a third prisoner training him, NEADS thought that would be too much confusion for a young pup to handle, so Bonnie graciously accepted Mo full-time instead of just for the weekends.

Bonnie is a teacher at the Warren, RI middle school, and Mike Carbone, her husband, is the principal there. He used to take Mosby out for breakfast (apparently, principals can do that). They're both active participants in NEADS programs. I've seen them at a few of the graduations since Mosby graduated, and Mosby, of course, was VERY excited to see both of them. I'm not sure if Bonnie teaches special needs kids, or if she just has a lot to do with them, because the last time we saw them at a graduation, they had three Down Syndrome kids with them. They really are dedicated teachers.

Bonnie held a dance (or holds an annual dance) to raise money for NEADS, and had a raffle basket of doggie supplies, and the music was so age-appropriately loud I thought it was going to deafen the dogs. In addition to Mosby, there was the dog that Bonnie was currently raising for NEADS and at least one more graduate dog. I think there was another that didn't stay too long.

This dance was held in the school cafeteria, and it was LOADED with middle school aged kids, most of whom remembered Mosby, so it was a great reunion time for all concerned. As Mike escorted us through the office area to get to the dance hall, the women stopped their work for a few minutes to greet Mosby, after Mike told them who he was. We have pictures of Mo spending time in the office when he was raised there.

In New Brunswick, where Mosby was born, the woman breeder there is apparently dedicated to donating puppies from more than one litter. Probably they've been evaluated and found not quite up to snuff for show quality and then she donates them to NEADS. Mosby's trainer, Christy, met them at the international border in Maine and transported Mosby and his litter brother, Micah, to NEADS in Princeton where they were placed in the puppy house to start their training. Micah graduated with Mosby, so they had a chance to connect once again, although I think they both had forgotten that they once shared their mother's womb. Of course, we think that Mosby is the handsomer, smarter brother, but then we're very prejudiced!

Sometime later in Mo's life, and I don't know why, Mosby moved up to Lebanon, New Hampshire, to be further trained by Glyn and Ginny Reinders. Coincidentally, Ginny also is a teacher. After that, around January or February of 2008, Mosby was returned to NEADS for further training and to be evaluated as to which kind of service he'd be best suited for. That's when God whispered in Christy's ear, and said, "I WANT HIM TO WORK FOR ME" and they decided that he'd be best suited for the Ministry. The rest is history.

Lynda

Chapter 89

MOSBY'S MUSINGS SEPTEMBER 2010

It's not MY fault I haven't composed anything in a looong while—it's entirely on Mom's shoulders. She's been so busy researching her ancestors, she hasn't paid any attention to my writings. Sheesh! It's not as though I don't have ancestors, also. My pedigree goes back just as far as hers, but she doesn't do anything about mine. Maybe her ancestors go back to Charlemagne, but she doesn't consider that he had a dog and I can probably trace my pedigree back to Charlemagne's dog! With many, many more names, since my generations turn over many more times than hers do!

Today in church, it being Labor Day weekend, when Pastor Deb was talking about our different jobs, I was thinking that my job isn't being done correctly 'cause Mom isn't writing down all my work-related activities. My work, visiting folks, is very important, to lots of folks. I was lying in my usual spot under their pew, and I almost bit Mom on her ankle, but being the sweet, gentle guy that I am, it was just a random thought. I think Mom felt my thoughts, though, and she told me on the way home that she'd really try to start writing down my activities again.

It's been such a dry spell without any writings that I'll have to just condense everything to a few simple pages, but I really HAVE been doing lots of interesting things and visiting lots of interesting folks, giving them my special kind of warmth and love, and putting smiles back onto their faces.

Pastor Debbie is busy gathering data for her upcoming children's books featuring—who else—ME! She had requested of Dad that she come with us on a visit, just to see how well I do my job, so we went to see Lois Grant at Pine Tree Park. However, after a short pat from Lois, I laid down beside Debbie, mostly because I know her better and she did have some yummy lotion on her legs that I kept on trying to lick off. I'm usually better behaved than that, but I just couldn't resist! Mom told Dad afterwards that she doesn't think Pastor Deb saw me at my best. Most times I pay better attention to the person I'm visiting. A few months later, when Don Lindgren was at the Apple Valley rehab, we were visiting him, laughing at his jokes, Pastor Debbie appeared in the doorway, and I'm happy to report that I did a better job of showing her how I work.

We've met Gloria Morris a few times at Donelan's, and I remember meeting her and Mel, her husband, who needed lots of my attention, and after that was accomplished, I laid down beside his recliner to be close to him. Gloria never fails to tell everybody how much Mel liked that. I was saddened to hear that he had gone to a nursing home, then went to live with our Heavenly Father, my Boss. That happens with a lot of folks I visit, and it makes my Mom and Dad kind of sad, but I know these folks are better off now, living with my Boss, even though we all miss them when they're no longer with us.

I heard my Mom tell somebody that this job is getting her down sometimes, and she much prefers visiting people in the hospitals who get better, go home, and resume their normal activities. Most of our visits don't end that way, and I wish I could get her to see that, by taking me around to different folks, she's making their days a little happier.

Once, when we were visiting Phyllis Wallace at Life Care Center in Littleton, we also visited Thelma Griffin, our former pastor's wife, who had taken a fall and needed some rehab. Even though she wasn't a dog person and didn't pay much attention to me, she did tell my Mom and Dad that she enjoyed reading about me in the church newsletters. That pleased me, as well as Mom and Dad, to hear that. We were very surprised, a month or so later, to hear that after arriving home, she was hospitalized and then went to her Heavenly Reward. Now she's rejoined with Pastor John, and they're probably walking together along the rocky coastal cliffs of Maine.

It seems we've visited Don Lindgren in a few different places—first, last year in his home, where I enjoyed snacks with their little girl, Cassie, even though we weren't allowed to play as we wanted to, since we were inside the trailer home. We've visited Don this year at the Ayer hospital and also next door at Apple Valley Rehab, a few times. I loved his funny sense of humor and the way he joked with all the nurses, aides, and maintenance folks as they passed his doorway. He always had a funny thing to say to everyone, and I enjoyed getting close to him for a good pat and scratch around my neck. What a nice guy, and now he's gone, too. But he won't be forgotten! Not by me, ever. I hope I can talk Mom and Dad into visiting Ellie sometime soon. I think she needs a visit, too.

Besides all these visits we make to folks who need a lift in their spirits, Dad and I have become minor celebrities around town. I usually get to walk Dad once in the morning and then again after supper, and it's a rare walk when someone doesn't pass us in their car and toot their horn and wave at us. I don't really recognize them, and neither does Dad, but he smiles and waves back at them, so they won't think he doesn't like them. I wave my tail at them—I hope they realize that. I continue to exchange greetings with Dapper, the border collie who guards his house across the street from the B & B, Littleton Inn. I don't think I mentioned that Dapper has his own pets, a bunny and a kitty, appropriately name Bunny and Kitty. It took me a while to make friends *with Kitty, but because she lived with her dog Dapper, I knew she wasn't afraid of me. When she'd lie down and roll on her back, I knew she was just teasing me. After a spell of not seeing her, Dad asked her owner about her and got the sad news that Kitty had become sick and died. So—I found out that it's not just human friends that I lose, but animal friends, too. Doesn't make me feel any better, but at least I'm happy that I knew them for a short while at least. Now I've become friends with the chickens, but they mostly stay around back where I can't see them.*

We meet Victor sometimes when he's sitting on the stone bench by the old cemetery, and Dad stops for a while so that Victor can pat me, and they chat about things that interest them. Sometimes when we get to the Congregational church parking lot, Dad will put me through my obedience commands, just to keep me aware of them in case I might need them. Often a car will pass us on the road, and besides honking their horn, a person will extend an arm out and give us a thumbs up sign, which pleases Dad.

So—even though I haven't always visited anyone that week, I'm still working at my job because I know I'm giving happiness to somebody when we're out and about. I'm doing my God-given job and spreading my love all around town.

When I was a wee baby at the puppy house and visitors would come to see us, I'd always run over to them to receive a pat or hug, and this didn't stop when I was old enough to go to the Rhode Island prison to start my obedience training. I loved all the folks over there, even the ones who wore the same clothes as everyone else. I could tell them apart easily, and I loved them all. When Bonnie would take me for the weekends, I just loved everyone I met, even while she was busy teaching me more commands and how to work with humans. I was everyone's friend, especially the school kids where she taught and husband Mike was the principal. Of course, I'll never forget those breakfasts that Mike used to bring me to. Later, I went to live in Lebanon, New Hampshire with Glyn and Ginny Reinders. Even though Glyn thought I'd make a grand Frisbee dog, my heart was with all the people I met. Ginny took me all over with other dogs who were also learning to be Service Dogs, and I was the one who was right up front to make new friends with people we'd meet. When I was old enough to return to the NEADS campus for additional training and evaluation, they could tell that I loved everyone and wanted to be friends with the whole wide world, not just one person. So—that's how I was chosen to partner up with my Mom and Dad. Mom came in to talk to the NEADS folks about acquiring a Therapy Dog for the Ministry, and they said, "Aha! We have just the right dog for that Calling!"

Now—does anyone think that it would have happened without my Boss nudging me and everyone else connected with my training? I don't think so. And neither do my Mom and Dad. I hear them talking sometimes about God's having planned this all along, to get me together with them so we could all work for God by visiting people and bringing them my special love and comfort when they need it most.

Manny and Marie Medeiros would often see me walking Dad past their White Street house, and one day on our way back, Marie stopped Dad to ask if he'd come in to visit her sister who also lives there. She was obviously in need of my special kind of loving, and I just couldn't wait to meet her. Marie said we could visit any time we were going by because it meant so much to them, so we've done that visit on occasion also.

Dad and I have our special times together when I take him on walks around town, and Mom and I have a different kind of special time together—grooming! That's when Mom makes me even handsomer than I naturally am. Every Saturday, usually late afternoon, Dad carries my personal grooming basket outside to the steps on the deck, and I know what's coming. Mom places me down on the grass and sits herself on the step facing me, then removes my clothes—my handsome red collar. The first part isn't so pleasant, and I try to get away from her, but she's firm, even though she's gentle, and I know she really wants me to stay still, so I mostly do. She squirts some stuff in my ears, rubs them around a bit, then takes out lots of ear wax and goo. Yuck! How come my Boss made my ears so superfluously filled with wax? I must say, when she's done, Mom slips me a wee piece of treat, which makes me forget about all that ear stuff. After the ears comes the Brushing of the Teeth—another yucky job, and as much as I try to keep my lips sealed, Mom somehow manages to get that brush into my mouth and then she starts scrubbing (gently, though) around my gums with the toothbrush which is loaded with doggy toothpaste. Actually, it doesn't taste all that bad, but I just don't like all that motion going on in my mouth. Next comes the Trimming of the Nails, which is equally as unpleasant to my mind, but I realize it's necessary. Due to the arthritis in her hands, Mom can't use the nail clippers any more, and when her son, Scott, suggested the battery-operated nail file, she decided to try it. At first, she didn't like it cause it takes so long to file each nail down, much longer than a quick snip of the clippers, but it doesn't hurt her hands, so that's what she uses now. I've heard that lots of dogs are afraid of the noise, but Mom approached me gradually with the file turned on near my paw, but not touching the claw, and since this was followed by a yummy treat, I quickly accepted it. Then it was on to actually touching the nail, and I didn't mind a bit. Of course, since Dad walks me so much on the sidewalks, my nails are really filed down by the friction, so Mom just makes a quick pass and only has to spend time on my dewclaws, which don't reach down to the sidewalk.

After the ears and nails comes the fun part—scissors are used to trim my stray hairs from around my ears and toes. This operation doesn't hurt and isn't noisy, so I accept this part quite readily, but Mom still gives me a wee treat when she's done with it. This is followed by The Rake, which is used to get my undercoat out, and I actually enjoy this, 'cause it feels good. This takes the most time of the whole grooming operation, I guess because I'm so hairy, but that's the way my Boss made me, so Mom doesn't mind. She usually hums or sings some pieces of church songs as she's working. Her favorite is "And He walks with me, and He talks with me, and tells me I am His own . . . ." I'm getting the message, but she keeps on repeating it, interspersed with "Shall we Gather at the River" and, of course, "Amazing Grace" which I'm familiar with, since my Scottish ancestors heard this song played on the bagpipes long before I was born, or my Mom and Dad, either. All the undercoat that Mom rakes out, and the guard hairs, too, are deposited into a large plastic bag, which Mom has saved—she's actually on to Bag #2 now, 'cause I'm so hairy. When she thinks she has enough bags full of my golden hairs, she's going to see about washing, then carding, then spinning until she has "dog yarn" and then she'll knit a scarf for herself! Imagine that! Then, when we go visiting, we'll be coordinated—Mom wearing her golden scarf, and me wearing my Golden coat. That'll be really a conversation piece, I bet.

So—the raking is done and Mom then takes out the brush to put every top hair in its place, even my beautiful tail. Mom tells me how handsome I am, offers another treat, and it's all over. We both enjoy this time together (except for the ears and nails), 'cause she's the only one who does it with me, and it's our own together time. I know, of course, that my Boss is there, listening to Mom sing, especially, and we both enter the condo feeling satisfied with time well spent, making me so beautiful. Both Mom and Dad want me to appear at my very best for my busiest working day—Sunday.

So—it's not just formal, planned, visits that make up my day. Sometimes it's just as we're walking around town God brings us to a place where I'm needed, and I always respond to His request. Life is good—all the time!

Mosby Mac Fisher, Church Dog

Chapter 90

MOSBY'S MUSINGS

October 7, 2010

Rain, rain, rain. I haven't been able to walk Dad this week because of all the rain, and haven't been able to go some places because of all the rain. My humans are under the impression that wet dog fur might smell yucky to some folks, so they tend to go places without me so they won't "turn anyone off" that doesn't like the smell. Personally, I like the aroma of wet dog fur. On the other paw, we certainly don't want to offend anyone.

Dad has observed that in the evening, I'm much more energetic than usual, and Mom replied that it's probably due to the lack of my usual walks during the day. Eventually, this rain must stop!

Yesterday, October 6, Mom and Dad finally listened to me and I took them to visit Phyllis Wallace at Life Care Center in Littleton, since it was only drizzling instead of pouring buckets of rain. So sad. She's slowly progressing downhill, such that her sentences don't always make much sense, and she's talking about her parents as if they're still alive, as well as some of her siblings whom we know have passed on. Still, when I carefully walked up to her, being mindful of her sickly feet, she reached out to pat me and smiled a bit when I placed my handsome head on her leg for a hug. So, even though her mind is sometimes off in a different place, she does receive a bit of pleasure from my visits, so Mom and Dad continue to go with me to visit her.

As usual, we stopped for outreached hands on the way to her room and on the way out. Phyllis' roommate was being wheeled back into their shared room, and I had to go over to her side and visit with her for a while, too.

After our goodbyes were said, on the way to the front door, a woman wheeling a man stopped us so that her husband (?) could reach out his "good" hand and pat me. He smiled while patting my velvety head, and the lady told us how much he loved dogs. I could tell!

Now, besides Lily, the director has a younger puppy, both of whom are kept barricaded in her office. Lily and pup immediately bounced over to the gate, barking a greeting to me and wagging their tails enthusiastically. Like the mature, true gentleman that

I am, I didn't return the bark since I knew Mom and Dad didn't approve of that behavior, even though I was tempted mightily. Maybe next time I can make their acquaintance without the barricade between us? I'd love that, and I know they would, too. Does the new pup mean that Charlie is no longer with us? It seems that God calls Home not only humans, but also canines, which makes us sad, but we reflect on their long lives, full of happiness, and try to not feel the loss so badly. We just try to spread happiness and joy wherever we are, as long as we are given, and when my Boss calls us home, we can go to Him with the confidence that we did the best we could do while here on earth.

On the way home, we stopped at my animal hospital to get my weight checked, since Mom had heard that their scales at last worked. Seventy-four pounds still! How satisfying! All those hungry, stomach-growling days worked, and I'm staying at the weight that Dr. Kilgore deems is ideal for me, even though Christy at NEADS thinks I should be slimmer yet.

Mosby Mac Fisher, Church Dog

Chapter 91

MOSBY'S MUSINGS—OCTOBER 2010

I have so much to say, it's hard to put it all down in one session.

First, I must say how much I loved participating with Pastor Debbie at my church's first ever Blessing of the Animals. The whole morning, 10:00 to 1:00, at least, was wonderful, starting with the worship service which opened with Mom doing the Invocation, a short story about a dog's patience, etc., which humans could learn from. Next was the Scripture reading from the Old Testament book of Genesis, where God creates all us animals and charges humans with taking responsibility for us. I always enjoy that passage so much because it reminds me that I do have to listen to my humans and obey them, since they're in charge of me.

Mr. John Moon, that nice guy from NEADS, my alma mater, talked about all the programs that NEADS runs to train dogs to give all kinds of services to humans. I feel that this is a canine pay-back to humans for taking care of all of us. He was accompanied by Rainey, a really cute, petite black lab, who is his Assistance Dog, whom he uses for many of his public relations events for NEADS. I really took to her, and wish she could come over to my pad sometime. I could show her my agility ring and tunnel, and we could run around together. Mom told me that it might just happen some day if John is in the area with her.

During worship service, we sat down in the next-to-the-front pew so that John would find us with no problem, and he did. There were, in our row, Mom sitting on a pew on the aisle side, then me on the floor, followed by Dad on a pew, then Rainey on the floor, next to John on a pew. During the Children's Story, with the children all gathered around Pastor Debbie in front of the altar, I saw a small hand reach under the front pew, trying to touch my paw. Having glimpsed the struggle, Mom pushed my head and paw closer to the hand, and soon my paw was patted and held by that small, enthusiastic hand. At that point, Mom looked over the top of the pew to see who was attached to that hand and was surprised to find David Court's smiling face looking at her. This is the little guy we've been told is afraid of dogs! Apparently, his desire to pat my paw overcame his fears, and I was very proud to have had a part in breaking the icy fear from his little being!

Then it was John's turn to step up, with Rainey at his side, and talk to everyone about NEADS, and I was so proud, listening to him talk about my alma mater, from which I graduated with Mom.

Then, after worship service, we creatures, human and others, gathered on the front lawn for the Blessing. There were six dogs, one kitty, and one bunny all waiting their turn to be blessed. Pastor Deb explained about the Blessing service, read a responsive reading, then asked my Boss's blessing on each individual critter and related human, walking around the circle of animals, followed by Mom, who gave each critter a treat. There were little milk bones for the canines, a kitty treat for the feline, and the bunny received a piece of carrot. Let's see, from my church's people, there were the Mackersie bunny and kitty, the Websters' dog Rico, Mr. Gibson (Blanchards) and Lizottes' dog, which is Aunt Bobby and Uncle Jack's granddog.

So—my church's first Blessing of the Animals. I hope there'll be more of them, 'cause it's a chance for me to meet some of the critters which the church folks have, but who can't come to regular worship services.

During the week I took Mom and Dad to Life Care Center in Littleton to visit Phyllis Wallace, who still remembers me, even though she couldn't remember my name or Mom and Dad's names, either. She's a bit confused, which is sad to see, but at least I know that when I lay my velvety head on her knee, she is comforted and enjoys patting me. So I consider there's still a value to our visits to her, even though she's not as sharp as she used to be.

This past Monday was another of those wonderful, exciting days at Grotonwood, the Baptist camp, for their Fall celebration and welcome-back to campers and other Baptists. There's so much to do at these Grotonwood Days, and so many people to greet, that I do get a little carried away with all the excitement and yip a bit, but Dad was very pleased that this year I was able to contain myself a wee bit and not pull too much on the leash until at last I settled down and behaved like the gentleman that they know I can be.

When we arrived at the temporary parking lot, there was a young lady there placing the orange traffic cones to direct the cars where to park, and when Dad used my name to tell me to calm down, this girl exclaimed, "Mosby's Raiders!" Mom asked her how she knew about Mosby's Raiders, to which she replied, "I'm related to Mosby. He was my ancestor!" When I heard that, I got very excited, almost as much as Mom was. She told the girl that I was named after Colonel John Mosby, and we all had a good chuckle over that. To think—I, a Baptist dog, have the name of her ancestor! That makes us cousins, sort of!

This year we took the little shuttle bus from the temporary parking lot in the woods to the main parking lot on the edge of the buildings, and I enjoyed the ride immensely. It gave me a chance to schmooz with the other riders, a little foretaste of all the people

I'd be greeting. Stepping down from the bus, the first thing we did was register so that we'd all be counted in the hopes of being the Super Church with the most number of attendees. As usual, Mom signed me in on a separate line, Mosby Mac Fisher, so that I'd be counted also. We think that's very appropriate, especially since I attend church almost every Sunday, and am as much a church person as the two-footed ones. The rules don't state that only humans are eligible to be counted!

Mom and Dad's first stop was at the apple pie booth, to buy one for our house and one for Thanksgiving at my cousins' home in Reading. They decided to have some apple crisp for lunch, so I took them over to a crowded picnic table to eat, and boy did I have fun there, greeting everyone at the table. One nice lady in a wheelchair almost got to give me some of her hamburger, but Mom caught her in time and told her that I only eat from my dish at home. Darn! I nearly had it! Anne Lee Ellis stopped by with her adorable grandchildren, and Alana's hands sure tasted good when I licked them. Griffin Poser came over to pat me, and Mom looked around to say hi to his mom, but couldn't spot her readily, so she chatted a bit with Griffin before he ran off for another game. We saw lots of church folks during our strolls around the place, and it was nice to chat with them, but soon it was time to retrieve our pies and walk back to the car. What a beautiful day we had, watching all the excited kids participating in the many games and rides available to them. I think God smiled down on us and gave us the sunny weather and happy people.

I want to make note of yet another contact with someone while Dad and I were on one of our many walks near the Common and down to Shattuck Street. While we were walking along near the Congregational Church, a woman stopped her car, got out and came over to us and asked Dad if she could pat me. "Of course," he replied, and she went on to say that she had just put her old Golden to sleep and missed him so much. She patted me for a while, then left us, as she said over her shoulder, "He's such a beautiful dog! Thanks—that made my day." I saw the tears sparkling in her eyes, and I'm glad that I could give her a little comfort. It's so sad when people lose their beloved four-footed family members. I'm just glad that I can be a little help for them.

I kind of figure that when Dad and I are on our walks, that I'm not "working" but am just a family member, but I guess my Boss has other plans sometimes and wants to remind me that I'm ALWAYS working for Him. I think it's the same thing with my folks—they're ALWAYS Christians, not just on Sundays when they go to church, but every day during the week also, and they should always remember that fact in everything they do and say. Mom says it's sometimes hard to remember that when she loses her patience about something or someone, but she says that by watching me give comfort to people even when I'm just walking with Dad, it helps her to remember that she's always a Christian and to act accordingly. I wonder if my Boss knows how tough it is sometimes, or if He plans it that way, just to see how well we'll behave in certain situations? Mom says she'll follow my example of always being ready to do my Boss's work, even when it's hard to do!

Today, Monday, October 18, I took Mom and Dad to Westford to visit Lois Grant, who is one of my all-time favorite humans to visit, because she's the one who always asks for a visit from me! It's so nice to know that I'm wanted. We almost missed Lois because her bed was empty and we found out from her roommate that she was in physical therapy. Mom and Dad decided to leave my business card on the altar plant which they had brought for her, and left her room. Luckily, they stopped at the nurses' station to inquire how long the PT session would last, and one of the nice male nurses told us he'd walk us down there, and it was no problem to interrupt her because she'd certainly want a visit from me. As we left the elevator to start walking down the corridor to the PT room, who should appear in her wheelchair but Lois—her session had just ended and she was going back to her room. We followed along behind her, although, as usual, we had to stop a half dozen times for various workers to pat me and talk to me. Lois is really an accomplished wheelchair driver! She zipped around corners, people, and equipment just as fast as I could travel on my four feet, and soon we all were back in her room. She was so happy to see me—she couldn't get enough of my handsome, velvety head on her lap and kept calling me over to her whenever I lay down or went over to Mom. It's so nice to be appreciated, and I could tell that Mom and Dad enjoyed talking to her, too. Of course, being a retriever, I was very interested in the birds flying to her window with the feeder attached to it by a suction cup. Her son had given her a bird book to identify all the birds, but I didn't care about that. As long as they had feathers and could fly, I was interested in them.

On the way to return to the car, it took the usual half hour to maneuver through the people riding in wheelchairs or pushing walkers, to say nothing of the nurses and aides, all of whom needed to pat me and talk to me. In the car on the way home, Dad told Mom that Lois is one of our more pleasant people to visit, because she obviously is so in love with me, and it gives them pleasure to visit her.

So—that's my last few weeks—lots and lots of people and their activities, all of which I'm grateful to my Boss to be able to take part in.

Arf!

Mosby Mac Fisher, Church Dog

Chapter 92

ANDREW #3 FLUNKS OUT!

Our enthusiasm for naming a Service Dog Andrew after Scotland's patron saint, hit a huge snag that fall. Doreen wrote us yet again about the third puppy to be named Andrew, with bad news:

Nov 11, 2010

Hi Lynda and Lawrence and Mosby,

I have some bad news about the pup named Andrew. Andrew did not have the temperament for an assistance dog. Andrew was released from the program due to low confidence. He will be placed as a pet.

The donation to NEADS to name Andrew will be used to partially sponsor Anastasia and Social Dog Chase. Anastasia is eight years old and lives with her family in West Peabody, MA. Anastasia uses a wheelchair for mobility. She loves school, books, music and being social.

Anastasia responds very well to dogs, she smiles, laughs and becomes engaged. Social Dog Chase will help Anastasia be more comfortable in social situations and be a companion. Dogs are very motivating and therapeutic for her.

Anastasia and Chase are scheduled for facility based training from November 29 through December 6. A Meet and Greet is scheduled for Thursday, December 2 from 6-8 pm on the NEADS campus. Anastasia and Chase are candidates for the Spring 2011 graduation, date to be decided.

We are always sorry when one of the pups does not make it through the program, but Andrew will enjoy being a pet.

Thank you for all your support and all you do for NEADS.

Doreen Sheridan

E-Mails From The Church Dog

Nov 13 2010

Mosby's response to Doreen:

Andrew #3 flunked out? That's unbelievable! I'm happy to read that my money has gone to help a little girl—kids are my favorite people.

Before my mom and dad heard about the NEADS program, they raised a puppy for the Guide Dog Foundation, based on Long Island. Georgie, a truly handsome Goldie, was so headstrong, they knew he wouldn't make it through the program, and as it turned out, the whole litter flunked out. Georgie was adopted by a young couple on Long Island, and Mom and Dad still get e-mails and picture attachments showing how happy Georgie is, and how happy the family is with him. So I know that Andrew #3, as well as Andrews #1 and #2 will be happy as just family pets.

Many thanks for your persistence in trying to raise an Andrew for the program, even though it didn't succeed. The picture of Chase shows that he's a very handsome young guy, just as my folks think I am!

Arf!

Mosby Mac Fisher, Therapy Dog for the Ministry, aka "The Church Dog"

Chapter 93

MOSBY'S NOVEMBER MUSINGS 2010

It's been over a week since my church celebrated Thanksgiving, so I thought I'd give Mom a little nudge to get going with my report for the end of Thanksgiving.

The March Forward Offering in church was awesome this year! Could it have been because I participated for the first time? Probably. Mom had been coaching me to carry a bag in my mouth, but I wasn't really cooperating. As soon as she took her hand away, I dropped it. Finally, Mom saw that it was going to be a tough sell, so instead she put a plastic bag around my neck and walked me around the living room. There was no adjustment period for that—I took to it right away, especially since I knew there'd be a treat coming very soon.

So on Thanksgiving Sunday, when everyone else was carrying their food for Loaves & Fishes up to the altar, Dad took my leash and directed us both up the aisle, Dad with canned goods in his hand, and I with a plastic bag containing Milk Bones around my neck. I was going to make some needy dog happy for Thanksgiving! The only problem was that my vest decided to malfunction! The strap in front quite frequently unhooks itself, and I thought it was tight enough, but it took that very minute for the straps to open wide, causing the vest to slowly begin a journey down my back to my tail! What a time for a wardrobe malfunction! Talk about embarrassing moments! Mom, tailing behind me, kept on hitching up the vest onto my shoulders, but immediately it began its journey again down to my tail. And, of course, the cameras were rolling and digital photos were recording the moment for posterity. Nobody noticed how well I performed at carrying the plastic bag to the altar—they were all noticing my wardrobe malfunction! I got over it quicker than Mom and Dad did.

That night, at the Ecumenical Thanksgiving Service, which we hosted, Dad was escorting me since Mom was working in the kitchen serving coffee and goodies to our guests. Marjorie Harvey approached us and petted my head while chatting with Dad about my Work. When she found out that we visit everyone we know who could use a little time with me, she walked over to the coffee counter to ask Mom if we could visit Grace Lindquist, who was at Life Care Center in Littleton.

That week, we made our way to Life Care Center in Littleton to visit Phyllis Caldwell, recovering from pneumonia, and learning physical therapy in preparation to going home. It's sad—I wanted to go to Phyllis Wallace's room, but I remember that Mom and Dad talked how she had gone Home to be with my Boss. We'll miss her, but we all know that she's in a really great Place now. When entering Phyllis Caldwell's room, we saw Vera already sitting in a chair chatting with Phyllis. We had a really good time, talking with both ladies, and were surprised when Phyllis said that Betty Lee had just arrived there, too. We knew she had been in a hospital for a broken hip, but were pleased to know that she had progressed to Littleton so that we could visit her. The room got a little crowded when Carolyn Webster quietly walked in to see Phyllis, so we left to allow more space for the ladies to chat, knowing that we had left Phyllis in good company, and we hoped, in good spirits. Upon arriving at Betty Lee's room, we found daughter Tracey sitting down with a nursing home attendant taking notes, but we were welcomed, and after a moment of confusion, Betty remembered us and we had a nice little visit with her. She was quite happy that I had come to see her and welcomed me with her broad, happy grin and hearty laugh.

Quite soon, Betty said, "Well, thanks for stopping by," and we knew it was time to leave her. She never needs a lengthy visit.

On the way out, we did stop by Grace Lindquist's room, and I found her to be a dog person, definitely. She patted my head and smiled, and since Dad knew her to be a real dog lady, and after asking if her feet were OK, he gave me the command, "Up" and I obediently placed both front paws on her lap so she could reach me easier. She gave my head a good hug and laughed delightedly. It's so nice to visit folks like her! We didn't stay too long with her and soon were on our way back down the aisle to the front door, stopping frequently so folks could get in a pat to my velvety head. They always end with a smile, then we know it's time to move on again, closer to the door. Right by the door, as Mom was pressing the correct buttons to unlock the door, Lily came over to the gated Director's office to greet me, followed by Indie, and we would have had a great time, three Golden Retrievers welcoming each other, but the door opened and Mom pulled me through. Reluctantly, I will admit. I don't know why we couldn't visit longer with my canine friends, but as soon as Lily started barking, I could feel Mom and Dad tense up.

So—another successful visit to Life Care Center in Littleton, and another month has flown by.

Mosby Mac Fisher, Church Dog

Chapter 94

MOSBY'S MUSINGS FOR DECEMBER 2010

A whole month has flown by, and what a busy month it has been. Since I am a Church Dog, one would expect it would have to be busy for me.

It started with the first Sunday in December with the town's Christmas Tree Lighting ceremonies at the Common, right adjacent to our church. Naturally, I had worn my fur coat, so I was ready to wait in the cold for Santa Claws to arrive on top of the fire department's ladder truck, but not Mom, so of course I stayed with her and watched the festivities from the doorway of the church. As usual, the fire truck's siren and the flashing lights announced Santa's imminent arrival at the Common, along Stevens Street, which the kind policeman had blocked off just for the fire truck. I was ready to run over there to greet the jolly man, but Mom held me back, which disappointed me, but I soon recovered when my little buddy, Mikey, arrived with his Mom, Laurie. They wasted no time in stripping off outer warm coats to get down to action with icing and decorating the Christmas cookies and eating same.

Dad was busy in the other room, running the train around the snow village. Pastor Debbie's village is always a big hit with the kids, and Dad was kept busy helping the kids who wanted to run the train, as he was trying to keep their hands off the track as well as the items strategically placed on same to purposely derail the train. This is not allowed, but as usual, there's always a kid or two who wants to cause a train disaster. It's a good thing that I'm not a wee bit taller, 'cause my tail could cause a huge derailment!

Surprisingly, this year Santa Claws dropped by for a visit with the kids, and I could hardly wait my turn to have my picture taken with the jolly old man. Funny thing about Santa—each time I smell him with my discriminating nose, it's like he's a whole new person. But I know he's Santa, because who else wears such fancy clothes?

This month we traveled a few times to Life Care Center on Foster Street to see Phyllis Caldwell, who always has a bunch of church ladies visiting her. We've never visited her when she isn't surrounded by company, but we manage to squeeze in for a short visit. Betty Lee has been moved to the Alzheimer's wing, and when we were let in by a kindly nurse, we found Betty zipping around the corridor in a wheelchair, buzzing everyone in her path. She did stop long enough to say hi, then said her usual: "Thanks for coming" and wheeled off down the corridor!

We saw Grace Lindquist again, sitting in her wheelchair in the corridor outside her room, and I really enjoyed visiting her, because she knows just the spot behind my ears to rub, which I love.

As we were on our way back down the corridor, Mom saw a name on one door which she recognized—Mary Ilsley, who used to live on New Estate Road, and whose son, Lloyd, used to see Laurie, back when they were quite young, she in high school and he a few years out of school.

So we stopped to visit Mary, who remembered Mom and Dad, and yes, she enjoyed a visit from me. They caught up on each other's family news while Mary was patting my head and scratching that spot behind my ears, quite thoroughly, I might add. Soon we left Mary with a promise to return, and started our walk back to the front door, with the usual pawses along the way for outreached hands to pat me. I love it so much that I can bring such happiness to folks, just by being a gentleman and letting them pat me.

As we approached the Director's office, that door was open, gate firmly in place, with Lily and Indie ready for me with a small yip instead of a bark, but when I responded with my deep, masculine bark, Lily started to turn it on before Mom could get me through the outside door. Don't these humans realize that we canines just want to say hello to each other with our voices and wagging tails? Mom and Dad think I should be the gentleman and lead the others by not voicing my exuberance quite so loudly, but I can't help it—I just want to shout my joy from the rooftop. Well, maybe I'll try to tone it down a bit next time.

Christmas Sunday in church is always a special Sunday, with the anticipated arrival of the baby Jesus, Christmas hymns sung throughout the whole month, kids getting so excited about all the gifts they'll receive. It's a fine balance for the kids between the anticipation of Santa's arrival and the true story about the birth of our Savior, Jesus Christ. The Chancel area was afire with all the poinsettias artfully placed by the Chancel Team, the glowing stained glass scene of the Three Wise Men approaching the Bethlehem stable, the star brightly shining above the Good Shepherd stained glass window, and the Advent wreath waiting for the fourth candle to be lit.

Dad and I were the Greeters for Christmas Sunday, so when we arrived a little late to our pew, everybody was standing singing the opening Christmas Carol hymn, and it was a wonderful, heart-warming sight to see. I heard Mom telling Dad that afternoon that she wished we could somehow attend one of the Christmas Eve services, either the children's at 7 o'clock, or the 11 o'clock candlelight service, but that's impossible if we go to Reading to cousin Jackie's house. The pull of family ties usually wins out, even though it means we can't attend our own church's services.

On Christmas Eve I usually ride with Mom and Dad to visit Jackie's family in Reading, but this year Laurie and Mikey rode with Mom and Dad, and doggone it all, there wasn't any room left for me! I would have tried to ride in the wayback, but it was full of presents, and Dad thinks it's not safe enough for me anyway, 'cause he says in a rear-end collision, I'd be smashed flat! So I stayed home and quietly hummed Christmas Carols to myself to while away the time until they returned. The first thing they did when returning was to put something under the tree, and I knew it was my gift from Tucker and Rosa, but, being the obedient guy that I am, I didn't touch it.

Christmas morning was exciting, let me tell you. Mikey came out of his guest bedroom upstairs, looked down the stairway at the lighted tree with all the presents laid out under it, and his eyes got big and round and his mouth dropped open and he just stood there looking down on the scene below. He had to be told to come down, and he ran so fast, his little legs were just a blur. Then it was quite a while of choosing a gift, tearing it open, and exclaiming about it, then on to the next one. I was so proud that Mikey would grab a wrapped gift from under the tree, then ask his Mom if it was for him before demolishing the wrapping paper. At each gift, he'd extend it to his Mom asking, "is this one for me?" Most times she'd say, "yes" and then he'd tear into it. Sometimes her answer had to be "no," and then he'd return it to its place under the tree and go on to the next one. Such a good little guy! Laurie had her cell phone turned on to "speaker" mode so that Daddy Steve, stationed in Kuwait, could hear Mikey while he was opening his presents.

But—where was mine? It turned out I had to wait for the grown-ups to assemble to get mine, which meant a lengthy wait through the yummy brunch that Mom and Laurie had prepared. When Uncle Charlie and Scott had arrived and everyone had eaten their fill (except for me, of course), then the presents were distributed and we all dug into them, including ME! Yippee! I got all kinds of chewie toys and tug toys, and I was quite happy with the Santa Claws stuffed toy. My Nazzaro cousins, Tucker and Rosa, had given me a nice, chewy braided tug toy, which I'm still enjoying.

Christmas Day was a huge success from my viewpoint, and I'm so happy because it recognizes the birth of my Boss, Jesus, who is God, along with the Holy Spirit, which I know is in me and guides me every day. Three in one—how neat! I know God lives in me and guides me because otherwise, I'd be a real rascal—I just know it! So this means that I have to try my very best to live up to the expectations that my Boss has for me, and sometimes, it's very hard, but I'm trying every day. Some days, I succeed.

One day, when I was walking with Dad on Shattuck Street, we were just in time to see some kids lined up to enter their school bus, so Dad stopped me so as not to cross the path of the kids, while the bus rumbled up, stopped, opened its doors, and the kids piled on. All this time I sat patiently waiting for the last kid to climb the stairs and the doors to close. At that point, Dad motioned me to go forward, and we continued on our walk, listening to the bus start to rumble along. As it came alongside us, the doors opened up, and the driver shouted to Dad, "That's some dog you've got there! I wish my kids behaved that well!" Then she closed the doors again and the bus continued on its way. As Dad and I continued our walk, I could hear Dad chuckling to himself, and he couldn't wait to get home to tell Mom.

It's moments like these that I know Mom and Dad love to experience, because it confirms what they have always felt about me, for quite some time now—that I'm something special, and I was chosen by my Boss to bring comfort and happiness to many people, not just people who go to our church, but everyone throughout the town who need a lift in their spirits.

This year has been a year of quite a few shining moments—the CBS visit in the spring, our annual trip to Loon Mountain for the Scottish Highland Games, the Blessing of the Animals in October, and our activities at Christmastime, but the most meaningful and inspirational moments for us have been those quiet times when someone in a wheelchair or in a car or just on the street has reached out and found my velvety soft head to pat and they've been comforted. These moments are what God has commanded me to do. The rest is just gravy.

Obediently Yours,

Mosby MacFisher, Therapy Dog for the Ministry

Mosby chats with Santa at church party.

Chapter 95

MOSBY'S MUSINGS—END OF THE YEAR 2010

I thought I was through talking about 2010 events, but Mom told me I should put down my thoughts on last night's visit to my alma mater—NEADS campus in Princeton.

Puppy House Lady Doreen told us that since Andrew #3 had flunked out, my money had gone toward a little girl, Anastasia, and her companion dog, Chase. They'd be getting through their training soon and we were invited to the traditional "meet-and-greet" where all the folks who had a hand in the training process would be there to greet the new team. There would be the puppy raisers, maybe trainers, and sponsors (that's us).

The Meet and Greet for Anastasia and Chase went off as scheduled on December 30.

Mom and Dad had checked off the date on their calendars, and I filed it in my mind which remembers all these important dates. In the meantime, Mom looked up the description list of clients on NEADS' website to learn a little bit about this new team. She found that Anastasia was a little girl with severe disabilities—she couldn't talk, couldn't walk, and sat up only with assistance, so she needed Chase to be her companion and to make her feel better. So we all hopped into the car last night, headed to Princeton. Mom told Dad that she's glad that my money was going toward a little girl, if it couldn't go to a disabled veteran, her other favorite choice.

After a short ride, we pulled into the NEADS parking lot in Princeton, and I knew, as soon as I hopped out of the car, I was at my old school. I was so happy, sniffing the yellow snowbanks, especially the roped-off canine outdoor bathroom area, checking to find any familiar scents. Nobody had been there that I remembered, but the new scents were very interesting, and Mom soon had to say, "Let's go!" to get me moving toward the building. As soon as we started through the double doors and I knew where I was, I started getting excited, and Mom had to remind me a few times to remember that I was a fully trained, obedient guy.

When we entered the lobby, two nice ladies exclaimed, "Here's Mosby!" and the cameras started clicking away. I didn't remember them, and neither did Mom, but they said they saw the CBS video of us and recognized me right away. We all discussed it, especially the uncivilized showing time of 5:30 in the morning. While we were waiting for Anastasia to arrive, Mom was very nice and walked with me around the whole floor area as I recalled happy memories of my time spent there. Then a nice man and his daughter wanted to pat me, and introduced themselves as Chase's weekend puppy raisers. I was very happy to find out they were from Rhode Island and worked with the prisoners at the Moran facility, because that's where I spent my puppy days.

Then someone announced that Anastasia had arrived, and soon her Mom came through the double doors pushing Anastasia in a special stroller, with Chase walking beside her. I got a little excited about meeting Chase and Mom had to keep me beside her until everyone had settled in, and she later commented to Dad that I behaved pretty well—not magnificent, but pretty good, for me. Whatever that means!

Soon, when everyone else had chatted with the trio, I walked over to them very quietly for an introduction. Chase and I checked each other out, nose to nose, then nose to the other end, and both our tails were creating a little breeze, wagging away. Anastasia was a cute little girl with lots of curly dark hair, big eyes, and a winning, ready smile. I could tell she was thinking about lots of things, but just couldn't speak to communicate. Her mom positioned her legs for her, then her arms, and she placed one of her arms on my velvety soft head so Anastasia could feel me. This was the only comfort I could give to her, and I was just as emotionally affected by that as Mom was, I think. Then Mom had an idea and asked Anastasia's mom if this sweet little girl would mind if I put my big head on her lap, to which her mom replied, "No, that'd be fine." So Dad brought me sitting closer to the wheelchair, Mom told me "hugs" and I put my huge head on her tiny lap, filling it up, and Anastasia smiled the widest smile I've ever seen!

Soon it was time for us to leave, and we rode home all thinking the same thing—"this is truly what my job is all about—comforting someone who truly needed it." How sad that some children are in such need of comforting and love, but how wonderful it is that we were in just the right place and time to reach out and give her what she needed! Maybe St. Andrew of Scotland isn't too miffed about the change in direction of our donation!

Obediently yours,

Mosby Mac Fisher, God's Dog

Chapter 96

MOSBY'S JANUARY MUSINGS—2011

The name for January is SNOW! No January thaw this year, so the snow keeps on piling up. We've done no visits to anyone this month mainly because of all the activities connected with snow. Although that's not really a valid excuse because there were some days with no snow falling, but Mom and Dad were so busy that we just didn't make any visits. Not that there were that many humans out there who needed our attention. Lets see, there's Betty Lee over at the Alzheimer's wing at Life Care Center, but that's only a one-minute visit because Betty just zooms along in her wheelchair after greetings are exchanged. Then there's Lois Grant in Westford, who is next on our list to visit. Hopefully, we'll see her soon. Dad has spent a LOT of time, without me, at the church, shoveling out the places that the plow or snow blower can't reach, like all the entrances with steps, the handicapped ramp, etc. That takes a lot of time and energy, and Mom frets about it and wonders when he's going to stop that activity. After all, in a few short months, he's going to be eighty years old. Let's see, in dog years, that's 560 years. Wow! That's OLD! I had to count on all my nails many times, plus those pesky dewclaws, too. The other activity that keeps Dad busy is snowshoeing with family friend Wayne. That can't be planned too far in advance, either. It has to be right after a good snowfall, before the snow starts thawing away. Wait a minute—there hasn't been a thaw this year. Maybe that's why there've been so many good snowshoe days. Without me, of course. Mom and I stay at home and wait for the guys to return, tired but invigorated.

January started off very nicely with a little ego-building experience for me. Not that my ego needs any building—Dad thinks I'm too conceited as it is, even though Mom thinks I'm just fine the way I am. She's the smarter one, I think!

Pastor Deb's Mom Shirley and step-dad Bud have friends who've seen my CBS video and were dying to meet me, so one Sunday morning I was standing in the doorway of Fellowship Hall, and in walked Shirley and Bud with their friends in tow. The nice lady oohed and aahed appropriately when she saw me and couldn't get enough of patting me, right there in the doorway. After the introductions were completed, the nice lady said that she had been in training to work with some NEADS weekend pups, but then some surgery put that on the back burner for a while, but she intends to return to it when she can. She knew all about NEADS and the good work that's done there, and she pawsitively couldn't get enough of me.

Lynda Reynolds Fisher

Dad and I were the official Greeters that day, and when we were done with that, we entered the sanctuary to find the row behind Mom taken up with Bud, Shirley, and friends so that they could be near me. How flattering! No wonder I'm so self-satisfied! I was thinking of all the recognition I've received from newspaper articles and television segments, but really, the thought of folks traveling to visit with me in my Boss's house is just so satisfying. I know I'm reaching out to folks and connecting, when they want to visit with me in this way. This is part of my job, as well as visiting nursing homes, hospitals, etc.

So, last year when I was reflecting on all the different ways I've been exposed to the public, I was wondering, "What next?" Maybe this visit is "what's next." People reaching out to pat my velvety head and saying nice things about me and my job. God is good—all the time!

Arf!

Mosby Mac Fisher, God's Dog

Chapter 97

MUSINGS OF THE MINISTRY DOG

March 1, 2011

It's certainly been a long while since I've set paw to pen to write about my activities, since I'm in a mindset of visiting ailing folks in hospitals or nursing homes as my main activity in life. But—when I think back on the first two months of the year (January and February), I actually HAVE been quite active, although not in my main role of Visiting Dog. The snowy days resulting in bad walking underfoot, combined with the scarcity of folks to visit, have caused me to have NO active visiting days so far this year, but notwithstanding that, I have been busy church-wise.

I've attended church almost every Sunday, lying quietly under the pew and listening to everything that's going on around me. I must admit to sleeping quietly through the sermons, but actually Pastor Deb doesn't mind that at all.

The coffee hours after church are when I turn on my charms to everyone who needs to pat my soft velvety head to cheer up their day. I love to see the smiles light up their faces, and know that it's my presence that put those smiles there.

Arf!

Mosby Mac Fisher, Church Dog

Chapter 98

MOSBY'S MEANDERINGS

Today, Tartan Day, April 6, I took Mom and Dad to Ayer to the Apple Valley Center to visit someone new—Marge MacMelville, who attends the Congregational Church. Mom had said that AnneLee recommended we should visit Marge sometime, even though she's not a Baptist, and we all were more than happy to spread our joy around to folks other than the church on the common.

Little did we know how many people in common we all knew. But I'm getting ahead of myself—upon entering the building Mom handed me over to Dad so that she could sign us in—Dad thinks that Mom's writing is more legible than his, so Mom always does that while Dad and I make everyone around us happy. It never fails, every time we enter a building to visit one person, the trip down the halls takes longer than the visit.

While mom was signing us in, a nice couple with a little baby talked to Dad about my Job, all the time patting my velvety head and receiving licks from my tongue. I tried to reach the baby, but never quite achieved that. They couldn't get enough of me! While all this was going on, nurses, aides, and volunteers passing the desk had to pat me, too. Doggone, if I weren't such a laid-back guy, I would have really had a swelled head, with all the attention I was receiving.

After a good ten minutes, we started the walk down the hall to Marge's room, only stopping five times for outstretched hands from people in wheelchairs. I can't pass by any of them without at least pausing so they can pat me and tell me how beautiful I am. Beautiful? Can't they tell I'm a guy, and they should say that I'm handsome, not beautiful! But Mom just smiles and lets them pat me to their hearts' content. It's such a nice ministry that I have, making people happy by just patting me. Such an easy Job!

At last we arrived in Marge's room, only to find her asleep. Mom was going to leave her my business card, but as she was reaching her hand into her pawcket, they saw her eyes opened and Mom introduced ourselves to Marge. When she saw me, she perked right up, sat up on her bed, and beckoned me over to her. She's definitely a dog person! I knew right away, before she said a word, that I had met my goal, to make her happy. Dad told her that AnneLee had suggested we visit her, and then he saw Millie Shaffer's picture in her mirror. They then had to tell her about our connection with the Shaffers, when the Fishers and Fentons lived near each other in Medford,

Dad's older sister used to be their sitter, and Dad and Buzz Thompson ran around together. Everyone grew up and Millie Fenton married Eddie Shaffer, then Lucy, Millie's younger sister, married Buzz, and Mom told Marge how she went through school with Lucy. Such connections! All the time, we could see that Marge was a little misty-eyed, and it came out that she and Millie were very good friends. It wasn't that long ago that Mom and Dad had attended Millie's funeral at the Congregational Church, and it made them feel bad, also, I think.

Then Marge told them that her daughter Carol works at the Littleton Animal Hospital and how much Carol loves Mosby. Oh, and then Mom had to tell Marge how her grandson Kevin, Carol's son, worked on the condo that we live in now. Such a small world, when we all live in a small town! They all had a good time talking about how much they love their churches. All the time they were talking, my head would go over to Marge's lap and she'd pat me. I could tell she was really enjoying my visit to her, and I know that Mom and Dad both did, too. She was such a nice lady to talk to, and they all had so much in common. This visit was a real howling success!

Then—Marge's phone rang, and we could tell it was a friend, so Mom placed my business card on the table, and we whispered goodbye so that she could chat with her friend on the phone. After the return trip down the corridor which took another ten minutes of patting, we returned to our car for the short trip home. I heard Mom and Dad talking about the nice visit, and what a pleasure it is to visit a dog person. There's an added pleasure to the visit, when we see the smiles I can put on people's faces.

I was reminded about last Sunday in church when Carol gave the Invocation and explained some of the reasons why people come to church: to sing in the choir, or to listen to the choir sing, or to hear the Scriptures read, or to pat Mosby, or to listen to the sermon—wait a minute—back up! TO PAT MOSBY? That caught my attention, and I raised my head from under the pew where I was resting. Do people come to church "to pat ME?" Really! Well, that's flattering. I never thought about that. I know I don't rank up there with the choir, or the Scriptures, or the sermon, but I'm really happy that my Ministry is pleasing to some folks. Especially with those words coming from Carol, who is allergic to my dog dander, and doesn't spend much time near me. I guess it's true what Mom tells Dad a lot—it doesn't matter where I take them, it'll make somebody happy. That's my job, and I'm happy to do it.

Arf!

Mosby Mac Fisher, Church Dog

Chapter 99

MOSBY'S MEANDERINGS

April 9, 2011

Today was another first for me, and for Mom and Dad, too. We went to Acton, next door to Littleton, to a school gym, for the Miracle League Spring Training event. What fun it was! After church one Sunday, Joe Vesey had asked Dad (don't know why he didn't go directly to me) if I could go there for spring training, just to visit around and be petted by any of the kids who wanted to pat me. Dad answered in the affirmative, as he does to most things which involve a visit somewhere to kids. When Joe explained that the Miracle League is a non-profit group of volunteers organized to help Special Needs kids (like Mikey) learn the basics of T-ball, which is the age-appropriate beginner of baseball, we were all for it. Joe thought my warm, comforting presence might be just what some kids might need who are a little nervous or overwhelmed by the whole experience of T-ball. As they knew, I was quite happy to be included in this event. After all, why not? It involved kids (my favorite humans) and activity which I love, and lots of rolling and bouncing balls.

Coincidentally, we found out that Laurie had signed up Mikey, but he couldn't go to this first session. So, on a bright, sunny day we drove over to the gym at one of the schools in Acton, and were blown away with all the kids who needed to touch my velvety head and hug me. Their ages were from about Mikey's age to almost-teenagers, and they were so enthusiastic about hitting the ball and running the bases. There were kids there with all kinds of disabilities, but they all wore big grins with an eagerness to participate. The ball was placed on the tee-stand, they were encouraged to hit it, with or without their buddy's assistance, then they ran the bases back to home plate with everybody clapping and cheering them on. What fun! In the meantime, the kids who weren't playing came over to me, some with adults, and asked to pat me. I was Mr. Popularity, and I loved it! So did the kids. I couldn't wait for the real games to start, in a couple of weeks. I really surprised Mom and Dad when I didn't bat an eyelash when a ball came rolling right to me a couple of times. They thought I'd be interested in chasing it, but I fooled them. I KNEW the balls were there for the kids, so I ignored them.

I must say that I've never seen so many Special Needs kids in one place, in all my life! With some of the kids, it was hard to tell that they weren't just typical kids, but with some of the others, you could definitely tell there was some kind of a need there, which I ignored. I just wagged my tail at all of them, licked their fingers with my wet tongue, and thoroughly enjoyed myself. There were lots of families with brothers and sisters and some were Special Needs, but some weren't. I could spot some of them who had Autism, just like my little buddy Mikey, and some had Cerebral Palsy, and some I couldn't tell what was their distinction, but it didn't matter. Each kid had a turn at the T-ball with Uncle Joe, and he handled each kid to the degree that was necessary. I watched as the hour progressed, as some kids wandered off with a parent and I didn't see them again, but some kids stayed, and I watched them progress from Uncle Joe helping them hit the ball, to the kids who learned to hit the ball without any help, then to run around the bases with their buddy. Uncle Joe helped them all—each according to their needs, around the three bases and back to home plate for a lot of applause from the adults and hi-fives. I even saw one kid who ended up not needing the T-ball stand and Uncle Joe gently threw the ball to him until he connected with the ball and the kid ran the bases successfully, skidded into home plate, and hi-fives were passed all around. What a great accomplishment for this boy! And for the coaches. And for the parents. And for all the adults and kids on the sidelines. Everyone was cheering. I do think that God was watching this, encouraging the kids to try their hardest, and making note of all the adults, parents and volunteers, who came together to help this bunch of kids have a good time playing and exercising to the very best of their abilities.

It wasn't all great fun for everyone, though. I could see some kids becoming frustrated, being hugged by their parents, and sometimes not bothering to come up to bat again. But I imagine their parents will encourage them to try it again, and maybe next time they'll do better. There was one little boy who walked out of the gym crying, and covering his ears with his hands, and I thought of our little Mikey, who sometimes is overwhelmed with noise and too many people, and I was glad to remember that the real games next month will be outdoors, I hope, where the noise and crowds of people will be lessened. I can't wait to go to watch Mikey play! It's going to be so much fun to watch him and all the other kids trying so hard. I guess that's one reason why Laurie and Mikey didn't attend this session—also because I heard her tell Mom that they already had something planned for today, but would certainly keep their Saturday mornings clear from now on, right through the Spring months.

I forgot to mention all the kids that came over to pet me! Not all the kids, but a good amount, first asked (or a parent asked) to pat me, then cautiously reached out a hand. The gym was divided in half and on the other side were the bigger kids, whom I visited a couple of times, and I made some friends over there, but I liked Uncle Joe's side, with the littler kids. One little guy, Ethan, kept coming over with his Dad but was too shy until about the fifth time when he finally patted my side and reached over to touch my ear. I hope I see Ethan again some time.

Lynda Reynolds Fisher

Uncle Joe was kept busy with the kids, but he found time to come over to say hello anyway. I found out something interesting—his voice sounds just like the voice of Santa Claws that I remember seeing at the church at Christmas time. What a coincidence!

Arf! Woof! Hurray for all the kids!

Mosby Mac Fisher, Church Dog

Chapter 100

A REQUEST FOR A VISIT

Last week, the week before my Dad's big (80th) birthday, I took my folks to see Lois Grant, who had been asking for me. On one of our many walks, Dad had encountered Gail, a neighbor and friend of Lois, when she lived in the Pine Tree Park group. Gail told Dad that Lois was always talking about me (how flattering), and was hoping for a visit soon.

So off we went, Dad driving us, to the nursing home in Westford, and of course we encountered lots of people in the halls on our way to Lois' room. But—we got to her room, and only her roommate was there. No Lois. Disappointment again! The roommate did say that Lois might be at the main dining room for an activity, so after leaving my card on her table, we wove our way back down the corridor, stopping for the outreached hands who just wanted to pat me and feel my velvety-soft head. We were in danger of getting completely turned around, with all these corridors branching this way and that, but at last we found the sign leading us to the main dining room, where we met folks in wheelchairs and others sitting in dining chairs, while the activities lady was helping them to bowl with these gigantic, light-weight balls, trying to hit the huge bowling pins. While Dad asked her if Lois had been here, Mom was busy walking me around to everyone who wanted to pat me. That took a while, only to find out that Lois had never been there. Wow! This little trip was turning into a first-class detective hunt! Someone else thought Lois might have gone to the main entrance, so we wandered around, trying to find the right corridor, eventually locating it, and as we started down the aisle, we saw Lois in her wheelchair, spinning the wheels trying to catch up with us. She had heard we were looking for her, and she was scooting all around trying to find us, but always just missing us.

With a broad smile breaking on her face, she led us back to her room, where we all enjoyed a really nice visit. She was just as happy to see us as we were to see her. We stayed an extra-long time, because we knew this lady was one who certainly enjoyed my visit. At last we told her goodbye and started our way to the main entrance, but of course had to stop a few times for out-stretched hands from wheelchairs, and even some of the nurses, aids, and maintenance people. One gentleman, sitting in a chair, surrounded by oxygen tanks, tubes, and what-nots, told us all about his Golden Retriever he used to have, and how special Goldens were. We couldn't agree with him more!

Lynda Reynolds Fisher

It's so heart-warming for me to belong to a breed of dog which is so beloved by so many people. Not that I have anything against other breeds, or mixed breeds, but I am sort of proud to be a Golden, and I know my Mom and Dad feel the same way. It makes our Assigned Job that much easier, I think.

Arf!

Mosby Mac Fisher, Therapy Dog for the Ministry

Chapter 101

DAD'S 80ᵀᴴ BIRTHDAY

Dad had said, for his 80ᵗʰ birthday, he adamantly DID NOT want a big event, in fact he wanted nothing at all, except for his own immediate family. Well, that didn't sit well with Mom, who believed it should be recognized as a huge milestone. So, after a bit of wheedling, Dad did say he'd be happy with a birthday cake in church, because he likes to celebrate with his church family. So, even though it wasn't a large enough celebration to suit Mom, she took off in high gear to get everything in place.

First, after checking the calendar, she found that the Sunday before Dad's Wednesday birthday would be Mother's Day, and she didn't want to interfere with anyone's plans for that special event, so after checking with Pastor Deb, she settled on the Sunday following Dad's birthday. OK. Cake to be ordered. Check. Paper products to be bought. Check. Birthday cards to be bought, one from Mom, one from me.

Back up. Paper products don't have to be purchased. Mom and Ellie had been up in the Deaconess supply closet searching for something else, and Ellie pulled out a plastic bag with blue plates and napkins, and made note of the box full of clear plastic forks. Perfect! Mom remembered those had been left over since Pastor Deb's Ordination Reception, held many years ago at this, her home church. Let's see—Debbie has been our pastor for ten years, so her Ordination occurred a few years before that—all these supplies have been sitting in the closet since then? Ellie and Mom looked at them and both made the decision to use them for Dad. "After all," Ellie said, he IS the Deaconerd, so dubbed for all the assistance he's given the Deaconesses over the years." How appropriate! Ellie took out a tablecloth, but Mom decided that she'd use one from home instead.

The next thing was to invite Wayne and Maria for the restaurant lunch, the only non-family people, but we knew Dad would like that, since he and Wayne are such good buddies. Mom was tickled that she could pull that off without Dad knowing!

Sunday, May 15 arrived and we all made our way to church, Dad and I being the chosen greeters, although most people weren't aware that it was Dad's special day. During the worship time of lifting up our concerns and celebrations, Pastor Deb told everyone that we were celebrating Dad's 80ᵗʰ birthday and everyone applauded and then sang a special Happy Birthday song to him, which made him a little uncomfortable, Mom thought. But, secretly, from my place under the pew, I thought Dad was touched to be singled out for this celebration.

During the coffee hour following the worship service, after Dad had cut the first slice of cake (following another round of Happy Birthday by everyone), Mom got busy cutting up and handing out the cake while Dad was busy shaking hands and receiving many well wishes from his church family and friends. I even managed to get a piece of icing from some kid's plate that tipped onto the floor, so I felt like I was part of the celebration, and in a very sweet way! I kept looking for more, but everyone else held on to their plates quite firmly.

As soon as that event was over and cleaned up, we hot-footed it across the Common to the Tre Amici Restaurant, arriving just as Laurie and Mikey, closely followed by Uncle Charlie, arrived. We all entered the restaurant mostly together and were led to a small private room which Mom had requested mostly for Mikey's benefit. He really does better without a lot of noise and clatter from the large public restaurant, so this was perfect for us.

Soon Scott arrived, and lastly, much to Dad's surprise, Wayne and Maria arrived, apologizing for being late, but having been tied up in traffic caused by the rain, they thought. The meal was really great, I heard. I wouldn't know because I didn't get any at all, even though I was under the table near Dad so that I could catch any drops. A guy can hope, can't he?

It was a quiet, small celebration, but we were all satisfied that it was what Dad wanted, and after all, it was for his birthday. My Dad's such a special guy!

Chapter 102

THE MIRACLE LEAGUE GAMES

This past Saturday was a busy day for us, as a family. Mom had committed to working at the polls for the town elections, but I hopped into the car and Dad drove us to Boxborough to see my little buddy Mikey play T-ball at the Miracle League's first game of this season. I remembered a lot of the folks from when we had gone to the spring training day a few weeks ago, even though Mikey wasn't there then.

On arriving at the field, I spotted Mikey with his mom Laurie, and immediately had to go over to them for a greeting and a bear hug. My job there was to mosey (not Mosby) around and chat up any kids who might need my attention. There was one girl in a wheelchair who kept coming over to me for a good pat, and lots of kids (and adults) who stopped by for a comforting pat.

When Mikey got up to bat, we were all hoping he'd do well, and DID HE EVER! To our surprise, he hit the ball on the Tee without any help, and he ran the bases so fast that his volunteer buddy who was assigned to him had to hustle to keep up with him. As he rounded third base to make it home, everyone cheered and hi-fived him when he reached home plate, sporting an ear-splitting grin and a little hop-skip step. He really enjoyed the experience, and we all were so ecstatically happy for him.

I can see that this Miracle League thing is a sure hit with everyone—all the kids are successful, their families enjoy watching their special kids achieve their successes, each according to their individual abilities, and all the volunteers know they're appreciated by the kids and their families.

Just like the game of baseball is a team effort, the Miracle League games are a LARGE team effort, and succeed they do! I can't wait for next Saturday to come so that we can go again.

<u>Visits made with Deb</u>

On May 24th we met Pastor Deb outside the Life Care Center of Nashoba Valley in Littleton so that I could get all my enthusiasm for her outside, before entering. Gosh! I can't help it! I just love her so much, and when I see her I can't contain myself for a while. I can hear Dad saying, "calm down, Mosby" but as much as I want to be obedient, there's a part of me that just has to be enthusiastic when I greet someone I know and love. Very soon, though, I did get that enthusiasm out of my system and we all walked in to the reception area to register. The Director had closed her door, because Lily had spotted me when we were outside, and she was greeting me very loudly, with Indie following close behind Lily in his enthusiasm. Some day, they're going to let me into that office so that Lilly, Indie, and I can romp, but that day hasn't happened yet.

After Mom had signed us all in, we made the usual foray down the corridor, stopping for every outreached hand. Pastor Debbie was watching my actions closely, because she especially asked to come along to see how well I perform my Ministry.

AnneLee had told Mom that Barbara Kamb was a resident, recovering from an automobile accident and that she was a dog person, so Barbara was our first destination. We found her at the end of a corridor looking out a window, and soon introductions were passed around, and they had a little laugh about the fact that Barbara had been the pre-Kindergarten teacher for Debbie's two girls, as well as our Scott's Kindergarten teacher. Not that anyone expected her to remember back to 45 years ago!

Barbara definitely was a dog person, bending over from her wheelchair to keep patting my head, after I had licked her hand and had settled down. The humans had a nice time chatting with Barbara, and I eventually dozed off, since human chatter doesn't always involve talk about me.

The next stop was to see a nice lady whom Mom has known for quite a while, first in Scouting and later in Town work. Jane had experienced a stroke and we found her in her room, sitting on her bed with two aides encouraging her to sit up. She greeted Mom with a wide, awkward smile, and was encouraged by the aide to pat my velvety head with her good hand. She seemed to enjoy me, but we didn't stay long because we could see she needed the assistance of the aides more than she needed me. I heard Mom tell Dad that we'd try another visit in a while, after Jane has had some therapy treatment and is feeling better.

Of course, no stop at Littleton Life Care Center is complete without a pause at the Alzheimer's wing. Our mission was to visit with Betty Lee, but of course, we had to stop at each wheelchair for a brief pause before continuing on our way. We met Betty in one of the little visiting rooms, and as always, as soon as she said hello, she was whizzing on her way in her wheelchair. A short pause in the dayroom to visit everyone turned into a longer visit than we anticipated, just because there were so many folks whose faces lit up with smiles when they saw me. I can really say that I "earned my keep" that day, with all the folks whose day I brightened a wee bit with my presence.

I wish Debbie could come along more times when we make our visits, but I know that she's very busy and can't spare all that much time. Mom told her she's always welcome to come with us and to just let us know when she wants to do it again.

<u>Littleton Animal Hospital</u>

In early June, I took my folks to my doctor's office for my annual Lyme Disease inoculation, and while standing at the reception desk, Carol, on the other side of the desk, told my Mom how much HER mom enjoyed our recent visit to her at Life Care Center in Littleton. Marge MacMelville had mentioned that her daughter Carol worked at the Littleton Animal Hospital, and my ears perked up at that, 'cause I love Carol. It's not just for the treats she usually gives me, but she's just a nice, friendly person who likes all animals. I was reflecting back on that visit with Marge as Carol was chatting to Mom and thinking what nice folks dog people are—actually, ALL animal people! Those are the people I like best in this whole wide world.

<u>Victor Rintoul</u>

For quite some time now, Mom and Dad have wanted to show my pal Victor the CBS video which he had a part in while he was at the Acton Life Care Center. At last, the day arrived, and Dad drove Victor to our condo so that he could view the show. Mom had me wait in the living room while Victor and Dad came in, and I must say that, although I was really, really happy to meet Victor in my home, I was quite calm after Mom had reminded me a few times.

So Victor sat on the sofa with me at his feet, and we all watched me, doing my job at church and then doing some visitations. Mom played back Victor's spot a few times so that he could see himself more than once, and he was most appreciative that he had the chance to see the show. It made me feel good that we could do this for Victor, because his visit was a large part of my Work.

<u>Memorial Day</u>

Dad was just starting to feel better from a bad cold, so decided not to march in the Memorial Day parade with the other veterans, much to Mom's relief. Since it was on the parade route, we decided to go to the front of the church to watch the parade come by. Soon Pastor Debbie arrived with my buddy, Mr. Gibson. After greeting each other, both ends, we wanted to play, but both handlers, Deb and Dad, frowned on that, telling us it wasn't the time or place for play, and we both had to behave like the gentlemen they know we can be. Soon we heard the band playing, and all heads on the sidewalk and lawn of the church turned to watch the marchers approaching. They

Lynda Reynolds Fisher

stopped short of the church, just at the Common, for ceremonies there for the Vietnam and Korea veterans and ended, of course with the firing salute as the flag was slowly raised. Now, I must mention that, a black Labrador Retriever and a gorgeous Golden Retriever, both bird dog breeds, should be relaxed around gunfire, being hunting dogs. Alas, no, not Mr. G. nor I. Mr. G. pulled Debbie up the front steps of the church and into the Narthex! I, being held by Dad on the steps, pulled mightily to escape the noise, and it was all Dad had, holding onto the railing, to resist being pulled up the stairs after Mr. G.! After every volley, Mom fed me a treat, hoping that maybe I'd associate the sharp shots with something good, but that'll take more practice, I'm afraid.

Mosby Mac Fisher, Church Dog—yes
  Hunting Dog—no

Chapter 103

MOSBY'S JUNE MEANDERINGS

July 2011

Where has the time flown? June is already over and we're well started on July. Today, being the day before Independence Day, is the Sunday when we like to be patriotic in church, and I did my part by wearing a patriotic neck scarf, imprinted all over with our American flag. I say "our" because, even though I started out life as a Canadian, I feel now that I'm all American, especially since I was welcomed into my church by Pastor Deb in a Commissioning service, designed especially for a dog.

Dad and I greeted today, and quite a few people mentioned how handsome and patriotic I looked, and wished they had remembered to wear something equally patriotic. Even Len's sermon today touched on Freedom and Independence, mostly from a religious point of view, rather than a country. Too bad there weren't more people in church to listen to our soon-to-be-ordained preacher, but it was the Independence Day long weekend, and many of our church family were away.

Just as sparse as the attendance was today, it was the opposite a few weeks ago when the Grotonwood summer staff of new camp counselors filled our pews to overflowing. On the first Sunday the counselors are at Grotonwood, they always attend our worship service, and from then on, I think they go to the Grotonwood Chapel. Don't actually know where they go—maybe to a lakefront service? But it's always a great time when they arrive at the Common in a couple of camp vans, then enter the sanctuary to fill one side of the church, only leaving empty a few pews in the front. We, the regular attendees, have to make do with the other side, which makes it filled up pretty well, being twice as many people as usual sitting on that side. I know that when Dad and I slipped into the pew beside Mom, there were a few startled stares in our direction. Pastor Debbie, in her Welcome, mentioned me—imagine that—and told the campers about me and invited them to pat me. I think she meant after church, but a few of them left their pews to come over to touch my velvety head.

During the postlude, Dad and I left before most other people, and as we went by the back pew, the Grotonwood staff, EACH and EVERY ONE, reached behind the pew to pat me as we went by! Of course, during the coffee hour, I was surrounded by the Grotonwood gang, as well as the usual folks who have to stop and chat with Dad and pat me. Mom had come over to us and noticed a nice young Grotonwood lady hanging back, but giving me the eye. Mom told her, "You can pat him if you like," to which she replied that she was really afraid of me. So Mom told her how friendly I was, even though I'm kind of intimidating because I'm such a big guy. Mom pulled a chair out from the table and asked the girl to sit down, then had Dad bring me a few steps closer, and I reached my head over to her thigh—not on her lap, 'cause that might have frightened her, but just beside her. When she accepted that and started patting my soft head, her smile broadened into a wide grin, and I knew I had another friend! What a great thing that was! I've made another Grotonwood pal! I hope she'll now feel better about all canines.

I can hardly wait for next June to bring another new batch of Grotonwood counselors that I can befriend.

One day last week, Pastor Deb brought Mr. Gibson to the church parking space to meet Dad and me and we all went for a walk together, as far as the Congo church. I was hoping that all my buddies would be out so that I could introduce Gibson to them, but we really didn't see many. Of course, Dapper was moseying around, and I did get to introduce them. They did the usual sniffing end-to-end and would have gotten along together quite well, but my Border Collie buddy can't walk with us because his human isn't around, so we left Dapper and continued on our way. Dad's friend John was just leaving Pine Tree Park and the humans stopped for a moment to be introduced to each other. When we continued on our walk, we saw nobody else. They must have been in hiding somewhere, because I usually see more folks on our walks. By then it was getting so hot and muggy that Mr. Gibson started to grumble so we all went back to the church and then came back to my air conditioned condo to meet up with Mom who was just returning from her doctor's visit. Dad's famous grilled cheese sandwiches were on the menu for the humans and a couple of puppy snacks for us canines were fine for us. Soon it was time for Pastor Deb and Mr. Gibson to leave, so we all said goodbye with a promise for another walk sometime soon, maybe on a cooler, drier day.

This past week I took Mom and Dad to Westford to visit Lois Grant and Barbara Hill, which activity was sort of successful. After the usual walk down the hall, stopping for all the outstretched hands to have their fill, we entered Barbara's room only to find her stretched out on her bed, sound asleep. And I do mean SOUND asleep! Mom started talking to Dad to see if that'd wake Barbara, but she remained asleep. Mom felt that if she'd been lightly asleep, just resting, the voices would have woken her up, but since she stayed asleep, she probably needed it, so there wasn't much point in waking her up just for a visit. After Mom went through her pawcket and left my business card, we trotted down the corridor to Lois Grant's room, but that was empty. We had passed the activity room where everyone was lined up in rows in their wheelchairs, singing along to a nice lady playing the piano and belting out old-time songs. As we entered that room, Mom started looking at everyone, and finally an aide retrieved Lois for us, and we started back down the corridor to Lois' room for a nice visit. Lois is always so happy to see us, and she mentioned that Pastor Debbie had been in recently to see her too. I got up quite close to Lois, because even though she only has one leg, it's not sick and I know I can't hurt her. She knows just the right spot behind my ears to scratch, and I just can't get enough of it. Lois loves to chat with us, and she tells the most interesting stories that I never get bored. Afterwards, when we arrived home again, I heard Mom tell Dad that it's always a pleasure to visit Lois, with all her stories, and the only thing that would have made it nicer would have been if Barbara had been awake. But we can't have everything just as we plan it, and we'll just make another trip back there sometime.

So—that's been my life lately. It's been a good combination of church activities, walking with friends, and visiting other friends. What more can a guy want? Life is good, when you're a Church Dog. God is good—all the time.

Arf!

Mosby Mac Fisher, Church Dog, and Dog-About-Town

Chapter 104

MOSBY'S MUSINGS ON MIRACLE LEAGUE

Spring 2011

The Miracle League games continued every Saturday morning, but soon it was the last day for the games, then followed the next week by TROPHY DAY! As we headed over to the school in Boxboro, we were thankful that our destination was so close to Littleton. We had found out that this was a state-wide event, so it could have been held somewhere that would be an hour's drive away. When the car entered the full parking lot, we had to hunt for a spot because of the folks whose kids had an earlier game than Mikey's. Eventually we all piled out of the car and over to the field, and boy, were we ever overwhelmed! There were kids everywhere, some walking and running by themselves, some in walkers, some in wheelchairs, and they were all waiting for their game to begin. Mikey was assigned to Team Youkilis, which was playing the last game that morning, against Team Papi, so we found a good seat on the bleachers and prepared to wait. No sooner had we sat down than the kids starting coming over to pat me and talk about my Job and how beautiful I am. Some kids had an adult with them, either parent or buddy, and needed help to pat me, and those were the kids with the widest grins and heartiest laughs when they achieved their goal. They couldn't get enough of me! Soon the announcer called for Team Youkilis to gather for their turn at bat, with their opposing team, Papi, out in the infield. A young guy named Evan had been assigned to be Mikey's buddy, so we watched them go over to the batter's area to wait their turn. All this time the announcer was telling everyone about what they'd be doing, hitting the ball and running the bases. Eventually it was Mikey's turn at bat, his name was announced and everyone clapped. Mikey didn't need his buddy's help, as some kids did. The bat made contact with the ball sitting on the tee, he threw the bat down and started running for first base! The announcer followed their progress as Mikey touched first base and headed for second, then third, then on to home plate as everyone cheered him on! When our fearless athlete landed on the plate, Coach Joe was there for a high-five, along with other people, and everyone was cheering for him— "Mikee, Mikee, Mikee." Each team had two innings, and when they weren't the team at bat, they were out in the infield, tossing balls with their buddies. It was a little confusing for me to watch, especially with kids coming up to pat me, but I did have a chance to remember some of the kids, especially as the weeks went on and I had a chance to sort them out. The announcer was a big help in keeping them straight, although I don't know how he did it. He'd be announcing Abby at bat, while Jordan was running to second or third, and Andy was headed for a home run, and he kept everyone's names straight, even to little nicknames he gave some of them.

Let's see, there was "Keep on Goin' Owen" and "Hammerin' Henry", to name a few. Abby and Lily, blonde twins, were the gutsiest players, one needing lots of help from her buddy to hit the ball, and two buddies ran the bases with her, one on each side to help her with her special walker. The other twin was in a motorized wheelchair, but she made all the bases accompanied by her buddy, to much cheering and encouragement from the announcer and the many volunteers who kept watch over all of them. There was Shannon, Addison, and Madison, along with Michael and our Mikey, and Connor, who had to be taken away from me for his turn at bat, and Thomas, who was a little bit afraid of me, I think. Each player was encouraged by the crowd's applause and hi-fives as they ran the bases, most succeeding in touching the plate for a home run. There were at least a dozen kids on each team, and they all played their hearts out, to the best of their individual abilities. Dad noticed a little girl in a wheelchair, watching me intently, and he thought she'd like a visit, so we walked over to her spot next to the infield. She smiled and reached out to pat my velvety head. She never spoke, but we could tell she was very happy to be able to touch me. That made my day. Dad's, too.

At last came Trophy Day, and wouldn't you know it—it was raining! An inning of play was scheduled, followed by the trophy awards, for each group of two teams, in the order which they had been playing this whole season, so Mikey's group was at the end. A little guy in a wheelchair (can't remember his name) entered the infield, assisted by his buddy, and the announcer said that he'd sing our National Anthem to start the game. Mom and Dad had stood up and prompted me to "stand" which I readily did. I had to nudge the elderly couple next to us because I thought they were never going to stand, but when Mom told Dad that I was so good standing, I think they took the hint and got out of their chairs. The rain had stopped, and we all thought an inning would be played successfully, but just when Mikey's team had almost completed batting and it would have been his turn up at bat, the light drizzle turned to a downpour, and everyone scrambled to get inside the gym. But, just as if it was planned, no matter who reached the stairs, they looked behind to let the kids in wheelchairs, crutches, or other aids ascend the steps first. I was touched to see that, even though it meant that my slightly damp coat became soggy wet before I entered the building. I was grateful that I could safely climb those stairs without assistance, and I wished it could have been true for all the kids, too.

Inside was a noisy bedlam, with all kinds of excited kids, Special Needs and their siblings, which made for a large crowd. I was wondering how Laurie was making out with Mikey, since he doesn't deal well with crowds, noisy ones especially, but he was so looking forward to that trophy, that he didn't mind the distractions. He had told Laurie at home that "This will be my first-ever trophy" and he was looking forward to it immensely. Again, the first-rate announcer had something personal to say about each kid before announcing his name and handing over the trophy to eager hands. Some kids ran up to him for their trophy, some kids were led by their buddy, some with crutches or in wheelchairs, but all wearing that same excited, triumphant grin, and I know their parents and relatives were thinking that it was worth all the extra fuss that was generated in getting their kids to each and every game. Just as in the batting order, Mikey was one of the last kids to be called, and I thought he was getting a wee bit tense, but when at last his name was called, he jumped up off the floor and ran up to the announcer for HIS TROPHY! Laurie has the neatest picture of him holding the trophy up over his head and smiling that face-splitting grin of victory—at last!

I think that all the many volunteers who put this event together and worked so hard on it will receive a special blessing from my Boss, because of their hard work in making this event the success it was. I looked around the room from my low position near the floor, and I could see smiles of gratitude on the many faces of the families of these Special Needs kids, and I couldn't help thinking that, in spite of the challenges some of these kids will experience in life, they'll have great memories of succeeding at the Miracle League games. My thanks, especially, to Coach Joe for including me in these games.

Arf!

Mosby "Play Ball" Mac Fisher, Special Envoy for the Miracle League

EPILOG

After three years of living with my Mom and Dad, I've generated a lot of publicity for my Calling as Church Dog, and I've been responsible for some nice things said about my alma mater, NEADS. Let's see—the local newspaper, The Littleton Independent, ran a nice story on me, as did the Boston Globe, and I've been interviewed by the local cable TV station, as well as hitting the big time with my network CBS bit. What's left, other than a starring role in a movie? Hmmmm. Maybe I should talk Mom into letting me dictate a book to her? That might go over well. We'll have to see what 2011 brings.

Mosby Mac Fisher, Therapy Dog for the Ministry
Aka The Church Dog
Aka Military Liaison Ministry Dog
Aka Special Envoy for the Miracle League

AFTERWORD

We thought we would just be visiting people in hospitals or nursing homes, to cheer up some patients, but what we found was that Mosby opened us up to many events and adventures which we otherwise would not have been exposed to. We found that, by giving some sick people the blessing of his affection, we, too, were blessed as a result of his ministry. Mosby soon led us along on many varied adventures, some happy, some inspirational, some humorous, but all very memorable, and we wouldn't have missed any of them for anything! What a blessed life Mosby has brought to us!

By his actions, Mosby opened our eyes to see others in a new light, as we believe Jesus wants us to—accepting everyone, willing to help everyone, and not being judgmental of anyone (I'm still working on that one, however). Mosby never loses his temper with anyone, and I'm still learning that lesson also. Being taught by a dog how to behave in a Christ-like way is eye-opening!

CPSIA information can be obtained at www.ICGtesting.com
Printed in the USA
BVOW010008071211
277665BV00002B/1/P